LONDO

BIZARRE &

CURIOUS

A Guide to Over 300 of the City's Strangest Sights

Graeme Chesters

Arab Hall, Leighton House

Survival Books • Bath • England

First published 2014

Copyright © Survival Books 2014
Cover design: Nicola Erdpresser
Cover photo: Cable Street Mural (www.flickr.com)
Maps © Jim Watson

Survival Books Limited
Office 169, 3 Edgar Buildings
George Street, Bath BA1 2FJ, United Kingdom
tel. 01225-462135
info@survivalbooks.net
www.survivalbooks.net

British Library Cataloguing in Publication Data
A CIP record for this book is available
from the British Library.
ISBN: 978-1-909282-58-2

Printed in China by D'Print Pte Ltd

Acknowledgements

The author would like to thank all those who helped with research and provided information for this book. Special thanks are due to Robbi Atilgan for editing; Peter Read for proof-reading; David Woodworth for final proof checking; Nicola Erdpresser for design, photo selection and cover design; Jim Watson for the superb maps; and the author's wife Louise for continuing with the pretence that writing is a proper job.

Last, but not least, a special thank you to the many photographers – the unsung heroes – whose beautiful images add colour and bring London to life.

NOTE

Before visiting anywhere without unrestricted access it's advisable to check the opening times, which are liable to change without notice.

Grant Museum

Contents

2. CITY & EAST LONDON **124**

3. NORTH LONDON 198

4. WEST LONDON   226

5. SOUTHWEST LONDON   256

6. SOUTHEAST LONDON   272

Murals from the tomb of Nebamun, British Museum

Readers' Guide

The notes below refer to the general information provided (in a panel after the header) for each entry:

- **Address:** Includes the telephone number and website (where applicable). You can enter the postcode to display a map of the location on Google and other map sites. If you're driving you can enter the postcode into your satnav.

- **Opening hours (where applicable):** These can change at short notice, so confirm by telephone or check the website before travelling. Note that the last entry to attractions is usually at least 30 minutes before the closing time. Some venues close periodically for private or official events.

- **Cost:** Liable to change. Many attractions – such as national museums and galleries – offer free entry. Ask about concessions and family rates if not indicated. Many museums have lower fees for groups, either per head or a fixed rate. Major attractions allow you to buy tickets online, thus circumventing queues, and prices may also be slightly lower.

- **Transport:** The nearest tube or rail station(s) is listed, although in some cases it may involve a lengthy walk. You can also travel to most venues by bus and to some by river ferry. Some places are best reached by car, although parking can be difficult or impossible in many areas. Most venues don't provide parking, particularly in central London, and even parking nearby can be a problem (and very expensive). If you need to travel by car, check the parking facilities in advance.

- **Allow:** The time required to see attractions varies considerably, from less than an hour for a small gallery to a number of days for national museums. If your time is limited it's advisable to check the website and decide what you most want to see. Don't forget to allow time for travelling, coffee/tea breaks and lunch.

Disabled Access

Many historic public and private buildings don't provide wheelchair access or provide wheelchair access to the ground floor only. Wheelchairs are provided at some venues, although users may need assistance. Most museums, galleries and public buildings have a WC, although it may not be wheelchair accessible. Contact venues directly if you have specific requirements. The Disabled Go website (disabledgo.com) provides more in-depth access information for many destinations.

Alfred Hitchcock Mosaics, Leytonstone tube station

Introduction

Researching and writing this book has been a pleasure and an education. Despite having lived in northwest, central and southeast London at various times, and happily pottered around the city for many years, I now realise how much I had (and still have) to learn, and how many unusual delights London has to offer. Not only had I failed to visit many of the over 300 places included in this book, I hadn't even heard of some of them.

London is a city with a cornucopia of bizarre and curious places and stories, being ancient, vast and in a constant state of flux. Newcomers have, of course, a wealth of world-famous attractions to keep them occupied for a month of Sundays, which are more than adequately covered in a plethora of standard guidebooks. What *London's Secrets: Bizarre & Curious* does is take you off the beaten path to seek out the more unusual places that often fail to register on the radar of both visitors and residents alike. It also highlights unexpected and often overlooked aspects and attractions of some of London's more famous tourist sites.

London's Secrets: Bizarre & Curious includes some of the city's most unusual buildings, striking public artworks, outrageous museum and gallery exhibits, hauntings (including by animals), legends and much more. The entries range from Britain's oldest door to the beginning of body-snatching, from dummy house façades to London's unluckiest spot, from a legal brothel to the capital's most haunted theatre, and from the original skull and crossbones to what has a strong claim to be London's campest statue.

Although this book isn't intended as a walking guide, many of the places covered are close to each other in central London – notably in the hubs of Westminster and the City – where you can easily stroll between them, while others are further out in the suburbs. However, all are close to public transport links and relatively easy to get to. And, conveniently for a city with a (largely unfounded) reputation for rain – London actually enjoys a lower annual rainfall than New York, Rome or Sydney – many of the attractions are indoors, meaning you can visit them whatever the weather.

So there's no excuse for not getting out and exploring. I hope you enjoy discovering the bizarre and curious secrets of London as much as I did.

Graeme Chesters
December 2013

CHAPTER I

CENTRAL LONDON

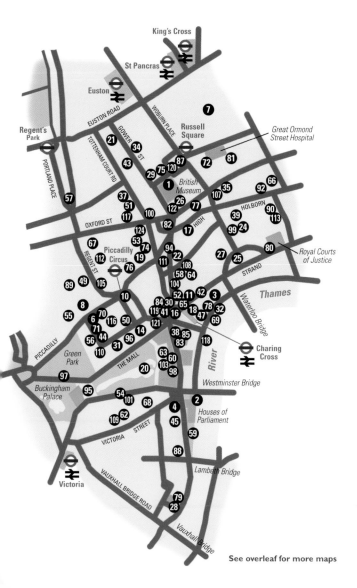

See overleaf for more maps

Land
G

Kensington

Gardens

Ke

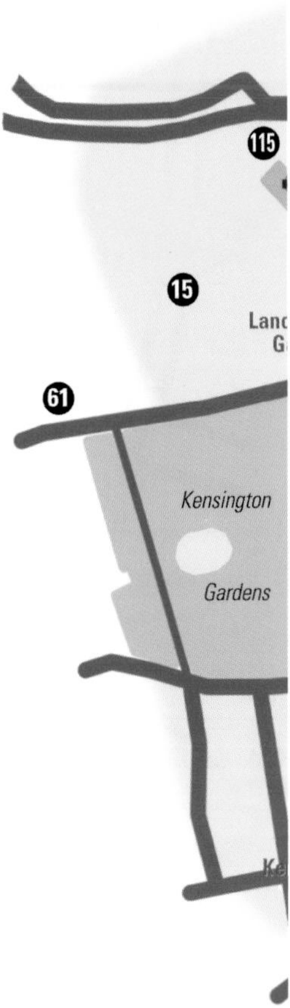

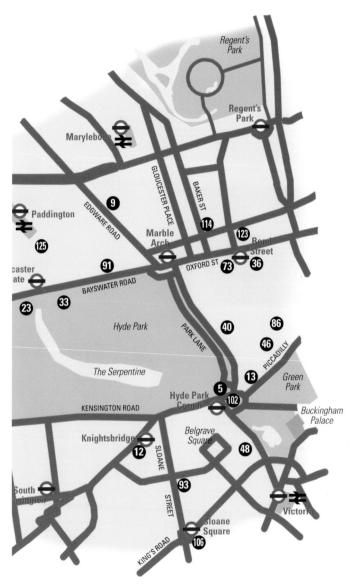

Regent's
Park

Regent's
Park

Marylebone

9

GLOUCESTER PLACE

BAKER ST

Paddington

125

EDGWARE ROAD

Marble
Arch

114

123

Bond
Street

caster
ate

91

73

36

23

33

BAYSWATER ROAD

OXFORD ST

Hyde Park

PARK LANE

40

86

46

PICCADILLY

The Serpentine

13

Green
Park

Hyde Park
Corner

5

102

KENSINGTON ROAD

Buckingham
Palace

Knightsbridge

12

SLOANE

Belgrave
Square

48

South
nsington

93

STREET

Victoria

Sloane
Square

106

KING'S ROAD

See previous page for more maps

I   THE BRITISH MUSEUM

Address: Great Russell Street, WC1B 3DG (020-7323 8181, britishmuseum.org).
Opening hours: Daily, 10am-5.30pm, but Fri, to 8.30pm.
Transport: Russell Sq or Tottenham Court Rd tube.

With a collection of over 8m items, the British Museum has more than its fair share of 'bizarre and curious' exhibits. The following are a few of my favourites:

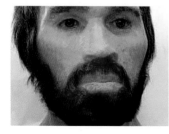

Lindow Man: This is the name given to the remarkably well-preserved remains of a man who met his death at Lindow Moss bog in Cheshire in the 1st century AD and was discovered by peat cutters some two millennia later in 1984.

The body has been extensively studied and it's known that he met a violent, unpleasant death: he was struck twice on the head with a heavy object and received a hard blow to his back, which broke a rib. A thin cord tied around his neck was probably used to strangle him and break his neck; once dead, his throat was cut and he was put face down in the bog. His death is thought to have been a ritual sacrifice.

The peat bog's acidic, oxygen-free conditions meant that Lindow Man's skin, hair and many of his internal organs were well preserved, although they gave him the appearance of having been pickled in tea.

Phallic Wind Chime: Also from the 1st century AD, this Roman wind chime is made of bronze and depicts a winged penis, from which five bells hang. Such chimes were hung in gardens and porches where they would tinkle in the wind – the sound was thought to ward off evil spirits – and bell chimes were often combined with a phallus, as the latter was viewed as a charm against evil and a symbol of good fortune.

To modern eyes, the wind chime is a challenging object, shocking and offensive to some. However, sexual and naked images were common in the

Greek and Roman worlds – neither of which was much influenced by the reservations and taboos of the Judaeo-Christian tradition – and it wasn't uncommon to see a phallus portrayed in paintings, jewellery and even furniture.

Warren Cup: This Roman silver cup originated near Jerusalem and dates from AD5-15, although it's named after a former owner, Edward Perry Warren (1860-1928). The images it carries will be even more upsetting to some people than the phallic wind chime above. One side of the cup shows two youths having sex, while the other displays a young man lowering himself onto the lap of an older, bearded man, while a slave boy looks on voyeuristically from behind a door.

Following Warren's death, the cup remained in private hands for many years and was only exhibited in public for the first time in the '80s, when social attitudes softened; it's had a permanent home at the British Museum since 1999.

Representations of sex acts are common in Roman art, on glass, pottery, terracotta lamps and wall paintings, in both private and public buildings. The Romans had no concept of – or word for – homosexuality. And for their mentors, the Greeks, the partnering of an older man with a youth was an accepted part of education.

2   THE HOUSES OF PARLIAMENT

Address: SW1A 0AA (020-7219 4272, parliament.uk).

Opening hours: Tours (75mins) for UK residents can be arranged through your MP and take place on Mon-Wed and Fri; the exact days and hours vary, so check the website. For all residents – UK and foreign – tours also take place on Saturday throughout much of the year, and Tue-Sat during the summer. Book by telephone (0844-847 1672) or you can buy tickets from the office near the Jewel Tower.

Cost: Free for UK residents if arranged through their MP. Saturday and summer tours: adult, £16.50; concession, £14; children 5-15, £7; under-5s, free.

Transport: Westminster tube.

The Houses of Parliament – or Palace of Westminster – are home to Britain's two Parliamentary Houses, the Lords and the Commons. They have a number of curiosities and quirks, including the following:

MPs' White Powder: A filled, communal snuffbox sits by the front door of the Commons. There's been one here since 1693, when smoking was disallowed in the Commons Chamber – a decision that was around three centuries ahead of its time – and snuff was offered to MPs instead. The current wooden snuffbox is a replacement after a World War II air-raid destroyed the silver original.

Remarkable Foresight: Westminster Hall is Parliament's oldest building and almost the only part of the ancient Palace of Westminster to survive in (almost) original form. It was built at the end of the 11th century,

The flamboyant, late Conservative MP Sir Nicholas Fairbairn is thought to have been one of the last Members to be a regular snuff user.

while its magnificent hammerbeam roof was commissioned in 1393 by Richard II. The roof measures 68 by 240ft and is the largest medieval timber roof in northern Europe.

When the roof was restored in 1913, several large timbers needed renewing. However, officials struggled to find oaks old and thus large enough, as many of the country's aged trees had been cut down. A bright spark decided to check where the original timbers had come from and it turned out that when they'd been cut in the 14th century from an estate near Wadhurst in Sussex, the estate's owners had realised that more timber would be needed for future repairs and planted a stand of oaks specifically for the purpose. These were ready by the early 20th century (520 years later) and were used in the restoration.

Taxi-lamp: On the top of a lamp standard outside Parliament on Parliament Square is a four-sided lamp bearing the word 'Taxi' on each of its panes of amber glass. This is the House of Commons Taxi-lamp – a light flashes on and off when an MP wants a taxi, thereby alerting passing drivers. It's clearly unacceptable for MPs to have to hail a cab on the street like the rest of us.

Toe the Line:
There are two sets of benches in the Commons Chamber. The Government sits on benches to the Speaker's right, while the Opposition occupies the benches to the Speaker's left. The red lines on the green carpet in front of the two sets of benches are two sword lengths and one foot apart, a throwback to the days when Members might have been tempted to settle disputes with swords.

Members still aren't allowed to cross the red lines during debates, and this is the origin of the expression 'toeing the line'.

3   THE SAVOY HOTEL

Address: Savoy Court, WC2R 0EU (020-7836 4343, fairmont.com/savoy-london).
Transport: Embankment tube.

It's often said that Savoy Court is the only place in London where you must drive on the right, but that's not the case: at Hammersmith bus station, the entrance and exit also force drivers on to the right side of the road.

cab drivers to reach out of the driver's door window to open the passenger's door (which opened backwards, having a handle at the front), without having to get out of the cab himself, and/or because the hotel's front doors are on the right of the street. Other people think the explanation is more prosaic: to prevent cars that are dropping people off or picking them up at the neighbouring Savoy Theatre from blocking the hotel's entrance.

Kaspar the Lucky Cat: The Savoy is the proud owner of a 3ft Art Deco black cat called Kaspar. It was specially

The Savoy is probably London's most famous hotel. It was built in 1889 by the impresario Richard D'Oyly Carte with the profits he made from staging Gilbert and Sullivan productions. It's long been a favourite with the glamorous and wealthy, and has a couple of notable oddities:

Driving Rules: Britain drives on the left-hand side of the road, but a Special Act of Parliament from 1902 requires traffic to drive on the right when entering Savoy Court from the Strand. For over a century, this has applied to all vehicles, be they horse-drawn or mechanical, and various explanations have been proposed for the anomaly.

It's said by some to be the result of the habit of the era's Hackney Carriage

commissioned in 1926 from Basil Ionides (1884-1950), an architect most famous for his 1929 redesign of the rebuilt Savoy Theatre. The cat is used as an extra guest when 13 dine at the hotel, to avoid the bad luck associated with that number; he's given a full place setting, has a napkin tied around his neck and is served each course. Otherwise, the cat sits in his own display case in the hotel's entrance hall.

This tradition dates back to 1898 when Woolf Joel, a South African diamond magnate, held a dinner at the Savoy. Due to a last-minute cancellation, only 13 people dined, which one of the guests deemed to be unlucky. He also claimed that the first person to leave the dinner would be the first to die. Woolf Joel laughed this off and, indeed, was the first to leave the table. A few weeks later, he was shot dead in his Johannesburg office.

Anxious that this wouldn't be repeated and worried about its reputation, the Savoy provided a member of staff to sit at tables of 13

Kaspar

for some years afterwards. However, this proved unpopular with guests, who often didn't want a stranger in their midst listening to their business, so a new solution was found: Kaspar the cat.

> Over the years, a number of the Savoy's famous patrons have become fond of Kaspar, including Winston Churchill, who frequently took his Cabinet to lunch at the hotel.

4   WESTMINSTER ABBEY

Address: SW1P 3PA (020-7222 5152, westminster-abbey.org).
Opening hours: Mon-Tue and Thu-Fri, 9.30am-4.30pm; Wed, 9.30am-7pm; Sat, 9.30am-2.30pm; Sun no tourist visits. Museum: Mon-Sat, 10.30am-4pm. Confirm via website.
Cost: Adult, £18; concession, £15; children 12-18, £8; under-11s, free accompanied by an adult; family, £36-44.
Transport: Westminster or St James's Park tube.

Much-visited Westminster Abbey has a number of unusual attractions:

O RARE BEN: IOHNSON

Ben Jonson's Curious Burial:
The dramatist and poet (1573-1637) is the only person in the Abbey buried in an upright position. Despite working as an actor and playwright – William Shakespeare was in the cast of Jonson's play *Every Man in his Humour* – as well as being tutor to Sir Walter Raleigh's son, becoming Poet Laureate in 1619 and receiving gifts from royalty, Jonson always seemed to be short of money.

Sadly, the great writer couldn't afford a standard 6ft by 2ft burial space and was interred on his feet (in a space taking up a mere 18 inches square) in the northern aisle of the nave

rather than in Poet's Corner, marked by a simple inscription: 'O Rare Ben Johnson'. Johnson's original stone was later moved to the base of the wall opposite the grave to preserve it.

It's said that Jonson's memorial was done at the expense of a certain Jack Young, who was passing when the grave was covered and gave the mason 18 pence to cut the inscription.

Britain's Oldest Door: A door opening into the Abbey's Chapter House dates from the 1050s, making it Britain's only surviving Anglo-Saxon door and the country's oldest. It measures 6.5ft high by 4ft wide and is made from a single tree; analysis of its rings shows that it grew between 924 and 1030. Fragments of skin found stuck to the door weren't from the stripped corpse of a criminal, nailed there to deter others – as was once

popularly believed – but are cow hide. This is slightly disappointing, we think.

Death Masks: With so much to see in the Abbey, some visitors overlook the museum, which is in the vaulted undercroft. This is one of the oldest parts of the building, dating from soon after the founding of the Norman church in 1065. The museum boasts a notable, curious and (to modern sensibilities) ghoulish collection of royal and other funeral effigies, some of them death masks. These wooden and wax images are some of the earliest likenesses of medieval monarchs, including Edward III, Henry VII and Elizabeth I.

Nelson's death mask

Later examples include Charles II, William III, Mary II, Queen Anne, Lord Nelson and Prime Minister William Pitt (the Elder).

England's Oldest Cultivated Garden: College Garden is one of the Abbey's three original gardens (along with the Garth and the Little Cloister) and is said to be England's oldest garden under continuous cultivation. It was the infirmary garden some 1,000 years ago, used for growing herbs and produce to keep the Abbey's occupants healthy, and to add flavour and interest to a diet that was often bland and stodgy.

College Garden

Until around 1300, London's climate sometimes approached Mediterranean-like warmth and a wide variety of plants would have been grown in the Abbey's gardens.

5   ACHILLES AS WELLINGTON

Address: Hyde Park, near Hyde Park Corner, between the Broad Walk and Lovers' Walk, W1.
Opening hours: 5am–midnight.
Transport: Hyde Park Corner tube.

The 18ft bronze statue of Achilles near Hyde Park Corner has a number of eccentricities. It looks too large – it stands 36ft high, including the base and mound – and although depicting the Greek hero of the Trojan War, it's dedicated to the Duke of Wellington. The statue is by Sir Richard Westmacott and was unveiled in 1822 to celebrate the Duke's victories in the Peninsular War and Napoleonic Wars, installed by order of George III. The entrance gates to Hyde Park were too low for it to pass through and a hole had to be knocked in the adjoining wall.

The statue was actually modelled on a noted classical study of a gladiator, although it's claimed that the head was based on Wellington's. It was London's first public nude statue since Roman times and there was an outcry over the penis, which had to be covered with a fig leaf to protect the public morals. The fig leaf has been chipped off twice, in 1870 and 1961. Wags have wondered whether the offending organ, like the head, was based on the Duke's.

> The figure of Achilles/Wellington stands on a Dartmoor granite plinth and carries a sword and shield. The bronze used for the casting came from cannons captured in the Duke's military campaigns at Salamanca, Toulouse, Vittoria and Waterloo.

Achilles as Wellington

THE BEAU WINDOW   6

> **Address:** White's, 37-38 St James's Street, SW1.
> **Transport:** Green Park tube.

George Bryan Brummell (1778-1840) – nicknamed Beau – was the foremost fashion icon of his age. Born in Downing Street – where his father worked as private secretary to Lord North – he later attended Eton, joined the Light Dragoons and became a member of the Prince of Wales's set. This was unusual for a commoner, but Brummell was renowned for his wit and fine dress sense.

Beau Brummell

When he came into his inheritance, Brummell resolved to become London's best-dressed gentleman, a splendidly shallow ambition. Gentlemen, including the Prince, would visit this iconic dandy to see how he was dressed. His style was one of understated elegance rather than the gaudy attire of the Georgian gentry. He claimed that it took him five hours to dress and, as well as taking scrupulous care of his personal hygiene, he recommended that boots be polished with Champagne.

As the ultimate reflection of his posing vanity, the bow window at one of his clubs, White's, became known as the Beau window. It was where he liked to sit, allowing passers-by on St James's Street to admire his incomparable fashion sense.

> Unfortunately, Brummell's rudeness (a counterbalance to his undoubted charm) and overspending eventually led to his downfall and he had to flee to France.

7 THE BIRTH OF THE BODY-SNATCHERS

Address: St George's Gardens, Heathcote Street, WC1N 2NU.
Opening hours: 7.30am-dusk.
Transport: Russell Sq tube.

Originally meadowland, this site was acquired in 1713 to serve as the burial ground for two new churches – St George, Bloomsbury Way and St George the Martyr, Queen Square – and became something of a curiosity, as the first church burial ground in London not to be situated next to its church (or churches in this instance).

It also has the dubious distinction of having experienced the first recorded case of body-snatching (the theft of corpses for medical research and teaching). This was in 1777 and was an 'inside job', carried out by a gravedigger, John Holmes, and his assistant, Robert Williams, who stole the body of a certain Jane Sainsbury.

Williams was stopped in the King's Cross area carrying a sack. When he was asked what was in it, he apparently couldn't manage anything better than 'I don't know'. The sack was opened to reveal the trussed-up corpse of the unfortunate woman. Her coffin was subsequently discovered to have been buried only just below the surface of the ground, to facilitate the theft of her body.

Holmes and Williams were sentenced to six months in prison and a severe whipping 'from Kingsgate Street, Holborn for a distance of half a mile to the Seven Dials'.

BURLINGTON ARCADE'S UNUSUAL ORIGIN   8

Address: Burlington Arcade, W1.
Opening hours: Mon-Fri, 10am-7pm; Sat, 9am-6.30pm; Sun, 11am-5pm.
Transport: Green Park or Piccadilly Circus tube.

Beadles

type of litter discarded, oysters being a cheap, popular 'fast food' of the day. As well as a barrier to litter louts, Burlington Arcade proved to be a retail success and remains so today.

> The arcade is patrolled by the Burlington Arcade Beadles, who wear traditional uniforms, including Edwardian frock coats and gold-braided top hats.

This upmarket shopping arcade opened in 1819 and was the precursor of the mid-19th-century European shopping gallery, as well as the modern shopping centre. Ironically, though, the impetus for building it wasn't primarily commercial but rather more prosaic.

It was built on the orders of Lord George Cavendish, the younger brother of the 5th Duke of Devonshire. He'd inherited the adjacent Burlington House, which was originally a private Palladian mansion. Since 1874, it's been famous as the home of the Royal Academy of Arts and five learned societies: the Geological Society, the Linnean Society, the Royal Astronomical Society, the Royal Society of Chemistry and the Society of Antiquaries.

Cavendish had the arcade built on what had been the house's side garden in order to prevent passers-by from throwing their rubbish over the wall of what was to be his home. Oyster shells were apparently the most common

9   THE CATO STREET DECAPITATORS

Address: 12 Cato Street, W1.
Transport: Edgware Road tube.

Decapitation was a punishment reserved for traitors. In less civilised times, they would have been hung, drawn (disembowelled) and quartered.

The blue plaque on this mews cottage in Marylebone marks the 1820 meeting place of a group of anarchists who were planning a curiously grisly mass murder. The Cato Street Conspirators, as they became known, were angered by the economic depression of the time – caused in part by industrialisation disrupting Britain's previously settled agricultural society – and resolved to enact something akin to the French Revolution.

They planned to begin by assassinating the entire British Cabinet while it dined at Grosvenor Square! But the police were tipped off and raided the cottage, to find around 25 men armed with guns and swords – as well as two sacks in which to carry off the severed heads of senior ministers.

The leader of the anarchists, Arthur Thistlewood, killed one of the arresting police officers before escaping but was recaptured shortly afterwards and, along with four co-conspirators, was sentenced to death. The five were hanged at Newgate Prison before a large crowd (some of whom had paid large sums to secure a decent vantage point), before their bodies were lowered and decapitated one by one. This was apparently met with boos and hisses from the crowd.

THE CONFUSED STATUE   10

Address: Piccadilly Circus, W1.
Transport: Piccadilly Circus tube.

The Shaftesbury Monument Memorial Fountain sits at the southwest corner of Piccadilly Circus and dates from 1892-3. It commemorates the philanthropy of Lord Shaftesbury (1801-1885) and is topped by Alfred Gilbert's winged nude statue of an archer. This statue has become an icon of London, even used as the symbol of the Standard newspaper, but it's actually misnamed and as such attracts confusion. It's popularly thought to depict Eros, the Greek god of sexual love – and is invariably called Eros – but it's actually of Anteros, his twin brother, the Greek god of selfless love. This is much more in tune with the worthy, benevolent Lord Shaftesbury.

Another popular misconception concerns where the archer is aiming his arrow. It's generally thought to be pointing either up Shaftesbury Avenue, as a visual pun to celebrate the philanthropist, or towards Lord Shaftesbury's country seat

Eros

in Wimborne Saint Giles, Dorset. However, photographs dating from the 1890s show it pointing down Regent Street towards the Houses of Parliament. And in the years since, it's been moved a number of times to point in various directions, something of a scattergun (or scatter arrow) approach.

If you take a moment to study the statue, you'll see that Eros/Anteros is holding his bow the wrong way round.

Piccadilly Circus illuminated signs

11   DEFACED SCULPTURES

> **Address:** Zimbabwe House, 429 Strand, WC2R 0JR.
> **Transport:** Charing Cross tube/rail.

Zimbabwe House on the Strand was purchased by the government of what was then Rhodesia in 1935, having previously been the headquarters of the British Medical Association. The building's façade has caused controversy for over a century, due to the installation of 18 larger-than-life naked figures. They were designed by the American-born British sculptor Jacob Epstein (1880-1959) in 1905 and were regarded by many people as far too graphic.

The male and female figures symbolise the Ages of Man; interestingly, they take inspiration from classical Indian art rather than the European tradition. However, whatever their aesthetic merits, the windows of a building opposite were apparently replaced with frosted glass so that the shocking spectacle couldn't be seen by those inside.

After the Rhodesian government took over the building, a piece of masonry fell off one of the statues onto the street below, almost hitting a passer-by. It's alleged that this was used as a convenient excuse – the health and safety mandate of the time – to chisel away all the statues' extremities (including, of course, the 'rude' bits), which is why today the statues are oddly defaced.

> Epstein had a track record when it came to provoking opinion. His work was often controversial and he regularly challenged taboos about what was and wasn't appropriate for public artworks.

THE DIANA & DODI MEMORIAL   12

> **Address:** Harrods, 87-135 Brompton Road, SW1X 7XL (harrods.com).
> **Opening hours:** Mon-Sat, 10am-8pm; Sun, 11.30am-6pm.
> **Transport:** Knightsbridge tube.

The former owner of Harrods, Mohamed Al-Fayed, installed two memorials to his late son, Dodi, and Diana, Princess of Wales, on the premises of the iconic retailer. The first dates from 1998 and consists of photographs of the couple behind a pyramid-shaped display. It includes a ring that Dodi had bought the day before they died (which some claim was intended as an engagement ring) and a wine glass from Diana's last meal, which bears a smudge of her lipstick.

Mohamed Al-Fayed (left), Dodi & Diana (right)

to your taste, either robust-yet-touching tributes or tacky, mawkish and conspiracy-theory-pandering. Whatever your view, they're unique!

> The Diana and Dodi memorials fit in with the Egyptian-themed decor of parts of Harrods (Fayed was born in Egypt) which includes hieroglyphics and a sphinx.

The second memorial, from 2005, is a bizarre 3m-high bronze statue of the couple dancing beneath the wings of an albatross. It's called Innocent Victims, a reference to the fact that Mohamed Fayed refused to accept the verdict of misadventure concerning the deaths of Diana and Dodi. He claims they were killed unlawfully and cites various parties as being responsible.

The memorials were designed by Bill Mitchell – the Harrods' architect for many years – and are, according

13

THE DOWN STREET GHOST STATION

Address: Down Street Mews, W1.
Transport: Hyde Park Corner tube.

London has around 50 abandoned (or 'ghost') tube stations, i.e. rather more than many cities have in actual service! A number of the surface buildings of these curiosities can still be seen today and one of the most interesting is Down Street, just off Piccadilly in Mayfair. It lies between Green Park and Hyde Park Corner on the Piccadilly Line and opened in 1907. It was never a busy station – its two more popular neighbours had the advantage of escalators rather than lifts – and it closed in 1932.

It's famous for having been the temporary home of Winston Churchill's wartime Cabinet, being 70ft

Temporary wartime Cabinet rooms

below ground level and protected by large, strong buildings on the surface. It was used until the new, heavily-fortified Cabinet War Rooms on King Charles Street in Whitehall (under the Treasury building) were ready.

The Emergency Railway Committee was Down Street's main wartime occupant. However, Churchill's bath is apparently still in situ, as well as some of the telephones and other communication equipment. Above ground, the station building remains.

Down Street's familiar façade is by Leslie Green (1875-1908), a short-lived architect best known for his designs of iconic London Underground stations.

THE DUKE OF YORK'S SOARING COLUMN   14

> **Address:** Waterloo Place, SW1Y 4AR.
> **Transport:** Charing Cross tube/rail.

when he died he was £2m in debt, a vast sum in those days.

Nobody was willing to fund the building of a monument to him, and the only way to raise the money required (around £25,000) was to dock the pay of the entire British army for a day. The great height of the subsequent column – which dates from 1830-33 – caused wags to suggest that the duke was still trying to escape his creditors.

> Others claimed that Frederick's statue was put atop a tall column so that Londoners (and presumably the country's soldiers) wouldn't have to put up with the sight and smell of him.

There's something not quite right about the statue-topped column at Waterloo Place, between the two elegant terraces that comprise Carlton House Terrace. Perhaps it's that the column is curiously tall. It reaches 124ft and perched high on the top is a 14ft bronze statue by Sir Richard Westmacott of Prince Frederick, Duke of York (1763-1827), second-oldest son of George III.

Frederick became commander of the British Army and is the duke referred to disparagingly in the nursery rhyme *The Grand Old Duke of York*. He developed a (somewhat unfair) reputation for military dithering, but he was undoubtedly feckless with money:

15   DUMMY HOUSE FAÇADES

Address: 23-4 Leinster Gardens, W2
Transport: Bayswater tube.

All is not what it appears to be in this upmarket residential street in Bayswater. Look closely and you'll spot an architectural illusion that dates back to the 1868 opening of the section of what later became the Metropolitan Line between Paddington and Bayswater. It necessitated the demolition of two houses, 23 and 24 Leinster Gardens, which formed part of a long residential terrace.

Rather than leave a gaping hole in the upmarket terrace, it was decided to build a 5ft thick façade to match the houses on either side – partly for aesthetic reasons and partly to ensure the structural soundness of the neighbouring properties. The 18 'blackened' windows on the façade are painted on and the doors have no letter boxes, which rather gives the game away.

The space behind the façade was originally used by trains to 'vent off', i.e. to dispose of fumes, which was essential to help keep the railway's tunnels clear of steam and smoke (the original trains were steam-powered). Today, the track is part of the District Line and trains can be seen running under the dummy houses.

There's a tradition of pranksters sending pizza deliveries, religious representatives and taxis to the 'entrance' at number 24.

THE ELEANOR CROSS 16

Address: The Forecourt of Charing Cross Station, WC2N 5HS.
Transport: Charing Cross tube/rail.

were originally wooden, later replaced with elaborately decorated stone crosses.

The original Charing Cross monument was demolished in 1647 during the Civil War, on the orders of Parliament. This replica was built in 1865 and is the work of the architect E M Barry. It's apparently more ornate than the original and was renovated in 2010; a striking, attractive sight that deserves more attention than it usually receives.

The Eleanor Cross was originally located on land that is now Trafalgar Square, on the site occupied by a statue of Charles I (see The Statue that Shouldn't be There on page 64).

As you rush in or out of hectic Charing Cross Station, it's easy to ignore the large, ornate monument in the taxi-menaced exterior forecourt. It's a 150-year-old replica of a 13th-century structure, the original built by Edward I (1239-1307) in memory of his late wife, Eleanor of Castile (1241-90).

It was one of a dozen crosses erected to mark the resting places along the route of Queen Eleanor's funeral procession, from Lincoln, where she died, to Westminster Abbey. Erected between 1291 and 1294, the crosses

17 FALSTAFF'S CURSE & LONDON'S UNLUCKIEST SPOT

Address: Around Seven Dials and St Giles, WC2
Transport: Covent Garden or Leicester Square tube.

A small area of central London seems to be inherently unlucky. Oxford Street is its northern boundary, Charing Cross Road marks the west, Endell Street the east and Long Acre the south. Businesses and other enterprises situated here often struggle, despite the high volume of passing trade.

The Shaftesbury Theatre, for example, apparently has a higher number of flops than other West End venues. Centre Point, the large, famously ugly office block at the area's northwest corner, was for many years regarded as a mixture of architectural joke and planning disgrace, as very few people wanted to lease

Centre Point

space in it. A newer addition to the area (completed in 2010), the brightly coloured Central St Giles, is similarly unpopular.

Why this seeming lack of fortune in what should be a prime location? Some people claim that it dates back to 1417 when Sir John Oldcastle – said to be the model for Shakespeare's Falstaff, who appears in three of the writer's plays – was burned at the stake in St Giles on the orders of Henry V. A legend says that as the flames engulfed him, Sir John cursed the land and surrounding area.

One of London's first 'skyscrapers', Centre Point has been Grade II listed since 1995

Sir John Oldcastle

Shaftesbury Theatre

FANLIGHTS & FAMOUS RESIDENTS   18

Address: Buckingham Street, WC2.
Transport: Embankment tube.

There's a definite whiff of history in Buckingham Street, where the houses date from the second half of the 17th century. Many had different builders and are therefore in a variety of styles; most are now used as commercial premises and some are listed buildings.

There must be something in the air here because the street has attracted a number of famous residents, as the hefty sprinkling of blue plaques attests. The most significant commemorate two great literary Londoners, Samuel Pepys, who lived at number 12 from 1679-88, and Charles Dickens, who lived at number 15 in 1834. The latter property was destroyed in World War II and later replaced.

The quirkiest aspect of Buckingham Street can be seen above the door of number 18, the house opposite the Pepys plaque: an original fanlight window. These date back to the time before a modern postal system was introduced. Until the 1840 invention of the penny post, houses didn't have numbers, and the recipients of letters were instead identified by a copy of the pattern on the fanlight window above their door.

Samuel Pepys

Charles Dickens

Buckingham Street also features link snuffers: upturned cones attached to the railings. These were used to snuff out the 'link', a bare-flame torch made of hemp dipped in pitch, used by travellers in the days before street lighting.

19   THE FIRST PERSON ON TELEVISION

Address: 22 Frith Street, W1D 4RP.
Transport: Leicester Square or Tottenham Court Road tube.

Unlikely as it seems, a Soho bicycle delivery boy was the first person to appear on television, in 1926. John Logie Baird (1888-1946) had invented the first camera and television set at his Frith Street workshop. He needed somebody to sit in front of the camera while he went next door to see if the image appeared on the crystal screen.

Jim Wallder was working locally as a delivery boy for a grocer (he lived nearby, in Meard Street, off Wardour Street) and happened to call on Logie Baird with a delivery at just the right time to be the first face on television. In another version of the story, Logie Baird approached Wallder on Old Compton Street to request his help.

Other people have claimed the distinction of being the first person on television, but Wallder's tale is regarded as the most authentic. A blue plaque at 22 Frith Street marks it as the scene of this ground-breaking television event, although Logie Baird's electromagnetic system was later replaced by purely electronic systems. Today, the ground floor of the building is occupied by Bar Italia (see Bar Italia's Gangland Past on page 74).

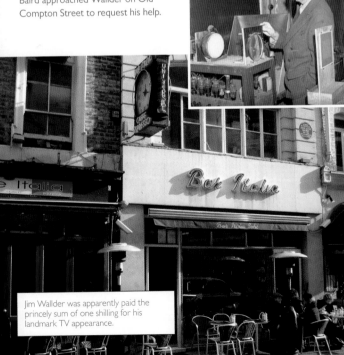

John Logie Baird

Jim Wallder was apparently paid the princely sum of one shilling for his landmark TV appearance.

THE GOVERNOR OF DUCK ISLAND   20

Address: St James's Park, SW1.
Opening hours: Daily, 5am–midnight.
Transport: St James's Park or Westminster tube.

This has a strong claim as London's most unusual job: the so-called governor of what is actually a bird sanctuary on a small promontory (it isn't really an island) in a lake (well, a canal) in a central London park. Birds have a long history in the area, having been kept in what is now St James's Park since 1612, when James I began the conversion of a once-swampy area into a formal garden.

Charles II continued the work and had it laid out like a French garden, including a canal which extended for around half a mile, most of the length of the park. The 'island' towards the east end of the canal became known as Duck Island, as it boasts a wide selection of birds, some of them gifts from abroad. Charles created the post of Governor of Duck Island (a sinecure with a modest salary) to give to his favourite, Charles St Denis, the seigneur de Saint-Évremond.

The 'post' of Governor of Duck Island was later revived by Queen Caroline (in 1733), who appointed a certain Stephen Duck to the position

(we're not making this up), adding another twist to the tale (or tail).

Charles St Denis had been exiled from France and is said to have introduced Champagne to Britain; it subsequently became the king's favourite tipple.

21 THE GRANT MUSEUM

Address: University College London, 21 University Street, WC1E 6DE (020-3108 2052, ucl.ac.uk/museums/zoology).
Opening hours: Mon-Sat, 1-5pm; Sun, closed.
Transport: Euston Square or Warren Street tube.

London's only remaining university zoological museum contains around 67,000 specimens covering the whole Animal Kingdom. It's a treasure trove for those in search of the curious and unusual and, as is often the case with London's museums, there are also a number of prurient curiosities, including a 3ft-long penis bone from a walrus and a rodent's barbed penis.

Strange, extinct species feature prominently, including an improbably designed giant deer whose massive antlers were almost twice as wide its height – little wonder it became extinct. There are also remains of the splendidly-named Quagga, an extinct South African zebra that sported fewer stripes than the familiar species; the Tasmanian Tiger or Thylacine, a dog-like carnivorous marsupial sometimes called the marsupial wolf, which died out in the '30s; and the iconic Dodo, that once lived on the Indian Ocean island of Mauritius – improbably, it was related to the pigeon.

Perhaps most unusually, the Grant Museum is home to the Blaschka collection of anatomically-perfect glass models of species that were hard to preserve – cephalopods, gastropods, jellyfish, sea anemones and sea cucumbers – made by noted 19th-century Czech jewellers.

One of the more bizarre and popular exhibits at the Grant Museum is a large jar crammed with whole preserved moles, 18 to be exact, possibly intended for dissection.

HARRIS'S LIST OF COVENT GARDEN LADIES   22

Address: Covent Garden, WC2.
Transport: Covent Garden tube.

As you wander around Covent Garden's trendy, tourist-choked fashion retailers, bars and restaurants, it might come as a surprise to discover that in the 18th century this was a well-known red-light district. So well-known, in fact, that this book – an annual directory of prostitutes working in the area – was published from 1757 to 1795.

specialities of between 120 and 190 prostitutes who worked in and around Covent Garden.

The author (or authors) wasn't known, but a Grub Street hack called Samuel Derrick is usually thought to have written the guide from 1757 until his death in 1769. He's said to have been inspired by the pimp Jack Harris, hence the book's title. After Derrick's death, the author is unknown. Eventually, public opinion began to turn against the sex trade and reformers petitioned for official action. The publishers of *Harris's List* were fined and imprisoned in 1795, the last year it was published.

Kitty Fisher, well-known 18th-century courtesan, by Joshua Reynolds

It was a small publication – conveniently pocket-sized – and was printed and published locally, retailing at two shillings and sixpence. In 1791, it was estimated that it sold 8,000 copies annually. Entries in the book described the physical appearance and sexual

The prose in *Harris's List* was quite spicy, lurid even, and some argue that the book was actually erotica, mainly designed for 'solitary sexual enjoyment'.

23   HUGGING BEARS & TEMPERANCE

> **Address:** Kensington Gardens, WC2.
> **Opening hours:** Daily, 6am-dusk.
> **Transport:** Lancaster Gate tube.

London's rapidly growing population, and the water was often contaminated, leading to severe outbreaks of sickness and, sometimes, death.

So the Association's fountains were much-needed and in time they became known as Temperance Fountains. Beer had long been the main alternative to water and was generally safer, but excessive alcohol consumption had a devastating effect on the urban poor and the drinking fountains were often sited opposite pubs to provide an alternative, teetotal thirst quencher. By 1936, the Association stopped building water troughs, as vehicles were replacing horses as beasts of burden, but more drinking fountains were built in parks, as here.

> Early drinking fountains were supplied with cups, but these were later replaced by jets of water, which were regarded as more hygienic.

An unusual drinking fountain near the northern edge of Kensington Gardens shows two bears embracing. It was installed here in 1939 (the original was stolen and replaced by a copy in 1970) to commemorate 80 years of the lengthily-titled Metropolitan Drinking Fountain and Cattle Trough Association. The Association had been set up in 1859 to provide free drinking water to the public, as well as water troughs for horses and cattle.

In the 19th century, water was provided by nine private companies, each with a geographic monopoly. However, the quantity supplied was invariably inadequate, especially for

Sunken Garden, Kensington Palace

THE HUNTERIAN MUSEUM 24

Address: The Royal College of Surgeons, 35-43 Lincoln's Inn Fields, WC2A 3PE (020-7869 6560, rcseng.ac.uk/museums/hunterian).
Opening hours: Tue-Sat, 10am-5pm.
Transport: Chancery Lane or Holborn tube.

Part of the Royal College of Surgeons, the Hunterian Museum is named after the 18th-century anatomist John Hunter, whose collection made up its original core, and has a number of curious and sometimes alarming exhibits.

Skeleton of Charles Byrne (left)

These include everything from an 18th-century sheep's gut condom (of a type memorably referred to as 'armour' by James Boswell, the lawyer, roisterer and biographer of Samuel Johnson) to a series of diseased penises, a faulty rectum and Winston Churchill's dentures.

One of the most poignant exhibits is the giant skeleton of the 7ft 7in Irishman Charles Byrne, who was exhibited as a fairground attraction during his lifetime. When Byrne fell ill in 1782, Hunter became obsessed with securing the body for his collection. Byrne feared becoming a permanent anatomical attraction and instructed that his corpse be put in a lead coffin, which he paid some fishermen to bury at sea. However, Hunter was ruthless, and after Byrne's death in 1783 he gave the fishermen £500 for the corpse. He boiled it in a copper vat to reveal the bones which he then exhibited, so poor Charles Byrne remains in death, as in life, a bizarre curiosity.

Researchers in the 20th century ascribed Charles Byrne's unusual height to a disorder of the pituitary gland.

25   THE INDIAN HIGH COMMISSION SWASTIKA

Address: India House, Aldwych, WC2B 4NA.
Transport: Temple tube.

the Nazi party flag, later becoming Germany's state flag. Thus the swastika has been greatly stigmatised, and is still outlawed in Germany and certain other places.

However, it remains a sign of good fortune in India, therefore it's apt – if initially unsettling – to see swastikas carved into the wall of the Indian High Commission in Aldwych: the front of the building displays a roundel with upright swastikas on either side of a tree.

Long before it was appropriated by Adolf Hitler, the swastika had been used by various cultures over thousands of years, invariably in a positive sense and often to bring good luck. The first archaeological evidence of swastika-like emblems is from the Indus Valley Civilisation (3,300-1,300BC), in what is now the northwest of the Indian subcontinent.

Swastikas were also used by a number of other ancient civilisations, including in China, Japan and parts of southern Europe, and in the early decades of the 20th century it was also seen in the west.

The Nazis adopted the swastika as a symbol in 1920, to denote the Aryan race (from the Sanskrit, arya, meaning 'honourable, respectable, noble', and promoting the Nazi idea of a Master Race). When Hitler came to power in 1933, a right-facing, 45° rotated swastika was incorporated into

THE LONDON BEER FLOOD   26

Address: 22 Great Russell Street, WC1B 3NN.
Transport: Tottenham Court Road tube.

What sounds like a joyful event was actually a tragedy. It occurred on October 17th 1814 when a huge vat of beer (containing around 135,000 gallons) ruptured at the Meux Brewery on Tottenham Court Road. This caused other vats to do the same, in a sort of domino effect, leading to around 325,000 gallons of beer gushing into the surrounding streets.

The resulting wave destroyed two homes and knocked down a wall of the Tavistock Arms pub (at 22 Great Russell Street, now a hotel), trapping a young employee, Eleanor Cooper, under the rubble. The flood spread around the slum area of St Giles where many families lived packed tightly together in basement rooms. These filled with beer and at least nine people died, either drowned or from their injuries; one victim is reported to have succumbed to alcohol poisoning.

The brewer was subsequently taken to court but the disaster was ruled to be an Act of God, leaving nobody responsible. It apparently took weeks for the strong smell of beer to fade from the area.

The flood was a bonus for some of the locals, who ran outside carrying kettles, pans and pots to scoop up as much free beer as they could.

27   LONDON'S MOST HAUNTED THEATRE

Address: Theatre Royal, Drury Lane, WC2B 5JF.
Transport: Covent Garden or Holborn tube.

Andrew Lloyd Webber's Grade II listed Theatre Royal boasts an interesting collection of ghosts. And 'boast' is the operative word, as the ghosts are thought to be benign, helpful even – their appearance is said to signal good fortune for a particular actor or production. The most famous ghost is the 'Man in Grey', who appears as an 18th-century nobleman, dressed in cape, riding boots and wearing a sword, his hair powdered under a tricorn hat.

It's claimed that he's the ghost of a man whose skeleton was found in a walled-up passage in 1848, a dagger still between his ribs. The theatre's history relates that in its early years a man bothering an actress was asked to leave the premises. He refused, a fight broke out and the man was killed – his body was walled up immediately to dispose of the corpse.

The ghosts of the actor Charles Macklin and clown Joseph Grimaldi (see Dancing on Grimaldi's Grave on page 218) are also thought to haunt the Theatre Royal. Macklin is said to appear backstage at the spot where he accidentally killed fellow actor Thomas Hallam in 1735 in a petty dispute over a wig (see The Contrite Memorial on page 81).

Grimaldi's ghost is reported to be a helpful apparition, guiding nervous actors about the stage.

Scene from Oliver!

MILLBANK PRISON   28

Address: Around Tate Britain and The Morpeth Arms, SW1.
Transport: Pimlico tube.

damp fostered disease to which many of the prisoners had reduced immunity due to their poor diet, and the huge prison's network of corridors was so extensive that even the warders got lost.

Today, a large circular bollard by the Thames stands where the prison's river steps used to be, with information provided on an inscription. Part of the

Odd though it seems today, the tourist-soaked area of Pimlico around Tate Britain was once the site of a vast prison, the Millbank Prison (or Penitentiary). One of the world's largest jails, it was in use between 1816 and 1890, during which it was a holding facility for convicts before they were transported to Australia.

There were problems with the building, which was constructed in the shape of a six-pointed star and built on seven acres of marshy ground. The

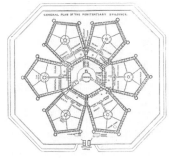

prison's perimeter ditch survives – it runs between Cureton Street and John Islip Street – while archaeological excavations at Tate Britain and Chelsea College of Art and Design have found significant sections of its external walls, courtyard watchtowers and drainage culverts. The Morpeth Arms pub has the remains of some of the prison cells in its basement, along with the ghost of a prisoner.

The prison provides the origin of the Australian slang term for an Englishman: Pom, i.e. Prisoner of Millbank.

29   THE MODEL FOR THE MINISTRY OF TRUTH

Address: Senate House, Malet Street, WC1V 7HU.
Transport: Goodge Street or Russell Square tube.

The building is undoubtedly monolithic, 210ft high and running to19 floors. It was designed by Charles Holden (1875-1960), who was responsible for a number of London Underground stations, and was planned as part of a much larger development, although World War II put paid to the rest of the scheme.

The structure's reception was mixed. Evelyn Waugh in *Put Out More Flags* described it as 'the vast bulk of London University insulting the autumnal sky'. Others have called it Stalinist or totalitarian due to its vast bulk and scale, something that Orwell obviously noted. However, the architect Eric Mendelsohn said he was 'very much taken and am convinced that there is no finer building in London'.

Senate House is the University of London's administrative centre and sits in the calm, academic surrounds of Bloomsbury. It's a large, Grade II listed, Art Deco pile – built 1932-7 – and was used by the Ministry of Information during World War II. It was also the inspiration for the Ministry of Truth in George Orwell's novel *1984*. Orwell was familiar with the building, as his wife worked there for the Ministry's censorship department.

Senate House was London's second-tallest building (after St Paul's Cathedral) when it was completed and one of London's first skyscrapers.

THE NATIONAL GALLERY   30

> **Address:** Trafalgar Square, WC2N 5DN (020-7747 2885, nationalgallery.org.uk).
> **Opening hours:** Daily, 10am-6pm (Fri to 9pm).
> **Transport:** Charing Cross tube/rail.

A number of curiosities lurk within the National Gallery's fabulous collection of paintings. Here are two of the more interesting:

The Ambassadors: This large, impressive painting dates from 1533 and is by Hans Holbein the Younger, a sometime court painter to Henry VIII. It's a portrait of two powerful young men: on the left, Jean de Dinteville, 29, French ambassador to England, and on the right his friend Georges de Selve, 25, Bishop of Lavaur.

Often overlooked in the foreground of the painting is its main curiosity: the distorted image of a skull, a symbol of mortality. It's an example of what's called anamorphosis or anamorphic projection, i.e. deliberate distortion. When viewed from a standpoint to the right of the picture, the distortion is corrected.

Mr and Mrs Andrews: Thomas Gainsborough's 1748 portrait of this land-owning couple shows off the landscape of their Suffolk estate; the background of changing weather and naturalistic scenery was a novelty at the time. The picture's main curiosity, however, is that Mrs Andrews' lap is unfinished. This wasn't laziness on Gainsborough's part – the space may have been left for a child for her to hold.

> In the top left of *The Ambassadors* a tiny crucifix peeps out from behind the hanging. Like the skull, it signifies an awareness of mortality and of where salvation supposedly lies.

31   NELL GWYN'S 'ROYAL' RESIDENCE

Address: 79 Pall Mall, SW1Y 5ES.
Transport: Green Park tube.

Nell Gwyn

owned by the Crown and the existing tenant was told to transfer the lease to her, which he did. However, she was unhappy at being merely a lessee and complained to the king. Her approach obviously worked, as in 1676 she was granted the freehold of the property, which remained in her family until 1693 and has been in private hands ever since.

Pall Mall gets its unusual name from a croquet-like game from Italy – *pallo a maglio*, i.e. ball to mallet –which became popular in London in Charles II's reign. The king himself could often be seen playing it with his mistresses in St James's Park.

The Pall Mall house that was once the home of Nell Gwyn (it's marked with a blue plaque accordingly) remains the only property on the south side of the thoroughfare that isn't owned by the Crown. This demonstrates the hold that she had over a king. Eleanor 'Nell' Gwyn (or Gwynn or Gwynne, 1650-87) was an actress and long-time mistress of Charles II. Her rags-to-riches story contains echoes of Cinderella and she's become regarded as something of a heroine.

In 1671 she moved into the townhouse at 79 Pall Mall. The property was

A CURSED OBELISK

Address: Embankment, WC2
Transport: Embankment tube.

Cleopatra's Needle is the popular, if inaccurate, name given to three Egyptian obelisks re-erected in London, New York and Paris in the 19th century. They have nothing to do with Cleopatra, however, being much older. She reigned from 51-30BC, whereas the London obelisk dates from the reign of Thutmose III (1,479-1,425BC).

It's made of red granite, is 69ft high and weighs 224 tons. Erected at Heliopolis around 1,450BC, it was moved to Alexandria by the Romans in 12BC. It toppled over into the sand some time later, thereby preserving most of its hieroglyphics from weathering. Presented to Britain in 1819 to commemorate Nelson's victory at the Battle of the Nile, it remained in Egypt until 1877, when its transport to London was sponsored, costing a substantial £10,000.

This is when rumours of the curse began. It was nearly lost in transit during a Bay of Biscay storm, during which six sailors died saving it. There are claims that mocking laughter and strange screams can be heard around the obelisk, which are thought to come from the lost sailors.

Occultist Aleister Crowley maintained that Rameses (who modified the original hieroglyphics around 1,300BC) had put a spell on the obelisk to preserve his soul inside it. Strange sounds said to come from within the needle are claimed to be the voice of Rameses.

Sphinx guarding obelisk

33   THE PET CEMETERY

> **Address:** Garden of Victoria Gate Lodge, Hyde Park, W2.
> **Transport:** Lancaster Gate tube.

Pet cemeteries are generally regarded as an American phenomenon, but London has a 130-year-old example of its own. The cemetery came about informally, as a favour granted in 1881 by the lodge keeper at Hyde Park's Victoria Gate. It continued to be used thereafter and eventually numbered some 300 graves.

The first burial was of 'Cherry', a Maltese Terrier, the pet of the children of a Mr and Mrs J Lewis Barned. The family often visited the park and had got to know the lodge keeper. When the dog died, they asked him if Cherry could be buried in the garden of the lodge, near the park that their pet had loved. The idea caught on with other locals and it gradually became an unofficial cemetery. Some of the inscriptions on the headstones are unstinting in their messages of love for the departed pets.

The lack of space and changing fashions saw burials decline after 1903 and only a handful have taken place since, the last being a regimental mascot in 1967. The cemetery isn't open to the public but you can view it through the park fence.

> The cemetery reveals some bizarre choices of names for pets, including Fattie, Freeky, Scum, Tally-Ho and, er, Nigger!

THE PETRIE MUSEUM OF ARCHAEOLOGY   34

Address: University College London, Malet Place, WC1E 6BT (020-7679 2000, ucl.ac.uk/museums/petrie).
Opening hours: Tue-Fri, 1-5pm; Sat, 10am-1pm; Sun, closed.
Transport: Euston Square or Goodge Street tube.

The Petrie Museum is named after the English Egyptologist Flinders Petrie and contains one of the world's great collections of Egyptian and Sudanese archaeology, dating from prehistory to the Islamic period. If the British Museum excels at Egyptology's 'big stuff', the Petrie's 80,000 objects focus on the minutiae and provides a vivid impression of what everyday life was like. It's full of curious exhibits, but the most obviously bizarre is the relief of the god Min in 'an excited state'.

Min originated in pre-dynastic Egypt (the 4th millennium BC) and is represented in various guises, but often, as here, in male human form with an erect penis. Unsurprisingly, he was the god of reproduction and male sexual potency, and was associated with a type of lettuce that produces latex when cut, probably because of its similarity to semen. At the beginning of the harvest, images of Min were taken to the fields and naked games were held in his honour, notably the climbing of a large tent pole, with obvious phallic symbolism. Christians regularly defaced Min's monuments and Victorian Egyptologists would only take photographs of the image from the waist up.

Other quirky objects include the oldest wills on papyrus; the oldest gynaecological papyrus; and socks and sandals from the Roman period (hopefully not worn together!).

35   A RIOTOUS DEVELOPMENT

Address: Red Lion Square, WC1R.
Transport: Holborn tube.

In the southeast of Bloomsbury, between Theobald's Road and High Holborn, is the site of one of London's more unlikely pitched battles. Red Lion Square was developed in 1684 by a controversial character called Nicholas Barbon (c 1640-98), although it proved to be a difficult exercise. Barbon was a man of many parts, an economist, surgeon and also a speculative builder, notorious for his dubious land purchases and shoddy buildings (some of which collapsed due to inadequate foundations).

Nicholas Barbon

When he proposed his development on the 17-acre Red Lion Fields site, the lawyers of adjacent Gray's Inn objected. They didn't want the countryside views they enjoyed to be blocked by buildings. As well as mounting a series of unsuccessful legal challenges against the development, the lawyers took direct physical action, including throwing bricks at the builders and fighting with them, temporarily halting construction.

In response, it's said, Barbon employed some of London's hardest-bitten thugs to protect his builders, and the next time the lawyers tried to interrupt the building work, they found the developer's heavies too much for them and were driven off. Today, only a few of the houses survive from Barbon's time.

To give Barbon his full — and truly bizarre name — he was christened Nicholas Unless-Jesus-Christ-Had-Died-For-Thee-Thou-Hadst-Been-Damned Barebon.

Bust of Bertrand Russell in Red Lion Square

A RIVER IN AN ANTIQUES CENTRE   36

Address: Grays, 58 Davies Street and 1-7 Davies Mews, W1K 5AB (020-7493 9344, graysantiques.com).
Opening hours: Mon-Fri, 10am-6pm; Sat, 11am-5pm (some of the dealers); Sun, closed.
Transport: Bond Street tube.

Based in an attractive, Grade II listed, Victorian terracotta building, Grays is an antiques centre with over 200 antique dealers. When the operation moved here in 1977, the basement in the mews part of the premises was found to be flooded by 6ft of water. The building is in the path of a running Thames tributary – the hidden River Tyburn – which rises at Shepherds Well in Hampstead and flows through Regents Park and the West End to the Thames via Davies Mews.

Before the 18th century, Oxford Street was called Tyburn Road and as the surrounding area became developed, the river was culverted and effectively disappeared from view. However, its clean, running water can still be seen today in the middle of the basement of Grays' mews site, where it has now been tamed and controlled.

Indeed, it's become a tourist attraction and is stocked with goldfish to add visual appeal. It's also said to be haunted by the ghosts of criminals hanged at the nearby Tyburn Tree.

Executions took place at Tyburn (modern Marble Arch) from 1196-1783, first from tree branches, subsequently from a gallows. Not all the hangings were successful, and the survivors were sometimes revived in the waters of the River Tyburn.

37   THE SATANIC COCKTAIL

Address: The Fitzroy Tavern, 16 Charlotte Street, W1T 2NA.
Opening hours: Mon-Sat, 11am-11pm; Sun, noon-10.30pm.
Transport: Goodge Street tube.

Crowley invented a suitably Satanic cocktail for the Fitzroy Tavern, the Kubla Khan Number Two – a heady blend of gin, vermouth and laudanum. The last is a tincture of opium, containing around 10 per cent powdered opium, which has been illegal in the UK since the 1920 Dangerous Drugs Act and today is classified as a Class A drug.

The Fitzroy Tavern can rightly claim to be one of London's great bohemian, intellectual and literary haunts, particularly from the '20s to the '50s. Its regulars included characters as diverse as visionary writer George Orwell, member of The Goons comedy troupe Michael Bentine, playwright and author George Bernard Shaw, artists Augustus John and Walter Sickert, Britain's last hangman Albert Pierrepoint, comedian Tommy Cooper and Welsh poet Dylan Thomas.

So famous was Fitzroy Tavern that it gave its name to the area: Fitzrovia. Nowadays, it's sometimes called the rather clumsy Noho, i.e. North Soho, to try to suggest a racier edge than it probably has.

Another of the hostelry's regulars, Aleister Crowley (1875-1947), was arguably its most notorious. He was a ceremonial magician, drug user (his 1922 novel was called *Diary of a Drug Fiend*), mountaineer, occultist, poet, self-publicist and bisexual erotic adventurer, who was sometimes dubbed The Great Beast 666.

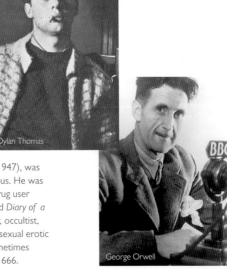

Dylan Thomas

George Orwell

SCOTLAND IN LONDON   38

Address: Great Scotland Yard, SW1.
Transport: Charing Cross tube/rail.

Scotland Yard is known worldwide as the headquarters of London's police force (though it subsequently moved to New Scotland Yard in Victoria and is due to move again in 2015). Interestingly, the name dates from a time when Scotland was a separate country.

local laws), this street off Whitehall, near Trafalgar Square, is still Scottish land in a sense. That's because bizarrely, after the Act of Union, nobody bothered to abolish Great Scotland Yard's foreign status. It's intriguing to reflect on this at a time when Scotland is shortly to vote on whether or not to become a separate country again.

It wasn't until the 1707 Act of Union that England and Scotland became joined as Great Britain. Before then, Scotland was a foreign country with a London embassy, and the name Great Scotland Yard harks back to that time. There were originally two other streets – Little Scotland Yard and Middle Scotland Yard – which no longer exist.

Because foreign embassies are deemed to be foreign territory (or rather, they are afforded special privileges, including immunity from most

Until the Act of Union, England and Scotland were totally separate countries, with their own customs, traditions and statutes. Evidence of that lingers even today; for example Scottish law and English law still differ in various significant ways.

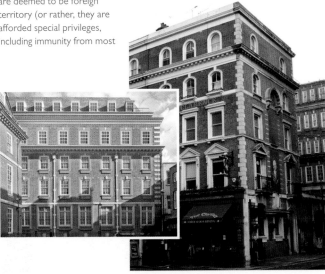

39 SIR JOHN SOANE'S MUSEUM

Address: 13 Lincoln's Inn Fields, WC2A 3BP (020-7405 2107, soane.org).
Opening hours: Tue-Sat, 10am-5pm.
Transport: Holborn tube.

The former home of the architect Sir John Soane is now a museum displaying the quirky and varied collection of art, archaeology and other intriguing items that he amassed. There's much that's curious and engaging here, including the following:

Casts: As in the British Museum (see page 20), Soane's collection reveals the early 19th-century craze for making casts of pieces from private and public collections. This allowed people to see copies of items they were unlikely ever to be able to travel to view. Unusual casts here include the rare face masks of the actress Sarah Siddons and the artist Thomas Banks; a collection of 91 casts made by Canova's workshop in Rome for the architect Lewis Wyatt, including casts from churches and temples and of sculptures; and a cast of the Henry Webber medallion 'The Judgement of Midas', which won him the Royal Academy Gold Medal for sculpture.

Seti I's Sarcophagus

Seti I's Sarcophagus: Dating from c 1,370BC, this is carved from a single piece of alabaster and is regarded as one of the finest Egyptian pieces outside Egypt. Soane bought it in 1824 for £2,000, after the British Museum had declined to pay so much.

Soane was so pleased to secure the Seti Sarcophagus that he threw a three-day party to celebrate. It was attended by 890 people, including Samuel Taylor Coleridge, Robert Peel and the then Prime Minister, Robert Jenkinson.

Riva degli Schiavoni, Canaletto

SKITTLES   40

Address: 15 South Street, W1.
Transport: Hyde Park Corner tube.

A blue plaque marks this Mayfair house as the home (from 1872 to 1920) of Catherine Walters (1839-1920), popularly known as Skittles and regarded as 'the last Victorian courtesan'. A courtesan isn't quite a prostitute but rather the mistress of a man (or men in this case) of rank, who receives gifts and/or payment for her 'attentions' — so still quite at odds with starchy Victorian morality.

Catherine Walters is thought to have acquired her nickname because she'd worked at a bowling alley in Chesterfield Street near Park Lane, skittles being the game that evolved into bowling. Skittles evolved also — becoming a woman of wealth and influence — and was rumoured to have numbered aristocrats, intellectuals, members of the Royal Family and senior politicians among her benefactors.

Skittles

Skittles' influential patrons are thought to have included the Prince of Wales (later Edward VII), Napoleon III and the Marquess of Hartington (later the eighth Duke of Devonshire).

Skittles managed to survive in her somewhat insecure line of work because she was renowned for discretion and loyalty, and never confirmed or denied rumours about her benefactors. This allowed her to enjoy a long and successful 'career'. She retired in 1890 and when she died in 1920, her estate was worth an impressive £2,764 19s and 6d.

CATHERINE WALTERS (Skittles) "The last Victorian Courtesan" lived here from 1872 until 1920

41   THE STATUE THAT SHOULDN'T BE THERE

Address: South of Trafalgar Square, WC2.
Transport: Charing Cross tube/rail.

The bronze equestrian statue of Charles I to the south of Trafalgar Square is a great survivor, as it should have been destroyed in the mid-17th century. It shows the king in a demi-suit of armour, but without a helmet, and was cast in the 1630s by Herbert Le Sueur on the orders of the 1st Earl of Portland. However, by the time of the English Civil War (1642-51) between Royalists and Parliament it had yet to be erected.

When the Parliamentarian forces won, the statue was sold to a Holborn metal smith called (appropriately) John Rivet (or Rivett). Parliament instructed

> KING CHARLES I
> 1625 - 1649
> THIS BRONZE STATUE WAS MADE IN 1633
> FOR LORD TREASURER WESTON
> BY HUBERT LE SUEUR
> IT WAS ACQUIRED FOR THE CROWN
> AND SET UP HERE IN 1675.
> THE CARVED WORK OF THE PEDESTAL
> BEING EXECUTED BY JOSHUA MARSHALL

him to destroy this Royalist symbol and recycle the metal. However, Rivet ignored the order and kept the statue on his premises (which must have been risky), producing some scraps

The bronze Charles I stares defiantly down Whitehall towards the Banqueting House, where he was executed in 1649.

of bronze as 'evidence' of having done as he was told.

After the Restoration in 1660, the statue was 'recovered' by the 2nd Earl of Portland – Rivet was apparently reluctant to give it up – and bought by the new king, Charles II. It was placed in its current spot in 1675 and marks the official centre of the capital, the point from which distances to London are measured.

STRAND LEY LINE

Address: The Strand, W1.
Transport: Charing Cross tube/rail.

If the mystical and pseudo-scientific aren't to your taste, you're advised to skip this and go to the next item. A ley line is an (alleged) alignment of a number of places of geographical and historical significance, including ancient monuments, natural ridges, religious and spiritual sites, and water-fords.

Leys were originally regarded as prehistoric in origin – usually Neolithic, i.e. New Stone Age – and were pathways used for trade and ceremonial purposes. More recently, modern pagans and New Agers have grafted on the idea that leys are sources of earth power or energy, possibly related to magnetic fields. There's no scientific evidence for this and an obvious criticism of ley lines is that, given the high density of prehistoric and historic sites in Britain, finding straight lines that 'connect' them is inevitable and has no mystical overtones.

The so-called Strand Ley is one of the best known in London. It runs, from west to east, from St James's Palace – St Martin's – St Mary-le-Strand – St Clement Danes – St Dunstan's – Bart's Hospital – Holy Well – Arnold Circus. Walk it and let us know if you become mystically attuned, or similar.

Another ley line is said to link such disparate London landmarks as the Tower of London, Houses of Parliament and Brompton Cemetery.

STRAND LEY, London

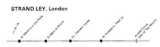

43   THE TEMPLE OF THE OCCULT

Address: 99 Gower Street, WC1.
Transport: Goodge Street tube.

This building on Gower Street was once the base of a most unusual and unnerving couple. It was here that Frank Dutton Jackson, a fake cleric, and his wife, Editha, established a temple of the occult in the early 20th century. Jackson dubbed himself 'Theo Horos' and debauched large numbers of young girls in mock religious ceremonies at the 'temple', having first set the scene with dimmed lighting and incense.

Editha

Jackson even told one girl – Daisy Adams – that he was Jesus Christ and that she would give birth to a divine baby. He and his wife were eventually brought to justice and he was convicted of procuring girls for immoral purposes and rape; he was sentenced to 15 years, Editha to seven.

Harry Houdini described Swami Laura Horos – one of the various nicknames and aliases that Editha used – as 'one of the most extraordinary fake mediums and mystery swindlers the world has ever known'. This is 'praise' indeed from the famous stunt performer and escapologist, who was a noted scourge of fake magicians and spiritualists.

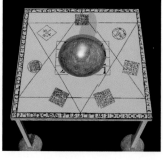

Number 99 Gower Street was occupied by The Spectator magazine from 1920 until the mid-'70s and now belongs to the Catholic Church, another religious institution that's had problems with sex scandals.

THE TEXAS EMBASSY IN LONDON   44

> **Address:** Pickering Place, off St James's Street, SW1.
> **Transport:** Green Park tube.

A plaque on narrow, wood-panelled Pickering Place in St James's reveals a little-known historical oddity. It marks the location of the Legation (a type of embassy) of Texas, which was a separate sovereign nation from March 2nd 1836 to February 19th 1846, after gaining independence from Mexico.

The plaque is on the north side of the premises of the noted wine merchant Berry Brothers and Rudd, as the Legation was located in the same building. St James's was a convenient location for an embassy, as ambassadors were presented to the Court of St James's at nearby St James's Palace.

> In the 18th century secluded Pickering Place was notorious for its gambling dens, bear baiting and duels.

Following independence, the Texans were worried about interference from Mexico and in a bid to protect itself from invasion, the Texas government sought to foster international ties.

It maintained a legation in London, as well as in Washington D.C. and Paris. However, attempts to curry favour with the British nearly backfired; when Texas sought to join the US in 1845 the British wanted to keep it independent, as a counterweight to the US. An independent Texas wouldn't have been financially viable, however, and today it's the second-largest of the 50 US states (after Alaska).

45   THORNEY ISLAND

> **Address:** Westminster Abbey and surrounds, SW1.
> **Transport:** Westminster tube.

As you wander the tourist-packed streets around Westminster Abbey, pause to consider the curious fact that the Abbey was originally built on an eyot (a small island) called Thorney Island. The island was formed by rivulets of the River Tyburn, which rose in Hampstead, ran through St James's and entered the Thames near the lowest point where it could be forded at low tide.

Thorney, or the Eyot of Thorns, is described in a charter of King Offa (reigned 757-796) as a 'terrible place'. This has amused generations of Westminster School pupils, who today comprise most of the permanent residents of what was the island. Over time, the monks cleared the brambles and by the time of Edward the Confessor (reigned 1042-66), it was apparently a 'delightful place, surrounded by fertile land and green fields'.

Today there's no sign that the area was once an island, as the land level has risen, the rivulets have been built over and the Thames has been embanked. The name, however, lives on in Thorney Street, behind the MI5 building.

> It's been suggested that Thorney Island was where King Canute (or Cnut, reigned 1016-35) demonstrated that even he couldn't hold back the tide.

UNLUCKY FOR ROCK STARS 46

Address: 9 Curzon Place, W1J.
Transport: Green Park tube.

In the '70s, flat number 12 in this Grade II listed, 18th-century building was owned by the American singer-songwriter Harry Nilsson. Strangely, considering the excessive world of rock and roll, the flat is a fairly nondescript pied-à-terre in Mayfair, a blue-blooded part of town. Nilsson often let friends stay in the flat when he was away and, bizarrely, both Mama Cass and Keith Moon died here.

Mama Cass

Mama Cass – real name Ellen Naomi Cohen – was a former member of the Mamas and Papas and died aged 32 in 1974. There have long been rumours that she choked to death on a ham sandwich but they're untrue. A heart attack killed her, brought on by prolonged obesity: at 5ft 5in, she weighed around 15 stone.

Keith Moon – the wayward but charming and talented drummer for The Who – died here in 1978, also aged 32. He was famously excessive in his behaviour, bingeing on drink and drugs, allegedly once driving his lilac Rolls-Royce into a garden pond used as a swimming pool. Ironically, he died from an overdose of a medicine prescribed to combat the symptoms of alcohol withdrawal.

Keith Moon

Harry Nilsson

Nilsson was upset by the deaths of two friends in his flat and subsequently sold it to Keith Moon's band mate Pete Townshend.

47 | THE YORK WATERGATE

Address: Embankment Gardens, WC2.
Transport: Charing Cross tube/rail or Embankment tube.

The York Watergate is curiously marooned in Embankment Gardens, sitting where the river used to meet its bank. It's an intriguing reminder of a time when a string of mansions lined the Strand and backed onto the Thames. The Watergate is all that remains of York House (as it later became), built as a London base for the Bishops of Norwich, probably in the 1230s.

In the 16th century, the house was acquired by Henry VIII; it took on its name when it was given to the Archbishop of York in 1586. Later, it was owned by racy royal favourite, the Duke of Buckingham.

The Watergate was built around 1625 to provide a place for the Duke to alight from his boat, but now sits 150 yards back from the river. This is due to the building of the Thames Embankment in the 1860s, a remarkable feat of Victorian civil engineering by Sir Joseph Bazalgette which reclaimed some 32 acres of riverside land, leaving the Watergate high and dry.

The Watergate is built of stone, in an Italianate style popular during the reign of Charles I. It has three bays, with bands on the side facing the river. The lions on top hold shields and anchors, symbols of the Duke of Buckingham's role as Lord High Admiral.

ALARMING SCULPTURES   48

Address: 33 Grosvenor Place, SW1.
Transport: Victoria tube/rail.

A rather bland '50s building on Grosvenor Place is much enlivened by six impressively disturbing sculptures. They're the work of sculptor Maurice Lambert (1901-64) and date from the time when the building was the headquarters of Associated Electrical Industries.

The sculptures depict angels triumphing over demons. The angels gaze into the distance, their faces calm, while inflecting grievous harm on the demons they hold: one tightens a rope around his demon's neck, another stabs his demon in the belly. It seems a clear representation of good versus evil, but the angels are obviously male and the demons are obviously female, so the sculptures might also be a comment on the battle of the sexes.

THE ARREST OF A DEAD MAN   49

Address: 14 Savile Row, W1.
Transport: Bond Street or Piccadilly Circus tube.

Savile Row is the home of traditional men's bespoke tailoring and number 14 is currently the outlet of the esteemed Hardy Amies. However, for a short time before his death, it was the home of the Irish-born playwright

Sheridan

and MP Richard Brinsley Sheridan (1751-1816).

Sheridan had serious financial problems in his later years which apparently continued even after his death. A visitor to see the corpse claimed to be a long-lost relative, eager to pay his respects, but when the coffin was opened, he revealed himself to be a bailiff and promptly arrested the dead man for non-payment of bills. And

Sheridan's funeral wasn't allowed to take place until his friends had paid his debts.

50   THE ATHENAEUM CLUB KERB STONES

Address: Waterloo Place, SW1.
Transport: Charing Cross tube/rail or Piccadilly Circus tube.

On the pavement outside one of the country's most famous gentlemen's clubs is an odd pair of kerb stones. They've been *in situ* since 1830 and were placed there to allow

the Duke of Wellington (1769-1852) to mount and dismount from his horse while visiting the club, of which he was a member.

The kerb stones were installed at the Duke's express request, the special treatment partly explained by the fact that he was Prime Minister at the time. He was thus favoured more than the club's many other famous members, who've included figures as diverse as Winston Churchill, Charles Darwin, Charles Dickens and Sir Arthur Conan Doyle.

Athenaeum Club

AUTHORITARIAN PERCY STREET   51

Address: Percy Street, W1.
Transport: Goodge Street tube.

Perhaps there's something in the air in this Fitzrovia street, as two of its properties have connections with authoritarian rule, one fictional, the other all too real. Number 4 was where Adolf Hitler's half-brother Alois (1882-1956) lived before World War I and it's claimed that the future Führer visited him here in 1912.

The upstairs room at number 18 was once home to George Orwell's second wife, Sonia Brownell (1918-80). They married in 1949 and Orwell (1903-50) apparently used the room as the model for the one in which Winston and Julia meet to conduct their doomed affair in his novel about the ultimate authoritarian state, *1984*. In the book, the room is above the duplicitous Mr Charrington's antiques shop.

THE BABY IN THE ROCK   52

Address: St Martin-in-the-Fields, Trafalgar Square, WC2N 4JJ (stmartin-in-the-fields.org).
Transport: Charing Cross tube/rail.

St Martin-in-the-Fields is a much-visited church that's well known as a concert venue, shop and award-winning café. It's on the northwest corner of Trafalgar Square and its external porchway is the unexpected site of a sculpture of a newborn baby that seems to emerge from a lump of rock. Indeed, the baby's umbilical cord disappears into the rock, which is a 4.5-tonne block of Portland stone.

It's called *The Christ Child* and is by Mike Chapman, designed to mark the millennium and dating from 1999. The Biblical inscription next to it is from John 1 14: 'In the beginning was the word and the word became flesh and lived among us.'

St Martin-in-the-Fields

53   BAR ITALIA'S GANGLAND PAST

Address: 22 Frith Street, W1D 4RF (baritaliasoho.co.uk).
Opening hours: Daily, 7am-5am.
Transport: Leicester Square or Tottenham Court Road tube.

This legendary, late-night/early morning Italian coffee bar on Frith Street is a reminder of the area's rugged past. The Soho of the '50s and '60s seems a curious and distant memory in today's upmarket district of trendy bars, destination restaurants and media offices. Indeed, it's become too safe and sanitised for some tastes.

But when Bar Italia opened in 1949 – it was one of London's first continental coffee bars – Soho was much sleazier and not just because of the sex trade. It also had a violent gang culture. A number of Bar Italia's regular customers had gang and mob connections, and notorious fights often erupted on the street outside.

BIRDCAGE WALK   54

Address: Birdcage Walk, SW1H.
Transport: St James's Park tube.

Duke of St Albans

later enlarged by his grandson, Charles II (1630-85, reigned 1660-85).

Unusually, only the Royal Family and the Hereditary Grand Falconer, the Duke of St Albans, were allowed to drive along the road until 1828, when it was opened to the public. The results of this were mixed: by the mid-19th century it had become notorious as a gay pick-up area.

This oddly-named street in Westminster is attractively sited, with verdant St James's Park to the north and the backs of the elegant buildings of Queen Anne's Gate to the south. Its unusual name comes from the Royal Menagerie and Aviary, which were located here in the reign of James I (1566-1625, reigned 1603-25) and

THE BISHOP'S MITRE   55

Address: Ely House, 37 Dover Street, W1S 4NJ.
Transport: Green Park tube.

Dover Street in Mayfair is noted for its Georgian architecture, clubs and art galleries. It also has a curiosity at number 37: a bishop's mitre in the middle of a roundel (a decorative medallion) above the first floor windows. The term mitre comes from the Greek for headband or turban and describes a tall hat traditionally worn by senior clergy

The mitre symbol marks the fact that this impressive townhouse was commissioned by Edmund Keene (1714-81), Bishop of Ely, as his palace. Built 1772-76 by renowned neoclassical architect Robert Taylor (1714-88), it has been described by Country Life magazine as 'one of the best houses in London'.

56   BLUE BALL YARD

Address: Stafford Hotel, SW1A 1NJ.
Transport: Green Park tube.

Blue Ball Yard is an attractive courtyard off St James's Street, with an unusual, almost rustic atmosphere, despite being right in the heart of London. It houses a block of 18th-century stables – built in 1742 – which were once part of the Royal Mews and stabled the aristocracy's thoroughbreds. Nowadays they shelter upmarket visitors of another sort, being an annexe of the adjacent Stafford Hotel.

The annexe buildings retain many original features, including split doors and wooden beams. The yard itself is one of two surviving 18th-century examples in the area, the other being Pickering Place (dating from 1731), which is across the road, next to the wine merchant Berry Brothers and Rudd.

THE BREATHING SCULPTURE 57

Address: Broadcasting House, 2-22 Portland Place, W1A 1AA.
Transport: Oxford Circus tube.

Also called the Memorial Sculpture, this eye-catching work sits on the roof of BBC Broadcasting House. It commemorates journalists and associated staff killed while working as BBC war correspondents. The sculpture is a 32ft glass and steel column, with a torch-like, inverted spire shape. It's the work of Spanish artist Jaume Plensa, the shape being based on the spire of the adjacent All Souls Church and the radio mast on the roof of Broadcasting House.

Breathing is etched with text and features a poem by James Fenton, poet and journalist. After dark, the sculpture glows, and at 10pm – during transmission of News at Ten – it shines a beam of light (reaching 900m) into the night sky for 30 minutes.

THE BUCKET OF BLOOD 58

Address: The Lamb & Flag, 33 Rose Street, WC2E 9EB (http://lambandflagcoventgarden.co.uk).
Opening hours: Mon-Sat, 11am-11pm; Sun, noon-10.30pm.
Transport: Covent Garden or Leicester Square tube.

The Lamb & Flag pub nestles in a short alleyway in Covent Garden, an area of upmarket retailers, creative types and tourists, therefore it's curious to discover that it has a rough and ready past. The poet John Dryden was beaten and nearly killed at the tavern in 1679. And at the beginning of the 19th century it became known as the Bucket of Blood because it staged illegal prize

fights in the back bar.

It's one of London's oldest pubs; the building dates from the 1630s and the first mention of a pub here is in 1772. It's also one of many London hostelries to claim Charles Dickens as a regular patron.

---

59   THE BUXTON MEMORIAL FOUNTAIN

Address: Victoria Tower Gardens, SW1.
Transport: Westminster tube.

The gardens next to the Houses of Parliament have an unusual, statuesque memorial and drinking fountain. It commemorates the 1834 emancipation of slaves in the British Empire and was commissioned by the MP and social justice campaigner Charles Buxton (1823-71). The memorial was dedicated to his father, Thomas Fowell Buxton (1786-1845), and to the abolitionists Henry Brougham, Thomas Clarkson, Stephen Lushington, Thomas Babington Macaulay and William Wilberforce.

Designed by the Gothic Revival architect Samuel Sanders Teulon (1812-73), it includes eight bronze figures representing different rulers of England from various eras. The gardens in which it sits are adjacent to the Victoria Tower, the south-western corner of the Palace of Westminster, which provides a majestic backdrop.

THE CADIZ MEMORIAL   60

Address: Horse Guards Parade, SW1.
Transport: Charing Cross tube/rail.

There's a curious memorial in the southeast corner of Horse Guards Parade. It consists of a large French mortar mounted on the back of a cast-iron Chinese dragon, and commemorates the lifting of the Siege of Cadiz in Spain in 1812 by forces led by the Duke of Wellington against the French.

The impressive French mortar was given to the Prince Regent by the Spanish government as a gesture of thanks. It could apparently propel a shell nearly three miles which was an

unheard of distance at the time. The mortar is mounted on a base built at the Royal Arsenal in Woolwich in 1814.

Horse Guards Parade

CAFÉ DIANA   61

Address: 5 Wellington Terrace, W2 4LW (020-7792 9606).
Opening hours: Daily, 8am-11pm.
Transport: Notting Hill Gate tube.

This neighbourhood café in Bayswater has become something of a shrine to the late Diana, Princess of Wales (1961-97). Its walls are extensively decorated with photographs and memorabilia, which is

fascinating to some people but a touch creepy to others. Apart from this, it's a fairly standard local café, friendly and full of light owing to its large windows; a few outdoor tables provide a good spot for people watching.

Apparently, Diana used to visit the café occasionally when she was in residence at Kensington Palace. It's a good place to take fans of the Royal Family and, perhaps, visiting foreign friends, although prices are a bit above average due to the novelty factor.

62   CAXTON HALL

Address: 10 Caxton Street, SW1H 0AQ.
Transport: St James's Park tube.

This elegant, striking, Grade II listed building has, alas, been a block of luxury apartments since 2006, but it has a more interesting and unusual past as an upmarket registry office. It was designed in 1878, in an ornate Francis I style with red brick and pink sandstone, by William Lee and FJ Smith. It was known as Westminster City Hall and was the venue for a number of high-profile weddings.

Among the many notables married here were figures as diverse as Donald Campbell (of *Bluebird* fame), Joan Collins, Anthony Eden (to Clarissa Churchill, Sir Winston's niece), Diana Dors, Adam Faith, Barry Gibb, George Harrison, Yehudi Menuhin, Roger Moore, Peter Sellers, Ringo Starr, Elizabeth Taylor and Orson Welles.

THE CITADEL   63

> **Address:** Horse Guards Parade, SW1.
> **Transport:** Charing Cross tube/rail or Westminster tube.

This curious lump of a structure was built for the Admiralty in 1940-1 by WA Forsyth to house and protect communications systems in the event of a German invasion. Under its leafy façade – the building is covered in Russian vine to soften its harsh appearance – it's made of compressed pebble and flint blocks and, iceberg-like, extends deep underground.

Churchill described it as 'the vast monstrosity which weighs upon the Horse Guards Parade' and said of it 'the demolition of whose 20-ft-thick steel and concrete walls will be a problem for future generations when we reach a safe world'. However, it survives in this still-unsafe world, used today by the Ministry of Defence. Underground passages are said to connect it with other parts of Whitehall.

THE CONTRITE MEMORIAL   64

> **Address:** St Paul's Church, Bedford Street, WC2E 9ED (020-7836 5221, actorschurch.org).
> **Opening hours:** Mon-Fri, 8.30am-5pm; Sat, varies, depending on events; Sun, 9am-1pm.
> **Transport:** Covent Garden tube.

A memorial in a Covent Garden church shows an actor's contrition over a man's death. Charles Macklin (c 1698-1797) killed Thomas Hallam, a fellow actor, at the Theatre Royal in 1735, during a

Charles Macklin

petty quarrel over a wig that Macklin had worn in a farce and which Hallam had taken. Macklin lunged at Hallam with his stick, which entered the man's left eye and killed him.

Macklin was found guilty of manslaughter, although he

seems to have escaped punishment, as he soon resumed acting. However, his memorial tablet at St Paul's – known as the Actors' Church due to its long association with the theatrical community – demonstrates his remorse, showing a dagger piercing the eye of a theatrical mask.

65 A CONVERSATION WITH OSCAR WILDE

Address: Adelaide Street, WC2N.
Transport: Charing Cross tube/rail.

This unusual sculpture shows Oscar Wilde rising from a sarcophagus while smoking a cigarette and inviting passers-by to sit down and have a chat. The base carries a famous quote from the writer's play *Lady Windermere's Fan*: 'We are all in the gutter, but some of us are looking at the stars.'

The statue by Maggi Hambling was installed in 1998 and is made of green granite and bronze. It was unveiled by comedian and actor Stephen Fry, who played the writer in the 1997 film *Wilde*. Oscar's cigarette has been repeatedly stolen, to the annoyance of Hambling, an ex-smoker who supports people's freedom of choice to smoke or not.

Oscar Wilde

We are all in the gutter, but some of us are looking at the stars.

THE CURFEW BELL   66

Address: Gray's Inn, 5-7 South Square, WC1R 5ET.
Transport: Chancery Lane tube.

Gray's Inn Gardens

At 9pm each night an ancient ritual is enacted at Gray's Inn, a centre of the legal profession since the 14th century. It's the ringing of a bell to mark the London curfew, a tradition that's been maintained with almost religious zeal.

The term comes from the Norman French *couvre le feu* – put out your fire – and was instigated by William the Conqueror (1028-87). It wasn't rung to tell people to stay indoors but rather to extinguish all candles and fires, as fire was a constant threat in a city with many timber and thatched buildings. Dozens of curfew bells would have been rung in medieval London. Today, there are just two, the other being at the Tower of London.

A DRINK IN PRISON   67

Address: The Courthouse Hotel Bar, 19-21 Great Marlborough Street, W1F 7HL (020-7297 5555, courthouse-hotel.com).
Opening hours: Mon-Sat, 11-1.30am; Sun, 11am-11pm.
Transport: Oxford Circus tube.

The Grade II listed Courthouse Hotel is situated in what was once the Great Marlborough Street Magistrates Court, where in 1835 Charles Dickens worked as a court reporter for the *Morning Chronicle*. The hotel's

bar is in the court's former cell blocks, which would no doubt have pleased Dickens who was an enthusiastic patron of London's drinking establishments.

Prisoners were held in the cells before and after court

appearances, and included such notable figures as Oscar Wilde and Mick Jagger. The three original holding cells remain intact – including their secure doors – and can each seat up to eight drinkers. They're available for private use and can be booked in advance.

68   THE DRUID'S LEGACY?

Address: Tothill Street, SW1.
Transport: St James's Park tube.

Modern pagans and New Agers are keen to demonstrate that the druids once had a presence in London. Tothill Street, they claim, is named after *tot*, meaning sacred mound. The mound has apparently all-but disappeared – it's supposed to have been at nearby Tothill Fields, surviving until Elizabethan times – but is said to have been an ancient place of assembly before the Saxon conquest of the 6th century.

Some say it's no coincidence that the surrounding area is the seat of the British government, as it's been a significant location for thousands of years. Another 'sacred' mound sits under Tower Hill, another important base for the British establishment (see The Tower of London on page 132).

EGYPTIAN STREET FURNITURE   69

Address: Victoria Embankment, WC2.
Transport: Westminster tube.

The ancient obelisk Cleopatra's Needle (see A Cursed Obelisk on page 55) arrived in London in 1878, after a difficult journey from Egypt, during which it was almost lost at sea. Before its arrival, the scene was set by the installation of some eye-catching, Egyptian-themed benches along the stretch of the Thames where it was to be erected.

Made of cast iron and dating from the mid-1870s, these unusual seats feature either sphinxes or camels at each end; the latter seated and laden. They were designed by George Vulliamy (1817-86), architect of the Board of Works, who was also responsible for the lampposts along this section of river and the Needle's pedestal and sphinxes.

THE FORTNUM & MASON CLOCK   70

Address: 181 Piccadilly, W1A 1ER.
Transport: Piccadilly Circus tube.

The ornate clock at upmarket grocer Fortnum & Mason is one of London's most singular, although it isn't as old as it looks, dating only from 1964. The then owner W Garfield Weston commissioned the clock to be installed above the main entrance as a tribute to the store's founders,

W Garfield Weston

William Fortnum and Hugh Mason, who established the business in 1707.

Every 15 minutes, the clock plays a selection of airs on 18 bells, but the main event takes place on the hour, when 4ft-high models of the founders emerge and bow to each other, accompanied by chimes and 18th-century music. They're dressed in period costume – one carries a candelabrum, the other a loaded tea tray – and they come to check that standards are being maintained!

71   FOSSILS AT THE ECONOMIST

Address: The Economist Buildings, 25 St James's Street, SW1A 1HG.
Transport: Green Park tube.

Regarded as a landmark of '60s architecture, this small development – which is in the 'tower and plaza' format – sits surprisingly comfortably in the 18th-century surrounds of St James's. Intriguingly, it's of interest to people wanting to see fossils as well as noted buildings.

The Grade II listed development is faced with a nougat-like type of Portland stone called roach. Portland stone is a limestone from the Jurassic period, quarried on Dorset's Isle of Portland, and roach is a fossil-rich type of Portland stone, containing generous numbers of small marine fossils from around 140m years ago. Plenty are in evidence here when you examine the buildings' façades.

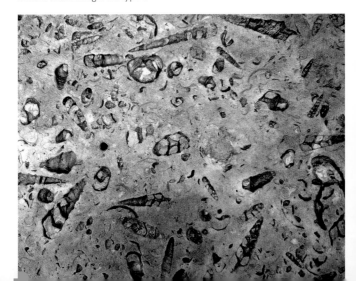

GARDEN POETRY   72

Address: Queen Square Gardens, WC1N 3AJ.
Opening hours: 7.30am-dusk.
Transport: Holborn or Russell Square tube.

Queen Square was laid out in 1716 and has a couple of quirks. The lead statue at the northeast corner is from around 1775. It's of a crowned queen in royal robes, but exactly which queen is uncertain: it could be Queen Charlotte, wife of George III, or it might be Queen Anne or Mary II.

There's poetry here, too. A memorial urn to commemorate the Queen's Silver Jubilee has the following inscriptions by the poets Ted Hughes and Philip Larkin respectively: 'A nation's a soul, A soul is a wheel, With a crown for a hub, To keep it whole'; and 'In times when nothing stood, But worsened or grew strange, There was one constant good, She did not change'.

A GLAMOROUS ELECTRICITY SUBSTATION   73

Address: Brown Hart Gardens, Duke Street, W1K 6WP.
Transport: Bond Street tube.

This electricity substation is unusually glamorous for such a functional building and is Grade II listed accordingly. Built in 1905 to C Stanley Peach's Baroque design, it's made of Portland stone and has a pavilion and steps at either end. There's also a balustrade, while Diocletian windows along the sides provide light for the galleries of the engine rooms.

Another notable feature is the extensive, 10,000ft² public garden that sits on top of the substation, in the paved Italian style, with trees in tubs. It closed for refurbishment in 2012 and reopened in 2013 with the addition of the Garden Café.

74   THE GOLDEN ARM

Address: Manette Street, off Greek Street, W1D
Transport: Tottenham Court Road tube

Manette Street in Soho was originally called Rose Street, taking its current name in 1895 after the character Dr Alexandre Manette in Charles Dickens' 1859 novel, *A Tale of Two Cities*. In the early 18th century Soho had a large French population – it was sometimes known as Petty France – and Dickens chose it as the location for Dr Manette's lodgings during the French Revolution.

In Victorian times, Manette Street was the site of a goldbeater who used cast-iron mallets to make gold leaf. Dickens describes this in the novel, likening it to being beaten by a giant with a golden arm. Hence the eye-catching golden arm sticking out of the wall above the entrance to Goldbeaters House, near the Pillars of Hercules pub.

GOLDEN INSECTS   75

Address: The London School of Hygiene and Tropical Medicine, Keppel Street, WC1E 7HT.
Transport: Goodge Street or Russell Square tube.

Keppel Street is in the heart of leafy, academic Bloomsbury, near the British Museum and Russell Square. Part of the University of London is housed here in an attractive Art Deco building dating from 1929. Designed by P Morley Horder and O Verner Rees, it's decorated with several unusual, eye-catching golden insects.

It's the home of the London School of Hygiene and Tropical Medicine, a public research university and leading postgraduate institution specialising in public health and tropical medicine. The gilt insects adorning the first floor window balconies are, appropriately, of creatures that do harm to man (usually as vectors of disease), including a bedbug, flea, fruit fly, louse, mosquito and tick.

HAIR-RAISING BURIALS   76

Address: St Anne's Churchyard, 55 Dean Street, W1D 1AF (020-7437 8039, stannes-soho.weebly.com).
Transport: Leicester Square tube.

The churchyard of St Anne's in Soho is raised around 8ft above street level – the consequence of having been the final resting place of over 60,000 souls since 1695. By the mid-19th century it had become notorious: the air was foul

with the stench of decaying bodies, buried too shallow and close together.

Joseph Rogers, a doctor called to treat cases of fever in the surrounding slums, found that liquid from decomposing corpses was seeping into the buildings' cellars and had contaminated a nearby well. Burials ceased here in 1853 when the Parish secured space at Brookwood Cemetery in Surrey. Since 1894, the churchyard has been a park, a hallowed spot of Soho greenery.

77 HALICARNASSUS IN LONDON

Address: St George's Church, Bloomsbury Way, WC1A 2SA (020-7242 1979, stgeorgesbloomsbury.org.uk).
Transport: Holborn or Tottenham Court Road tube.

The tower of this Nicholas Hawksmoor church is a piece of the Near East in London. Built 1716-31 and Grade II listed, the tower is influenced by Pliny the Elder's description of the Mausoleum at Halicarnassus (modern Bodrum in Turkey), a tomb built 353-350BC for Mausolus, a provincial governor in the Persian Empire. It was one of the Seven Wonders of the Ancient World.

The tower is stepped like a pyramid and topped by a statue of George I in Roman dress, posing as St George. It's also adorned with statues of fighting lions and unicorns, symbolising the recent end of the First Jacobite Rising. The church portico also has an eastern influence, based on the temple of Bacchus in Baalbek (in modern Lebanon).

THE IMPERIAL CAMEL CORPS STATUE

Address: Victoria Embankment Gardens, WC2.
Transport: Embankment tube.

An oddly-undersized statue in Embankment Gardens is a memorial to the unusual, now-forgotten Imperial Camel Corps Brigade. A camel-mounted infantry brigade raised for service in the Middle East during World War I, the Corps was active from January 1916 until May 1919.

The brigade grew to become four battalions, one each from Great Britain and New Zealand, and two from Australia; it comprised around 4,150 men and 4,800 camels. The memorial shows an infantryman mounted on a camel set atop a stone plinth with commemorative bronze plaques. The names of around 350 members of the brigade who died during the war are listed.

JETÉ

Address: 46-57 Millbank, SW1.
Transport: Pimlico tube.

An intriguing statue sits near Tate Britain on the north bank of the River Thames, opposite the monolithic MI6 building. It's by the Italian-born British sculptor Enzo Plazzotta (1921-81) and dates from 1975. An elegant bronze, it's modelled on the ballet dancer David Wall (1946-2013), who's in mid-leap and seemingly aiming at the Thames, while he looks skywards. The statue is cleverly anchored to its pedestal by a trailing cloth tied to the dancer's waist.

Jeté is French for 'thrown' and is a ballet leap in which the dancer's weight is transferred from one foot to the other. The *grand jéte* is a broad, high leap with one leg stretched forward and the other back, like a 'split' in the air, as here.

80   JUSTICE FOR THE HOMELESS

> **Address:** The Royal Courts of Justice, Strand, WC2A 2LL.
> **Transport:** Temple tube.

The vast, sprawling complex of the Royal Courts of Justice was built on a 6-acre site where 450 homes were demolished to make way for it. So it's nicely ironic that a homeless man was once found living in the Courts' basement, having been there for several years, happily undetected.

The rambling Gothic Revival pile was completed in 1882 and has over 1,000 rooms, explaining why it was relatively easy for him to remain concealed. Its construction was primarily paid for with money left by those dying intestate (without a will) – around £700,000 – a more tenuous connection with those who fall slightly outside the mainstream of society.

LAMB'S CONDUIT STREET 81

Address: Lamb's Conduit Street, WC1N.
Transport: Holborn or Russell Square tube.

This is another of London's curiously-named streets, although it has nothing to do with veterinary science. It's named after William Lamb who, in 1577, improved an existing conduit (channel) to bring clean water down from Holborn as an act of charity. He also provided 120 pails for poor women.

Today, it's an attractive shopping street with an elegant, Grade II listed Victorian pub, also named after Lamb. The pub retains its frosted glass snob screens, which were popular in the 1890s to hide customers from the landlord and drinkers in the other bars. The conduit itself no longer exists but there's a statue of a woman with an urn on a drinking fountain in Guilford Place at the top of the street.

A LAST DRINK FOR THE CONDEMNED 82

Address: St Giles-in-the-Fields, 60 St Giles High Street, WC2H 8LG.
Opening hours: Mon-Fri, 8.15am-6pm.
Transport: Tottenham Court Road tube.

St Giles was the last church on the route between Newgate Prison and the gallows at Tyburn, where the church wardens paid for the condemned to have a final drink at the pub next door, The Angel, before they were hanged.

The current church, Grade I listed, was built 1731-3 in the Palladian style, but there's been a church on the site since at least 1101. The custom of the last drink is thought to date from the early 15th century, and became known as the 'St Giles Bowl'.

There's a remnant of this in the name Bowl Yard, which is on the south side of St Giles High Street. And there used to be a nearby pub called The Bowl.

83 A LEGAL BROTHEL

Address: The Silver Cross, 33 Whitehall, SW1A 2BX (020-7930 8350).
Opening hours: Mon-Sat, 11am-11pm; Sun, noon-10.30pm.
Transport: Charing Cross tube/rail.

There's potentially rather more on offer at this pub than a pie, a pint and a chat about the football. It was granted a licence to operate as a brothel by the unfortunate Charles I (1600-49) and this has never been revoked.

Although the Silver Cross is now just a regular hostelry, its days as a brothel are marked in a curious way – with a ghost, thought to be that of a young prostitute who was murdered here. She apparently makes her presence felt by uttering strange noises and causing pictures to fall off the wall. People have also reported feeling strangely cold and a sensation of being watched.

LONDON'S CAMPEST STATUE   84

Address: Trafalgar Square, WC2.
Transport: Charing Cross tube/rail.

In the front 'garden' (it's more of a strip of grass) of the National Gallery to the north of Trafalgar Square is a fine statue of James II (1633-1701). It's the work of England's pre-eminent wood carver, Grinling Gibbons (1648-1721) – or one of his pupils – and forms a pair with the statue of Charles II (James's brother and predecessor) at the Royal Hospital, Chelsea; both were commissioned by Tobias Rustat.

The statue of James is surely London's campest, with its left arm on hip, the right pointing down and the legs posed in a way a modern model would approve of. Moreover, he's dressed as a Roman Emperor, toga and all, and wears a suitably effete expression on his face.

LONDON'S FIRST PAVEMENTS   85

Address: Craig's Court, SW1.
Transport: Charing Cross tube/rail.

A small, obscure alley near Trafalgar Square is where London's pavements were first conceived. Although we take them for granted today, until the mid-18th century pavements didn't exist. Instead, carriages, carts, horses and pedestrians all jostled each other on the dirt roads that ran right up to the front of buildings.

In the 1760s, Arthur Onslow, Speaker of the House of Commons, found himself in an embarrassing position when trying to get his carriage into Craig's Court: it became stuck. His predicament would have been alleviated had there been footways to separate the road

Arthur Onslow

from surrounding buildings. Soon after, in a splendidly self-interested way, he was instrumental in passing a bill to introduce pavements to London.

86 LONDON'S LONGEST PUB NAME

Address: I Am the Only Running Footman, 5 Charles Street, W1J 5DF (020-7499 2988, therunningfootmanmayfair.com).
Opening hours: Mon-Fri, 7.30am-11pm; Sat, 9.30am-11pm; Sun, 9.30am-10pm.
Transport: Green Park tube.

It says The Only Running Footman on the sign outside this pub just off Berkeley Square in Mayfair but the full name is actually 'I Am the Only Running Footman'. It's London's longest pub name and England's second-longest. Behind the verbose moniker lies an interesting snippet of history.

It dates from the time when aristocrats' carriages were preceded by manservants on foot whose duties included clearing a route through the streets, which were often cluttered with animals, carts and people. They carried a stick to help clear the way, and also paid toll-keepers and carried lights after dark. The good and the great of Mayfair employed a lot of these servants, who used to meet at this pub.

LONDON'S MOST CHATEAU-LIKE HOTEL   87

Address: The Hotel Russell, Russell Square, WC1B 5BE (020-7837 6470, principal-hayley.com/ph-hotels/hotel-russell.aspx).
Transport: Russell Square tube.

Russell Square is the site of one of London's most unexpectedly flamboyant hotels. It was built in 1898 by the architect Charles Fitzroy Doll (1850-1929), who specialised in designing hotels, and is based on the early 16th-century Chateau de Madrid, which was on the edge of the Bois de Boulogne near Paris.

Grade II listed, it's unusually clad in brick and distinctive, decorative thé-au-lait (tea with milk) terracotta. The sculptor Henry Charles Fehr (1867-1940) was responsible for the life-size statues of four British queens above the main entrance: Elizabeth I, Mary II, Anne and Victoria. The hotel's restaurant – named after the building's architect – is almost identical to that on the Titanic, which Doll also designed.

LONDON'S MOST INTERESTING DOOR   88

Address: Nobel House, 9 Millbank, SW1.
Transport: Pimlico tube.

What used to be the headquarters of ICI (Imperial Chemical Industries) was built in 1928-31 by Sir Frank Baines in the neoclassical style and is Grade II listed. However, it's the unusual, striking doorway and its surrounds that draw the eye, the work

of William Bateman Fagan (1860-1948).

The massive bronze doors are surrounded by architectural carvings with a maritime theme – including mermen – made of granite. There are six relief panels on each door, showing advances in technology.

Stone Age technologies are on the left – including people dragging a log down to the river, to be made into a boat – with modern ones on the right.

LONDON'S OLDEST OUTDOOR STATUE

Address: Sotheby's, 34-35 New Bond Street, W1A 2AA.
Transport: Tottenham Court Road tube.

SEKHMET
18TH DYNASTY CIRCA 1320 BC

An aged curiosity is mounted above the main entrance to the premises of the esteemed auction house Sotheby's: an ancient Egyptian black basalt effigy of Sekhmet, the lion goddess. It's eye-catching but often missed because it tends to be obscured by the flag flying above it.

The statue dates from around 1,320BC and has been Sotheby's mascot of sorts since the 1880s, when it was sold at auction for £40 but never collected by the buyer. Sekhmet's name means 'She who is powerful' and the goddess is associated with destruction and warfare, but also protection. Sotheby's has certainly prospered under the gaze of London's oldest outdoor statue.

THE LONDON SILVER VAULTS

90

Address: 53-64 Chancery Lane, WC2A 1QS (020-7242 3844, thesilvervaults.com).
Opening hours: Mon-Fri, 9am-5.30pm; Sat, 9am-1pm; Sun, closed.
Transport: Chancery Lane tube.

home to a number of silver dealers. So secure are the underground vaults that even a direct hit by a bomb to the building above during World War II didn't damage the vaults at all – although the building was destroyed. There's apparently never been a robbery here.

In the heart of London's legal district and close to Hatton Garden, centre for the capital's jewellery trade, is this curious, labyrinthine vault of treasures. It describes itself as 'the home of the world's largest retail collection of fine antique silver' and includes such oddities as a full-size silver armchair.

It opened as the Chancery Lane Safe Deposit in 1876, renting out strongrooms, and soon after became

LONDON'S SMALLEST HOUSE

91

Address: 10 Hyde Park Place, W2.
Transport: Marble Arch tube.

Opposite Hyde Park is a property so small you have to look twice to check that it's actually there. It's a little over a metre (3ft 6in) wide and was built in 1805, probably to block a

passageway to St George's graveyard and to serve as a watch house. Both measures were necessary to protect the burial ground from grave robbers, who were commonplace in London at the time.

The house is now part of Tyburn Convent and the ground floor is just a passageway behind a front door, while the first floor houses a miniscule bathroom. It's one and only tenant was a certain Lewis Grant Wallace.

92 MEDIEVAL OR MODERN?

Address: The Cittie of York, 22 High Holborn, WC1V 6BN.
Opening hours: Mon-Fri, 11.30am-11pm; Sat, noon-11pm; Sun, closed.
Transport: Chancery Lane tube.

This Grade II listed pub doesn't just look old but is on an inventory of historic pub interiors compiled by the Campaign for Real Ale (CAMRA). Moreover, a copper sign outside states that a tavern has been on the site since 1430. The date is accurate, but the current building is vastly younger, being a rebuild for the '20s.

Much of the material from the medieval tavern was apparently used in the reconstruction, but does that count as genuinely aged? Still, the interior is enjoyably wonky, with a markedly long bar and massive wine vats that hold 1,000 gallons each. And the pub has a series of small cubicles that resemble church confessionals, designed for lawyers from nearby chambers to have confidential discussions with clients.

MRS JORDAN'S PITHY PUT-DOWN   93

Address: 30 Cadogan Place, SW1.
Transport: Knightsbridge tube.

A blue plaque in Knightsbridge celebrates an actress who was the source of one of her era's better put-downs. Mrs Dorothy (or Dorothea) Jordan (nee Bland, 1762-1816) was an Anglo-Irish actress and courtesan, renowned for her wit on and off stage. She was the long-time lover of the Duke of Clarence, later William IV, and during a 20-year affair they had at least ten illegitimate children together.

When the Duke suggested reducing the allowance he paid to Mrs Jordan she sent him a succinct reply. It took the form of the bottom part of an advertising flyer for a play and it read, 'No money returned after the rising of the curtain'.

MYSTERIES   94

Address: 9-11 Monmouth Street, WC2H 9DA (020-7240 3688, mysteries.co.uk).
Opening hours: Mon-Sat, 10am-7pm; Sun, 1-6pm.
Transport: Tottenham Court Road tube.

This stalwart curiosity on the edge of Covent Garden is a one-stop shop for all things New Age and mystical. As well as books on a variety of weird and

wonderful subjects, it supplies candles, crystals, dream catchers (always useful), essence, gemstones, incense and yoga CDs and DVDs, among other things.

It also hosts readings by astrologers, psychics and tarot card practitioners (booking is recommended), and

celebrity customers apparently include Anne Hathaway and the alarmingly trout-pouted Jackie Stallone. In short, this is the place to cleanse your aura or realign your chakra. Or just soak up the slightly other-worldly atmosphere.

95   MYSTERIOUS COWFORD LODGE

Address: Spur Road (diagonally opposite Buckingham Palace), SW1.
Transport: St James's Park tube or Victoria tube/rail.

Nobody seems to know the purpose of Cowford Lodge standing opposite Buckingham Palace. This is odd in itself, but all the more so given its sensitive location. The building is thought to date from around 1912, when the Mall was renovated and the palace re-faced, and is built from the same Portland stone used for the palace.

The lodge manages to be striking and rather anonymous at the same time. The latter is probably partly because of its proximity to Buckingham Palace – it's

often ignored as a result. However, why it was built here is a mystery: it isn't logically sited to be either a proper lodge or a guard post. Ignominiously, it's now used for storage.

THE 'NAZI' DOG MEMORIAL   96

> **Address:** Waterloo Place, outside 9 Carlton House Terrace, SW1Y 5AG.
> **Transport:** Charing Cross tube/rail.

This can lay claim to be one of London's more bizarre, if modest, sights. It's a small gravestone in a tiny patch of garden outside what was the German Embassy in the '30s. The inscription reads Giro: *Ein Treuer Belgeiter* (Giro: A True Companion). Giro was the Alsatian dog owned by Dr Leopold von Hoesch, German Ambassador in London 1932-6. The dog died in 1934, accidentally electrocuted by an exposed wire.

Von Hoesch himself died in 1936 aged only 55. He predated the Nazi rise to power in 1933 and wasn't an enthusiastic supporter. Indeed, he was liked and trusted by the British. His replacement was the notorious Joachim von Ribbentrop, a Hitler favourite later hanged for war crimes.

NOT SO GOOD FOR YOUR HEALTH   97

> **Address:** Constitution Hill, SW1.
> **Transport:** Hyde Park Corner tube.

Constitution Hill is a road that connects the western end of the Mall (in front of Buckingham Palace) with Hyde Park Corner. The 'hill' part is misleading; it's such a gentle slope that most people don't even notice. It acquired the name in the 17th century, from Charles II's habit

of taking 'constitutional' walks here, often with his spaniels.

So far so healthy, but Constitution Hill was also the scene of three assassination attempts on Queen Victoria: in 1840 by Edward Oxford; in 1842 by John Francis; and in 1849 by William Hamilton. And in 1850, the former Prime Minister Sir Robert Peel was thrown from his horse here, suffering an injury from which he died three days later.

98   NUMBER TEN'S DOOR

Address: 10 Downing Street, SW1A 2AA.
Transport: Westminster tube.

The front door to Britain's seat of political power has a couple of interesting quirks. Until quite recently made of oak – thought to date from around 1735 in Robert Walpole's time – it was replaced by a blast-proof steel door following the IRA's February 1991 attack. The terrorists used a van they parked in Whitehall to launch a mortar at the Prime Minister's residence. It exploded in the back garden while the then PM, John Major, was holding a Cabinet meeting.

The wooden door's replacement wasn't just more secure, but much heavier: when it's removed to be repainted, it requires several men to lift it. The letter box is solid. The door cannot be opened from the outside, although there's always someone inside to unlock it.

THE OLD CURIOSITY SHOP   99

Address: 13-14 Portsmouth Street, WC2A 2ES (curiosityuk.com).
Opening hours: Mon-Sat, 10.30am-7pm; Sun, closed.
Transport: Holborn tube.

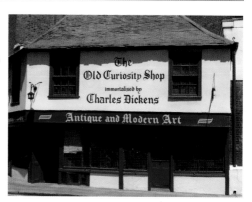

This quirky survivor is tucked away just south of Lincoln's Inn Fields and is almost certainly central London's oldest shop. It was built in around 1567 and gives an idea of how a high street would have looked before the Great Fire of 1666. The building has an overhanging upper storey, sloping roof, wooden beams and uneven floorboards. At one time it was a dairy on an estate given by Charles II to one of his various mistresses.

Today it has reverted to being a shop and is popularly thought to have been the model for Little Nell's home in the 1841 Charles Dickens novel of the same name. Sadly, there's little or no evidence to support this.

THE PAOLOZZI MOSAICS   100

Address: Tottenham Court Road tube station, Oxford Street, W1D 1AN.
Opening hours: Around 5-12.30am.
Transport: As above.

London's public art is often hurried past, particularly this example in Tottenham Court Road tube station. It's one of London's more crowded and annoyingly laid out stations, but is improved by the unusual mosaics of Eduardo Paolozzi (1924-2005), a Scottish artist and sculptor of Italian heritage.

They were commissioned in 1979, installed in the early '80s and draw their themes from places near the station and everyday life in London. The mosaics vary in their colour, form and degree of abstraction, with red important in the design of the mosaics on the (red-coloured) Central Line, while black dominates those on the (black) Northern Line. Some mosaics have been removed due to work on the Crossrail project (scheduled to finish in 2016) but will be reinstated.

101   QUEEN ANNE'S UNUSUAL HAUNTING

Address: Queen Anne's Gate, SW1.
Transport: St James's Park tube.

Queen Anne's Gate is a short, elegant, architecturally-significant street in Westminster. It was originally two streets which have had many distinguished residents over the years, including Jeremy Bentham, Lord Palmerston and John Stuart Mill. It's named after the last of the Stuart sovereigns, Queen Anne (1665-1714), who reigned 1702-14. She had an unfortunate life, plagued by ill health and enduring the heartache of conceiving nearly 20 children, none of whom survived her.

There's a statue of Anne here and her ghost is reported to walk the street three times at midnight on July 31st/ August 1st, the anniversary of her death. Some stories make grander claims: that the statue itself steps down and walks around its plinth.

THE QUEEN ELIZABETH GATE   102

Address: Hyde Park Corner, SW1.
Transport: Hyde Park Corner tube.

Sitting behind Apsley House and also known as the Queen Mother's Gate, this is attractively camp in style. It was inaugurated in 1993 by Queen Elizabeth II to celebrate the 90th birthday of Queen Elizabeth, the Queen Mother. The architect was Richard Rogers and the design – featuring a red lion and white unicorn – was the work of sculptor David Wynn.

The cost of £1.5m and the design were criticised – one commentator compared it to one of the Queen's hats – but attitudes have softened and most people now like it. The whole consists of six gates, railings and lamps, made from forged stainless steel and bronze. The overall design is intended to span the various styles of the 20th century.

QUEEN MARY'S STEPS   103

Address: Horse Guards Avenue, SW1A 2BE.
Transport: Charing Cross tube/rail.

Lurking incongruously behind the Ministry of Defence are rare surviving fragments of the old Tudor Whitehall Palace, built by Henry VIII. In 1691, Sir Christopher Wren added a terrace for Queen Mary in front of the palace's river wall. It overlooked the Thames and had steps to provide access to the State Barge – the present position of the steps is a reminder of how much wider the river used to be.

The old palace burned down in 1698, with only the Banqueting House surviving. Excavations in 1939 revealed the river wall and the northern flight of steps, both of which are now Grade I listed. The upper section of the steps has been repaired and their elegant sweep (typical of Wren) can be enjoyed today.

104   THE REAL DIAGON ALLEY

Address: Cecil Court, WC2.
Transport: Leicester Square tube.

Cecil Court is a pedestrian street linking Charing Cross Road and St Martin's Lane, and is said to have inspired Diagon Alley in the *Harry Potter* stories. For the few people unfamiliar with the Potter books and films, Diagon Alley is a fictional high street, accessible only to wizards and their kin.

Cecil Court is old, dating from the 17th century, and has a connection with Mozart. It was the temporary home of the eight-year-old composer for four months during his 1764 tour of Europe – marked by a blue plaque. Today, it's a centre for antiquarian booksellers and is admired for its original Victorian shop fronts.

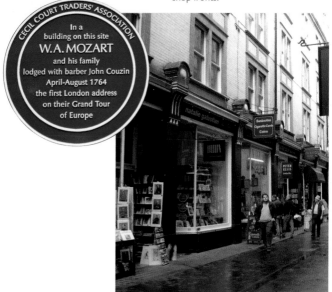

CECIL COURT TRADERS' ASSOCIATION
In a building on this site
W. A. MOZART
and his family lodged with barber John Couzin
April-August 1764
the first London address on their Grand Tour of Europe

THE REJUVENATED ART DECO BARBER   105

Address: Tommy Guns, 103/113 Regent Street, W1B 4HL (020-7734 5700).
Opening hours: Mon-Sat, 10am-8pm; Sun, noon-6pm.
Transport: Piccadilly Circus tube.

If you want to have your hair cut in what resembles an early Hollywood film set, this is the place to come. Originally a barber shop designed and built by Percy Westwood and Joseph Emberton, it opened in 1929 in what was then the Austin Reed store. The building is now the flagship outlet of the Superdry clothing company, and the barber shop has been restored to its former glory by Tommy Guns, remaining true to its Art Deco roots.

Modern twists have been added to the existing elements, with original Art Deco serpent style lighting and mirrors, authentic '30s barber chairs, stainless steel cabinets and travertine marble floors with a spider web footprint. The premises are deservedly Grade I listed.

THE RIVER IN A TUBE STATION   106

Address: Sloane Square tube station, SW1.
Transport: As above.

At ceiling level above the platform at upmarket Sloane Square's tube station runs a large pipe, over 4m (13ft) in diameter. Unexpectedly, and rather alarmingly, it's the conduit for what was once the River Westbourne. This is one of London's so-called 'lost rivers' – enclosed, often underground and channelled through pipes – and now part of the city's sewage system.

The Westbourne flowed from Hampstead Heath through Hyde Park (where it was dammed in the 1730s to form the Serpentine) to Sloane Square and into the Thames at Chelsea. In its current form, it's most easily seen at Sloane Square tube, still flowing through the original iron pipe built in the 19th century. The pipe is obviously robust, having survived the station being badly bombed in 1940.

107 THE ROAD TO NOWHERE

Address: Southampton Row, WC2B.
Transport: Holborn tube.

Near the junction of Southampton Row and Theobald's Road is a street leading underground – a 170ft open cutting with a one in ten gradient. It's the Kingsway Tram Subway, a 'cut-and-cover' tunnel built to join two tramway systems. It opened in 1906, closed in 1952 and ran from Theobald's Road to the Embankment under Waterloo Bridge.

Part of the subway is now the Strand underpass, but the rest remains largely intact and still has double tram tracks on the roadway and inside. It's now Grade II listed and has recently been partly reinvigorated, being the location for some of Crossrail's hidden enabling works. The intention is to leave the surface area as it currently is… as a historical curiosity.

THE ROYAL BALLET SCHOOL TWISTY BRIDGE

Address: 46 Floral Street, WC2E 9DA.
Transport: Covent Garden tube.

The bridge was installed in 2003 and is the work of Wilkinson Eyre Architects, who are responsible for a number of other striking bridges and buildings, including the distinctive, space-age London 2012 Basketball Arena.

If you look up to the fourth floor level of 46 Floral Street in Covent Garden, you'll see an unusual, award-winning footbridge which links the Royal Ballet School with the Royal Opera House. It's called the Bridge of Aspiration – although it's commonly known as the twisty or bendy bridge – and has what technical types call a 'skewed alignment', in the form of a concertina of 23 square portals with glazed intervals, all supported by an aluminium spine beam.

THE ST ERMIN'S HOTEL SPIES

Address: St Ermin's Hotel, 2 Caxton Street, SW1H 0QW (020-7222 7888, sterminshotel.co.uk).
Transport: St James's Park tube.

This stylish, horseshoe-shaped hotel has a long association with Britain's secret services. It's so-named because it's built on the site of a

15th-century chapel to St Ermin; the building was designed by E T Hall in 1889, becoming a hotel a decade later, and is now Grade II listed.

In 1940, Churchill held a historic meeting here, setting up the Special Operations Executive (SOE), which carried out covert operations from its headquarters at the hotel, while MI6 was stationed two floors above. In the '50s, members of the Cambridge Five – including Guy Burgess and Kim Philby – passed secret papers to the Russians in the hotel's Caxton Bar. A tunnel is said to run from under the hotel's grand staircase to the Houses of Parliament 600m away.

110   ST JAMES'S PALACE CHAPELS

Address: Pall Mall, SW1A 1NP.
Opening hours: The Chapels aren't open for visits, only for services, usually held at 8.30 and 11.15am on Sundays, except August and September. In the Chapel Royal they're held from the first Sunday in October to Good Friday, inclusive. In the Queens Chapel they're from Easter Sunday to the last Sunday in July, inclusive.
Transport: Green Park tube.

attend a service at one of its two chapels.

The Chapel Royal was built by Henry VIII and decorated by Hans Holbein in honour of the king's (short) fourth marriage, to Anne of Cleves. The Queen's Chapel was built by James I for his daughter-in-law, wife of Charles I. It was designed by Inigo Jones, the first notable British architect of the modern era.

It's widely held that St James's Palace is the only London royal palace closed to the public. However, a religious quirk means this isn't quite true: visitors can see a small part of the palace if they

THE SEVEN DIALS PILLAR

Address: Junction of St Giles Passage, Monmouth Street, Shorts Gardens, Earlham Street and Mercer Street, WC2.
Transport: Covent Garden tube.

Seven Dials is a small road junction in Covent Garden, where seven streets converge. At the centre is a pillar bearing six (not seven) sundials; it was commissioned before a later alteration to the building plans added a seventh street. The term Seven Dials also refers to the surrounding area, which was originally laid out in the 1690s.

Once a salubrious area, by the 19th century it had degenerated into one of London's most notorious slums, part of the rookery of St Giles. Today it's once again a prosperous district, noted for its fashion retailers. The current sundial pillar dates from the '80s and is built to the original design. Its placement was supervised by an astronomer to ensure its accuracy.

THE SOHO MURAL

Address: The corner of Broadwick Street and Carnaby Street, W1F.
Transport: Oxford Circus or Piccadilly Circus tube.

London has a number of murals – of varying quality – but the city has never quite taken to them. Perhaps they don't sit well under the grey skies, their vibrant colours being better suited to warmer climes. One of London's best and most eye-catching murals is in Soho – one of the city's more vibrant areas.

It dates from 1991 and depicts St Anne – to whom the local church is dedicated – presiding over some notable Soho denizens, including George Melly and Dylan Thomas; wags have suggested that they're trying to look up her skirt! The saint's skirt and petticoats display a map of Soho and London landmarks. The mural also has dogs and hares, a nod to when the area was a royal hunting ground.

113 SPENDING A PENNY IN STYLE

Address: Star Yard, WC2.
Transport: Chancery Lane tube.

Star Yard is off Chancery Lane and boasts a Grade II listed urinal, in the style of a Parisian pissoir – a common sight in 19th-century London. It's near the premises of Ede & Ravenscroft, London's oldest tailor, which was established in 1689 and specialises in legal wigs and gowns.

The urinal's exterior is a green rectangle of cast iron, with latticing and attractive patterned designs. The manufacturer's name (McDowall Steven & Co – Milton Iron Works) can be seen on one of the external panels. The structure featured in an episode of the comedy drama *Rumpole of the Bailey*, when the late actor Leo McKern is seen to enter it, but has been disused since the mid-'80s.

SPYMASTER

Address: 3 Portman Square, W1H 6LB (020-7486 3885, spymaster.co.uk).
Opening hours: Mon-Fri, 9.30am-6.30pm; Sat, 10am-5pm; Sun, closed.
Transport: Bond Street tube.

including body armour, body cameras, bugging devices, computer monitoring equipment, covert cameras, drug test kits, encryption equipment, handcuffs, home security equipment, night vision devices, phone recording equipment, and devices for radar detection and vehicle tracking. There's a full list of items on the website.

This is the flagship store of a retailer that does exactly what its name suggests: it sells everything a modern-day spy might need. Its other two outlets are in upmarket department stores – Harrods and Selfridges – which reinforces the rather obvious fact that the wealthy have the most to lose by not being properly protected.

Spymaster was established in 1991 and stocks a wide range of surveillance, counter-surveillance and personal protection equipment,

STANDING MAN & WALKING MAN

Address: Venice Walk, Paddington Basin, W2.
Transport: Edgware Road tube or Paddington tube/rail.

From a distance, these two sculpted figures look like real people. They're by the British sculptor Sean Henry (born 1965), whose work combines ceramics and sculpture, and portray two convincing male figures, one walking towards the other. A little larger than life-size, they're cast in bronze and painted in oils. Henry's figures are invariably painted, which makes a change from most contemporary sculpture and is a throwback to previous eras.

Referred to as 'Paddington Installation' on Henry's website, they were installed in 2004. They add interest to an otherwise uninspiring section of canal-side Paddington Basin, which is unfortunate enough to be situated adjacent to the Westway flyover.

116   THE STATUE WITH A MOLEHILL

Address: St James's Square, SW1.
Transport: Charing Cross tube/rail or Green Park tube.

The bronze statue of William III (1650-1702) has been in its present position in St James's Square since 1808. It's by John Bacon and portrays the king as a Roman general; this was clearly a popular guise as there are similar statues of William in Bristol, Glasgow and Petersfield (Hampshire).

Unusually, the St James's statue includes a small molehill at the feet of the horse on which William is sitting. The king died of pneumonia, a complication arising from a broken collarbone he suffered after a fall from his horse, Sorrell, which had tripped on a molehill while the king was riding at Hampton Court. Due to the mole's 'involvement' in the king's demise, his detractors toasted 'the little gentleman in the black velvet waistcoat'.

TERRACOTTA BEAVERS

> **Address:** 105-9 Oxford Street, W1D 2HQ.
> **Transport:** Tottenham Court Road tube.

Beavers grace the top of this Grade II listed building on Oxford Street. It dates from 1887-8 and was designed by Christopher and White for the hatter Henry Heath. Built in a Franco-Flemish Renaissance style, the front is faced in beige terracotta and includes a bas relief frieze representing the hat-making process – the last is by Benjamin Creswick, a protégé of the leading critic John Ruskin.

But it's the unusual gables (both small and large) that draw the eye, with decorated finials in the form of realistically modelled beavers, which are curious and striking against the skyline. They, too, are the work of Creswick and are a reference to the beaver fur used in the making of felt hats.

THE THAMES LIONS

> **Address:** The Victoria and Albert Embankments, WC2 and SE1.
> **Transport:** Westminster tube.

Striking lions' heads with steel mooring rings in their mouths line both sides of the Embankment, facing the river. They were designed by Timothy Butler (c 1806-85) as part of Sir Joseph Bazalgette's sewage project in 1868-70. However, they aren't just ornamental features but also serve as a flood warning.

It's said that if the lions 'drink', London will flood. Any police officer walking along this stretch of the Thames is supposed to keep an eye on them and if the water level reaches the mooring rings, the alarm is raised and the tube system and Thames tunnels are closed. The chances of flooding have been reduced since the building of the Thames Barrier, although climate change means that London might soon require more substantial protection.

119   TRAFALGAR SQUARE'S EMPTY FOURTH PLINTH

Address: Trafalgar Square, WC2.
Transport: Charing Cross tube/rail.

There's a plinth at each of the four corners of Trafalgar Square, but one has never had a permanent monument. It was originally intended to bear an equestrian statue of William IV but the money ran out. Over the next 150 years there was much discussion about what to do with the plinth but it wasn't until 1999 that it was decided to use it to display a sequence of contemporary artworks.

Some people want a permanent statue – suggested subjects have included Nelson Mandela and Margaret Thatcher – but the temporary occupants of the Fourth Plinth continue to amuse, inspire and, occasionally, annoy. A sculpture of a (very) blue cockerel by Katharina Fritsch in 2013 led to controversy: a national symbol of France in a square celebrating a victory over that country!

TS ELIOT'S TROUBLED MARRIAGE

Address: 24 Russell Square, WC1.
Transport: Russell Square tube.

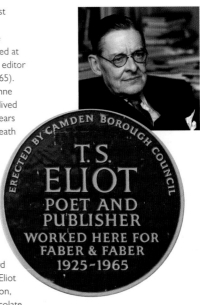

A blue plaque at the northwest corner of Russell Square commemorates the fact that the poet TS Eliot (1888-1965) worked at number 24 when he was poetry editor of Faber and Faber (from 1925-65). Eliot married his first wife, Vivienne Haigh-Wood, in 1915, but they lived together for only 18 of the 32 years between the wedding and her death in 1947.

Vivienne had physical and mental health problems, and sometimes came to Russell Square to plague Eliot for his shortcomings and ill-treatment of her. She famously once paraded up and down outside Faber's offices carrying a sandwich board declaring 'I am the wife that TS Eliot abandoned'. On another occasion, she poured a tureen of hot chocolate through the office's letter box.

THE TWO CHAIRMEN PUB SIGN

Address: 1 Warwick House Street, SW1Y 5AT (twochairmen.com).
Opening hours: Mon-Thu, 11.30am-11.30pm; Fri and Sat, 11.30am-midnight; Sun, closed.
Transport: Charing Cross tube/rail or Piccadilly Circus tube.

The Two Chairmen pub dates from 1683, the current building being from 1755, with 19th-century alterations. It has an unusual, eye-catching sign which shows two men carrying a sedan chair, in reference to the chair-carriers who could be hired here in days gone by.

It's a reminder of the curious origin of pub signs, which have been compulsory since a Royal Act of 1393 during the reign of Richard II. It declared that 'whosoever shall brew ale in the town with intention of selling it must hang out a sign, otherwise he shall forfeit his ale'. This was so that inspectors could identify and visit the premises to check the ale's quality. A pictorial sign was essential, as most people were illiterate.

122   VICTORIAN SHOPPING

Address: James Smith & Sons, 53 New Oxford Street, WC1A 1BL (020-7836 4731, james-smith.co.uk).
Opening hours: Mon-Fri, 10am-6pm; Sat, 10am-5.30pm; Sun, closed.
Transport: Tottenham Court Road tube.

This shop is unusual because it has retained its Victorian frontage, original and unspoilt. It appears to be from another age, which indeed it is: the shop was established in 1830 at Foubert Place and moved here in 1857. James Smith & Sons sell umbrellas, seat sticks and walking sticks, the first something of a banker in the unpredictable English climate, which perhaps explains its longevity. The firm has also prospered because it's renowned for products that are made to last.

The shop's interior resembles the old-school emporium that it is, packed with every type of umbrella and stick imaginable, while the exterior is striking, particularly the graphic Victorian typography.

THE WELBECK STREET CAR PARK

Address: 74-77 Welbeck Street, W1G 0BB.
Transport: Bond Street tube.

Resembling both a giant bee hive and a car radiator grill (the latter, appropriately), this multi-story car park sits in Marylebone and dates from a time when car parks were treated as significant structures, monuments in themselves. It's in the form of a giant grille (an angular diagrid, in architect-speak), open to the elements, which allows exhaust fumes to escape from the structure, so it's practical as well as integral to the design.

The car park was designed for Debenhams in the late '60s by Michael Blampied and still looks impressively futuristic. Indeed, it's one of the under-appreciated – if not forgotten – classics of the capital's architectural heritage.

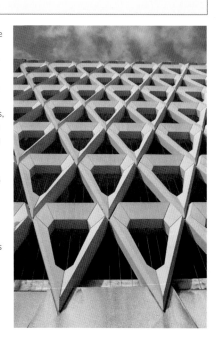

THE WELSH-SWISS-HUNGARIAN RESTAURANT

Address: The Gay Hussar, 2 Greek Street, W1D 4NB (020-7437 0973, gayhussar.co.uk).
Opening hours: Mon-Sat, 12.15-2.30pm and 5.30-10.45pm; Sun, closed.
Transport: Tottenham Court Road tube.

For a restaurant that sounds thoroughly Hungarian, this noted Soho eaterie isn't quite what it seems. Named after the Hungarian cavalrymen who were known to ride up to inns and demand buckets of wine for their horses, you might expect its founder to be more Hungarian than *goulash*.

But Victor Sassie, who opened the Gay Hussar in 1953, was actually from Barrow-in-Furness, of Welsh and Swiss heritage. His Hungarian 'connection' came from having been sent to Budapest by the British Hotel and Restaurant Association at the age of 17 to study catering. Still, this tenuous link didn't stop the restaurant becoming and remaining a success, much beloved by London's left-wing intelligentsia.

125 THE WORLD'S LARGEST HANGING BASKET

Address: Hotel Indigo, 16 London Street, W2 1HL.
Transport: Paddington tube/rail.

A boutique hotel in Paddington boasts what is claimed to be the world's largest hanging basket. And what an unusually big beast it is, measuring 20ft by 10ft, containing over 100 varieties of flower and plants, and weighing over a quarter of a ton. It took over three weeks to create and now hangs 25ft off the ground, not perhaps the most comfortable object to walk under.

Its inspiration is a lofty one, said to be the Hanging Gardens of Babylon, one of the ancient Seven Wonders of the World. And it's a work in progress, with the 'decor' of the basket changed in line with the evolving seasons.

Paolozzi mosaic, Tottenham Court Rd tube

CHAPTER 2

CITY & EAST END

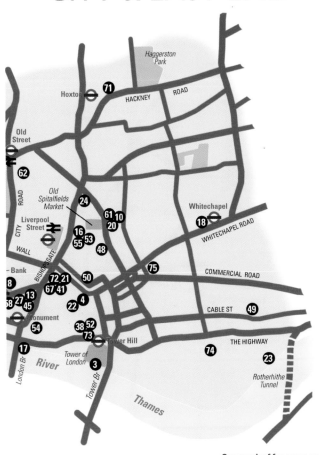

Haggerston
Park

Hoxton

HACKNEY   ROAD

71

Old
Street

62

Old
Spitalfields
Market

24   Whitechapel

61 10
20   18

Liverpool
Street   WHITECHAPEL ROAD

16
55 53
48

WALL   75

Bank   COMMERCIAL ROAD

8   72 21
67 41

27 13   22 4   CABLE ST   49
58 45

Monument   54

17   38 52
73   THE HIGHWAY

74   23

Tower Hill

River   Tower of
London   3   Rotherhithe
Tunnel

Thames

See overleaf for more maps

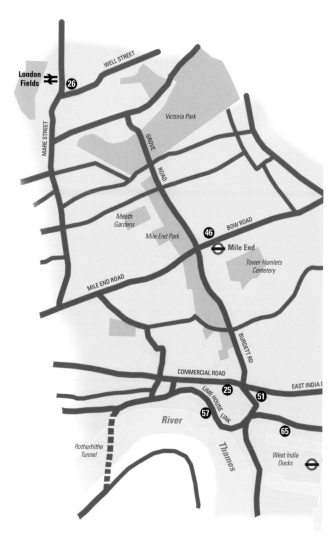

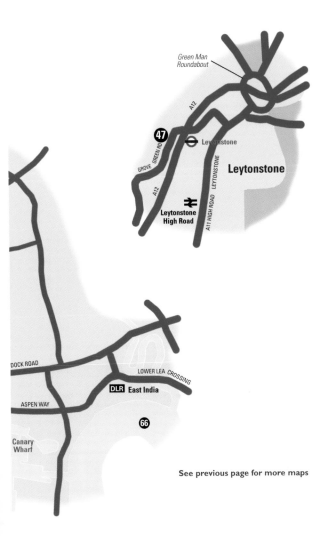

Green Man
Roundabout

A12

47 − Leytonstone

GROVE GREEN RD

A12

Leytonstone

A11 HIGH ROAD   LEYTONSTONE

Leytonstone
High Road

DOCK ROAD

LOWER LEA CROSSING

DLR East India

ASPEN WAY

66

Canary
Wharf

See previous page for more maps

I   COCK LANE, GOLDEN CHERUB & GHOST

Address: Cock Lane, EC1.
Transport: St Paul's tube.

With such an overtly suggestive name, you might expect Cock Lane to have a more humdrum history, perhaps as the former site of a poultry market. But you'd be wrong! For Cokkes Lane, as it was called in medieval times, derives its name from the frank and honest fact that it was one of the few places – perhaps the only place – in 14th-century London where brothels were legal. So hope lingers for the mucky-minded.

Cocks Lane is where writer and preacher John Bunyan died from a fever in 1688 – an inappropriate place of death for the devout Christian who wrote *The Pilgrim's Progress*, said to be England's first best-seller.

The junction of Cock Lane and Giltspur Street – the latter so-called because gilt spurs (what else?) were once made here – is known as Pye Corner and marks the westernmost extent of the Great Fire of London of 1666. This is commemorated by the eye-catching, gilt cherub known as the Golden Boy of Pye Corner, which is set high on the wall. The figure was originally built on the front of a pub called The Fortune of War, which was demolished in 1910.

The cherub is supposed to be chubby, to reinforce

Cock Lane, 19th-century illustration

the moralistic idea that the Great Fire was sent to punish Londoners for their gluttony (it began and ended at food-related locations, Pudding Lane and Pye Corner). In these well-fed times, however, he doesn't appear to be especially plump. Some people argue this is a sign that London is due to be ravaged by another conflagration.

Cock Lane was also the site of the so-called Cock Lane Ghost which manifested itself in 1762 and was known by the delightful nickname 'Scratching Fanny'. It attracted mass public attention, with people queuing and paying money to a young girl called Elizabeth Parsons, who was said to make contact with 'Fanny', a deceased young woman from Norfolk. Alas, a commission (which included the Duke of York and Samuel Johnson) set up

to investigate the supposed haunting concluded that it was a fraud.

The perpetrator of the ghostly hoax was Elizabeth's father, Richard Parsons, who was put on public display in the pillory as part of his punishment. Surprisingly, he was treated with kindness by the people he had tried to fool; they showered him with small change rather than the usual rotten fruit and vegetables.

'Scratching Fanny' had a number of famous fans. William Hogarth made reference to the ghost in two of his prints, while Charles Dickens was one of several Victorian writers who later alluded to the hauntings.

2   THE MUSEUM OF LONDON

> **Address:** 150 London Wall, EC2Y 5HN (020-7001 9844, museumoflondon.org.uk).
> **Opening hours:** Daily, 10am-6pm.
> **Transport:** Barbican or St Paul's tube.

The splendid Museum of London is the world's largest urban museum and concentrates on the social history of London and its people, from prehistory to the present. Its collections boast a number of striking, curious exhibits, including the following:

Ancient Bikini Bottoms: Most of the surviving evidence of Roman clothing consists of leather shoes, but an almost perfect pair of 1st-century leather bikini bottoms was found in 1953. It was down a Roman well in Queen Street, an example of how well leather survives in waterlogged conditions. A more decorated example of bikini briefs was subsequently found at Shadwell and other fragments have come from various locations in the City, which corresponds with the area covered by Roman London.

All but one of the surviving examples of Roman bikinis were found in London (the other was found at Mainz in Germany). The London bikinis have deep stretch marks across the front panels showing that they've been worn; their size suggests that they were worn by teenage girls – or that Roman women were much slimmer than their modern counterparts!

Bone Ice Skates: We sometimes think of medieval life as an almost unremittingly grim struggle for survival, but these 12th-century bone ice skates show that there was time for leisure and sport. Children and adults used animal limb bones as ice skates,

Depictions of bikini-like garments on pottery and murals indicate that they might have been worn by acrobats or other athletes (without bikini tops). Some archaeologists think they might simply have been everyday underwear or sanitary garments.

employing leather laces threaded through holes in the bones to attach them to their feet. A pole or pair of poles (iron-tipped if you could afford it) was used to propel yourself across the ice.

Lord Mayor's Coach: This splendidly and unexpectedly camp exhibit resembles something from a '50s Hollywood epic or an upmarket pantomime (possibly staged in Brighton). Designed by architect Sir Robert Taylor, it was built in 1753 by a Holborn manufacturer for £860. A number of the coach's features reflect the importance of London's port and of the City's business: the coachman's seat is supported by tritons (mythical

The procession of the Lord Mayor of the City of London dates back to the early 13th century and has its roots in the (justifiable) paranoia of King John. He insisted that each year, the newly elected Mayor – one of England's most powerful figures – be required to present himself (there has been only one lady Lord Mayor) at court and swear loyalty to the Crown.

sea creatures) and his footrest is shaped like a scallop shell. The coach is supported at each corner by cherubs representing the four then-known continents – Africa, America, Asia and Europe – and the City's coat of arms, including fire-breathing dragons, decorates the back of the coach.

3   THE TOWER OF LONDON

Address: EC3N 4AB (0844-482 7777, hrp.org.uk/TowerOfLondon).
Opening hours: Sun and Mon, 10am-4.30pm; Tue-Sat, 9am-4.30pm; last admission, 4pm.
Cost: Adult, £19; concession, £16; child, £9.50; family, £50.
Transport: Tower Hill tube.

One of London's most popular tourist attractions, the Tower of London is well-known for its strange and often violent history. Some of the more peculiar and unexpected facts about the 'Bloody Tower' include the following:

Prehistoric Base: The Tower was built by the Normans, who began construction in 1066. It's said to sit on a man-made prehistoric mound (it was common Norman practice to build on the sites of previous cultures) called the Bryn Gwyn in Welsh – the White or Holy Mound – which was used by druids for equinox and solstice ceremonies.

Ravens: It's said that the Tower and the kingdom will fall if the resident ravens leave. There must be at least six of them – they currently number seven. Charles II was the first monarch to insist that the ravens should be protected. This didn't please his astronomer, John Flamsteed, who complained that the

birds interfered with his observatory in the White Tower.

Although the birds have one wing trimmed by the Ravenmaster, some do go missing and others have to be 'sacked': a raven called George was dismissed in the '80s when he began to eat television aerials.

> The ravens' diet is appropriately bloody: 6oz of raw meat and bird biscuits soaked in blood each day. They also have the odd rabbit, as the fur is said to be good for them.

Soft Prison: Despite its reputation as a place of incarceration, there are no dungeons at the Tower and probably never were. Most of its prisoners came from society's upper echelons, and many lived in comfort, enjoying good food and alcohol, although they had to pay for the privilege. Sir Walter Raleigh,

Sir Walter Raleigh

> Ronnie and Reggie Kray were among the last prisoners to be detained at the Tower. They were held there in 1952, for failing to report for national service.

for example, who spent 13 years in the Tower, lived there with his wife and two children, and grew tobacco on Tower Green.

Spooks: The Tower is one of Britain's most haunted sites and the Queen's House is a spectral hotspot, haunted by Arbella Stuart, James I's cousin – there's reported to be particular activity in the Lennox room, where guests have reported feeling strangled.

Anne Boleyn

Anne Boleyn, beheaded at the Tower in 1536, is said to haunt the chapel of St Peter ad Vincula and apparently carries her head under her arm. Sir Walter Raleigh wanders the grounds, smoking his pipe from his decapitated head, while the Two Princes walk hand-in-hand. Other notable ghosts include Henry VI, Lady Jane Grey and Margaret Pole.

There's also the ghost of a huge bear, which appeared at the Martin Tower in the 19th century and scared a guard so badly that he died from shock. Bears (and other animals) have a history at the Tower: the King of Norway gave Henry III a polar bear in 1251, which was attached to a long chain so that it could fish in the Thames. And George III was presented with a grizzly bear in 1811.

Tower of London courtyard

4   THE ALDGATE PUMP

Address: The junction of Aldgate High Street, Fenchurch Street and Leadenhall Street, EC3.
Transport: Aldgate tube.

Sitting at a busy City junction and therefore sometimes overlooked, this Grade II listed, obelisk-like structure is ancient. It's first mentioned in the reign of King John (1199-1216), although it could, of course, be rather older. Now a drinking fountain, it was originally a water pump, having been moved here from a nearby location during street widening. The tapered Portland stone obelisk seen today dates from the 18th century.

There's a brass wolf's head on the drinking fountain, which is said to signify the last wolf shot in and around the City of London. This indicates the age

Today, the Aldgate Pump marks the official point at which the East End of London begins, while the road to Southend – the A13 – also starts from here.

of the various types of water outlet on this site.

It hasn't always been a healthy place to drink and its water source had to be switched to the mains supply in 1876. The previous source, an underground stream, had begun to taste unpleasant and was found to contain liquid human remains which had seeped into the stream from cemeteries in other parts of London. This led to the Aldgate Pump Epidemic during which several hundred people died.

ALSATIA, SANCTUARY FROM THE LAW   5

Address: Around Magpie Alley, off Whitefriars Street, EC4.
Transport: Blackfriars or Temple tube.

Alsatia was the name of the extensive precincts of the former Whitefriars Monastery, which existed from around 1253 until the Dissolution of the Monasteries by Henry VIII in the mid-16th century. Alsatia covered an area around what is today Magpie Alley (where a small section of the monastery crypt remains and can be seen, behind glass), spreading south of Fleet Street and adjacent to the Temple.

From the 16th to the late 17th century, Alsatia had the privilege of a sanctuary, which meant that it was exempted from the rule of law except against a writ of the Lord Chief Justice or of the Lords of the Privy Council. As a result, it became a refuge for all sorts of criminals. Many so-called sanctuaries were nothing less than places without law.

Alsatia was one of England's last places of sanctuary, all of which were abolished by an Act of Parliament –

The Escape from Prison Act – in 1697 and a further Act in 1723. Its lawless past is a curious contrast with today, as the area is part of the legal and financial heartland of London.

Alsatia was so-called after the old name for Alsace – today part of eastern France – which itself was outside juridical and legislative writ.

Remains of Whitefriars Monastery

6   AMEN COURT'S GHOSTS

Address: Amen Court, EC4.
Transport: St Paul's tube.

Unlikely as it seems, this attractive, tranquil court is said to be one of the City's most haunted locations. It was built to provide accommodation for nearby St Paul's Cathedral's canons and scribes, but behind the large wall visible through the main archway is a narrow passage known as Deadman's Walk. Condemned prisoners in the adjacent Newgate Prison were taken along it to be executed and many were buried beneath the wall, which is the focus of the supernatural activity.

The most famous of the hauntings is by the so-called Black Dog of Newgate. This is said to be a large black shape which can be seen slithering along the top of the wall, its appearance accompanied by a nauseating smell. The Black Dog is thought to originate from an incident of cannibalism in the jail during a famine in Henry III's reign.

The victim is claimed to have been a portly prisoner, whose ample, meaty frame proved too tempting for other prisoners, who were starving, and they killed and ate him. He subsequently took on the form of a dog to return to haunt his murderers and the place of his death.

Amen Court is approached via Ave Maria Lane. Many of the streets in this area, close to St Paul's, have ecclesiastical names.

AN AMPHITHEATRE IN OUTLINE   7

Address: Guildhall Yard, EC2.
Transport: Moorgate or St Paul's tube.

The black inlaid stones in the paving of the Guildhall's forecourt are overlooked by most people. That's a pity, as they mark the outline of London's Roman amphitheatre and provide a graphic picture of how large it was.

It was Britain's largest amphitheatre, with an external size of around 100m by 85m; the arena's area (marked by the black stones) measured some 60m by 40m. The amphitheatre would have held between 6,000 and 7,000 spectators, at a time when London's population was only 20,000-30,000. People would have gathered here to watch professional gladiatorial combats (although quite rarely, as such shows were expensive to stage), wild animal fights, public executions and religious ceremonies.

The first amphitheatre was built from timber around AD70, and in AD120 the wooden walls were replaced with ragstone (a hard, bluish-grey limestone), although the seating would still have been wooden. The amphitheatre was abandoned in the 4th century; it might subsequently have become the town's rubbish dump and much of its stone would later have been recycled for use in other buildings.

A few of the actual remains of the amphitheatre – which are scant – are displayed imaginatively in the basement of the adjacent Guildhall Art Gallery. The site was excavated in the late '80s ahead of the gallery's construction.

8   THE BANK OF ENGLAND'S BLACK NUN

Address: Threadneedle Street, EC2.
Transport: Bank tube.

le-Stocks, behind the Bank. The church, which dated from 1282, was demolished in 1781 and the land on which it had stood – including where Sarah was buried – became part of the Bank's gardens. Her ghost is said to have been seen walking in the gardens by staff many times and she apparently also finds time to haunt nearby Bank underground station.

Sarah would also accost the Bank's wealthy customers; at one point, it's said, she accused Baron Rothschild of stealing £2,000 from her.

The Old Lady of Threadneedle Street, as the Bank of England is fondly known, has an unusual lady of its own. The Bank is said to be haunted by the ghost of Sarah Whitehead, usually called the Black Nun because of its thick black clothes and dark veil.

Sarah Whitehead's brother, Philip, worked at the Bank, and in 1812 he was found guilty of forgery and executed, the usual punishment for the crime in the early 1800s. The shock of this apparently unhinged Sarah's mind and each day for the rest of her life (another 25 or more years) she would call at the Bank, dressed in black, and ask for her brother.

When she died, she was buried in the graveyard of nearby St Christopher-

BLEEDING HEART YARD   9

Address: Bleeding Heart Yard, EC1.
Transport: Chancery Lane tube or Farringdon tube/rail.

This cobbled courtyard off Greville Street is one of London's more bizarrely and gruesomely titled locations. Legend has it that it's named to commemorate the murder of Lady Elizabeth Hatton, society beauty and second wife of Sir William Hatton, whose family once owned the area around nearby Hatton Garden.

Lady Elizabeth's body is said to have been found here on 27th January 1626, 'torn limb from limb, but with her heart still pumping blood'. The Spanish ambassador was suspected, as she'd recently ended a relationship with him. After the break-up they were spotted together at a ball and she disappeared soon after.

But if a murder victim **was** discovered here, it wasn't Elizabeth, as she lived for another 20 years and died in 1646. It's thought that the story's confusion arose because there were a number of Hattons with the same names in the family tree. Even less satisfactorily for those in search of real blood-letting, some people think that the yard gets its name from a 16th-century inn, The Bleeding Heart, whose sign showed the Virgin Mary's heart pierced by five swords.

> The location is mentioned in Charles Dickens's *Little Dorrit*, with Bleeding Heart Yard being the home of the novel's Plornish family.

10   THE BRICK LANE JAMME MASJID

Address: 59 Brick Lane, E1 6QL (020-7247 6052, bricklanejammemasjid.co.uk).
Transport: Aldgate East tube or Liverpool Street tube/rail.

On the corner of Fournier Street and Brick Lane in vibrant, recently-revitalised Spitalfields is the only building in the world outside of Israel to have been a church, synagogue and mosque. It's currently the Brick Lane Jamme Masjid, which means Brick Lane Great Mosque in Bengali.

Georgian in style and Grade II* listed, it was built in 1743 as a Protestant chapel (*La Neuve Eglise*) by the French Huguenots who'd settled in the area, having fled France to avoid Catholic persecution. In 1809 it became a Wesleyan chapel and a decade later a Methodist chapel. In the late 19th century, it was converted into the Machzike Adass or Spitalfields Great Synagogue, the area having become home to Jewish refugees from Russia and Eastern Europe.

As the Jewish settlers became more prosperous, they moved elsewhere, many to north London, and it declined as a synagogue, eventually closing. The '70s saw an influx of Bangladeshi immigrants to Spitalfields – the restaurants they opened are the reason for Brick Lane's claim to be one of the UK's curry capitals – and the building was refurbished and opened as a mosque in 1976.

The eye-catching sundial on an exterior wall dates from the building's Huguenot period. Its inscription – *Umbra Sumus* – means 'we are shadows'.

BRIDEWELL VOYEURISM 11

Address: New Bridge Street, EC4.
Transport: Blackfriars tube/rail.

New Bridge Street is the site of what remains of a building that saw a remarkable example of officially sanctioned voyeurism. It was originally Bridewell Palace, which was built 1515-20 in an area known today as Bridewell Place, and was named after a nearby holy well which was dedicated to St Bride.

In 1555, the palace became a poorhouse and a year later a jail, Bridewell Prison. Many of the old buildings were destroyed in 1666's Great Fire and later rebuilt. The prison was closed in 1855 and the buildings demolished, except for the original gatehouse, which is now incorporated into the front of an office block at 14 New Bridge Street, near Bridewell Place.

What gives the area its prurient past is that from the 16th century onwards, new inmates arriving at the prison were routinely flogged – 12 lashes for adults, six for children. By the 18th century, the sight of semi-naked prostitutes being whipped had become such a popular attraction that a balustraded gallery was built for spectators. The spectacle ceased by 1791, however, when the flogging of women was abolished.

> Bridewell Palace was one of Henry VIII's residences and the scene of Holbein's famous painting *The Ambassadors*, now in London's National Gallery (see page 53).

12   THE CHURCH CAMEMBERT

Address: St Stephen Walbrook, 39 Walbrook, EC4N 8BN (020-7626 9000, ststephenwalbrook.net).
Opening hours: Mon-Fri, 10am-4pm.
Transport: Bank or Cannon Street tube.

The altar at St Stephen Walbrook Church is notable for having been unfavourably compared with a cheese. It's also the only piece of church furniture to have been designed by the great sculptor Henry Moore (1898-1986), having been commissioned by Peter Palumbo (later Lord Palumbo), a London property developer and financier with an interest in contemporary sculpture and architecture.

Palumbo was one of St Stephen's church wardens and invested much time and money on the church's restoration after World War II bomb damage. It was his decision to have Moore design a new altar and the sculptor was appointed in 1967. The carving didn't begin until 1973, however, and wasn't completed for a decade.

It was controversial from the start and even led to a hearing at the Court of Ecclesiastical Causes Reserved (only the second in over 20 years) with the aim of having it removed from the church. The court found in favour of the altar, but it still has its detractors and traditionalists have nicknamed it the Camembert cheese, owing to its shape and colour.

Unusually, the altar stands in the centre of the church and is made of pale cream travertine marble, with a diameter of 2.55m (just over 8ft). It's not so much sculpted as subtly rounded by Moore.

THE CORNHILL DEVILS   13

Address: 54 and 55 Cornhill, EC3V 3PD.
Transport: Bank tube.

The three devilish terracotta figures (two large and one small) that leer down from the upper storeys of this building on Cornhill are an unusual example of long-lasting revenge. They're intended to mock worshippers next door at St Peter upon Cornhill, an old City church now virtually submerged at street level by office blocks.

The story of the devils dates from the late 19th century, when one of St Peter's vicars scored a victory over the City's property developers. He discovered that plans for a neighbouring building (54 and 55 Cornhill) intruded by around a foot onto the church's land. The vicar complained and the architect was forced to review and change his plans, a costly and time-consuming exercise.

The architect gained a measure of revenge over the meddlesome cleric by adding the three terracotta figures to his building, which glare down to this day on people entering the church below. One of them (the closest to street level) is claimed to have been modelled on the offending reverend.

St Peter is said to be built on Britain's earliest place of Christian worship. This claim is probably untrue, but there's certainly been a church on the site for a long time. The present structure is a Wren rebuild after the Great Fire.

14   THE CROSS-EYED STATUE

Address: Fetter Lane, at the junction with New Fetter Lane, EC4.
Transport: Chancery Lane tube.

An accurate if unflattering bronze statue by James Butler (1988) stands on this City corner, commemorating a colourful character called John Wilkes (1725-97). He was a journalist, politician and radical who was once called 'the ugliest man in England'. This was partly because he was cross-eyed, which this statue clearly shows – it's thought to be London's only cross-eyed statue.

Wilkes – who became an MP in 1757 – was regarded as a champion of English freedom and was elected Lord Mayor of London in 1774. He was the first MP to propose universal suffrage in the Commons, introduced the first motion for parliamentary reform (in 1776), and led a campaign for press freedom that saw him imprisoned in the Tower of London.

Wilkes was also something of a libertine (fathering a number of children) and a member of the notorious Hellfire Club, so he obviously didn't let his ugliness hold him back. Despite his unsightly squint, protruding jaw and other physical quirks, he had plenty of charm and wit, once claiming that it 'took him only half an hour to talk away his face'. Later in life, he's said to have extended the required period of time.

Abraham Lincoln's assistant John Wilkes Booth is said to have been named after John Wilkes, and may have been a distant relative.

John Wilkes

DINING IN THE DARK   15

Address: Dans Le Noir, 30-31 Clerkenwell Green, EC1R 0DU (020-7253 1100, london.danslenoir.com).
Opening hours: See the website for full details, which are liable to change.
Transport: Farringdon tube/rail.

This has a strong claim to be London's most bizarre eating experience. Diners eat in total darkness, an experience which is intended to change their perception of the world and allows them to re-evaluate their perception of taste and smell.

Orders are taken in the fully lit bar where you choose from four different menus: White (exotic and unusual), Blue (fish and seafood), Red (meat) and Green (vegetarian). Before entering the completely dark dining room, all bags, coats and anything that produces light – mobile phone, lighters etc. – must be stored in a locker. You're also recommended to use the bathroom first, as to leave the room during the experience spoils it. You have a registered blind guide throughout your time in the dining room and shouldn't try to move around without being led by him (or her); you hail the guide by calling their name.

Your 'blind dining' experience lasts around an hour and a half, after which you repair to the bar to view pictures of your meal and wine, which you can compare with your own perceptions of what you ate and drank.

Despite its inherent weirdness, Dans De Noir isn't a cheap venue and you must book, as tables are often reserved weeks in advance.

16   DIRTY DICKS

Address: 202 Bishopsgate, EC2M 4NR (020-7283 5888, dirtydicks.co.uk).
Opening hours: Mon-Thu, 11am-midnight; Fri and Sat, 11-1am; Sun, 11am-10.30pm.
Transport: Liverpool Street tube/rail.

Established in 1745, this pub opposite Liverpool Street Station used to be called The Old Jerusalem. It changed its name to Dirty Dicks at the beginning of the 19th century to celebrate and perpetuate a strange local tale. Dirty Dick was a real person, called Richard (some sources

say Nathaniel) Bentley, a prosperous City merchant who lived nearby from the mid-18th century.

He owned a hardware shop and warehouse, and had been quite a dandy in his youth. However, following his fiancée's death, he henceforth refused to clean his home, shop, warehouse or, indeed, himself. As a result, he became a strange sort of 'celebrity of filth' and his business premises became known as The Dirty Warehouse – mail addressed thus would be successfully delivered.

Dirty Dick is said to have been the inspiration for the eccentric Miss Havisham in Charles Dickens's *Great Expectations*. Dickens was a great patron of London's pubs, and would almost certainly have been to this one.

He stopped trading in 1804 and died in 1809, but for long years afterwards, the pub lived up to its name and the cellar bar was covered in dust, grime and cobwebs, even playing host to dead cats. It's now been tidied up and is part of the Young's chain.

DOGGETT'S COAT & BADGE RACE

17

Address: From London Bridge to Cadogan Pier (www.doggetsrace.org.uk).
Transport: Monument tube.

This is the world's oldest rowing race, staged annually since 1715; it's probably also the world's oldest continuously-run sporting contest of any kind. It takes its name from Thomas Doggett (c 1640-1721), an Irish actor who became joint manager of the Drury Lane Theatre. The genesis of the race is said to have been when Doggett was rescued by a waterman after falling into the river while crossing the Thames near Embankment and his desire to express his gratitude – though others claim that there's little evidence for this.

Whatever the reason, Doggett arranged a race involving up to six apprentice watermen along a four mile and five furlong (7,400m) course between London Bridge and Cadogan Pier, Chelsea. It was originally held on 1st August against the outgoing (ebb) tide in boats used to ferry passengers across the Thames. Today it's staged in July at a time that coincides with the incoming (flood) tide, in modern, single sculling boats.

Doggett arranged for a winner's prize of a traditional watermen's orange coat furnished with a large silver badge, to commemorate the 1st August 1714 accession of George I – hence the coat and badge.

In his will, Thomas Doggett left instructions for the continuance of the race, and it's now overseen by the Fishmongers' Company (a City Livery Company).

18   THE ELEPHANT MAN DISPLAY

Address: 259 Whitechapel Road, E1.
Transport: Whitechapel tube.

Incredible though it seems today, in Victorian times people with deformities, disabilities and physical oddities were sometimes treated like a combination of museum exhibit and circus attraction. That's what happened to Joseph Merrick (1862-90) – better known as the Elephant Man and sometimes erroneously called John Merrick – who was put on display to paying customers in various parts of Britain.

He had a condition that led to severe physical deformities and strange growths (the exact cause is still unknown), giving him a bizarre appearance that was deemed worthy of presenting to paying customers. After touring the country so that he could be gawped at, he was put on display in what had been a vacant greengrocer's at 123 Whitechapel Road. Due to a road renumbering, it's now number 259, and currently (and prosaically) houses a sari retailer on the ground floor and a taxi firm upstairs.

The display of 'human oddities' was becoming unpopular by the 1890s and in 1894 the police closed the display at Whitechapel Road, only a few weeks after it had opened.

There are exhibits about Joseph Merrick's short, difficult life at the nearby hospital where he received treatment. Visit the Royal London Hospital Museum, St Philip's Church, Newark Street, E1 2AA (Tue-Sat, 10am-4.30pm, free entry).

John Merrick

THE EXECUTIONER'S BELL   19

Address: St Sepulchre-without-Newgate, Holborn Viaduct, EC1A 2DQ
(020-7236 1145, st-sepulchre.org.uk).
Opening hours: Mon-Fri, 11am-3pm; Sat and Sun, closed to visitors.
Transport: Farringdon tube/rail or St Paul's tube.

The infamous Newgate Prison was built in 1188 and remodelled many times during its long history, which lasted until 1902. The prison was renowned for its terrible conditions and its executions (held just outside) which drew large crowds until 1868, when public executions were discontinued. In all, over 1,000 people were executed here.

St Sepulchre's Church was close to Newgate and is the largest parish church in the City, dating from 1137, although the present structure is a 1670 Wren rebuild after the Great Fire. A curious, morbid connection between the prison and the church is displayed in a glass case in the church: a handbell that was rung on the eve of Newgate executions.

At midnight before an execution, St Sepulchre's bellman would go to the prison via an underground passage and ring 12 double tolls to the prisoners, while he chanted: 'All you that in the condemned hold do lie, prepare you, for tomorrow you shall die...' A certain Robert Dow donated money to the parish in 1604 or 1605 to ensure that this unpleasant ritual continued to be performed in perpetuity.

St Sepulchre's bells are among the 'Cockney bells' of London, named in the nursery rhyme *Oranges and Lemons* as the 'bells of Old Bailey'.

20   FIRE PROTECTION BADGES

> **Address:** 37 Fournier Street, E1.
> **Transport:** Aldgate or Aldgate East tube.

Badges and plaques embossed with the crests of insurance companies were once common on London buildings. They're a throwback to the days before the capital had a public fire service, when individual insurance companies often had their

own fire-fighting crews. These only extinguished fires in buildings insured by their company – which were identified by badges – or, for a fee, those insured by other companies.

Made from copper or lead, the badges are very collectable and many have been removed (or stolen) over the years. They were first used in the late 17th century, by the Sun Fire Office, and were common in the 18th century. They were placed prominently on the front of the insured building.

By around 1825 their use began to fade. Insurance companies started to co-operate with each other and allow their fire fighters to tackle any fire – not just those in buildings they insured – in an attempt to avoid the spread of fire. Thus badges increasingly served as advertisements for the insurance companies, rather than as a way of identifying the buildings they insured.

> On January 1st 1883, a number of individual fire brigades was combined into the London Fire Engine Establishment, which fought all fires and was the forerunner of today's London Fire Brigade.

THE GHERKIN'S POETIC BENCHES   21

> **Address:** 30 St Mary Axe, EC3A 8EP.
> **Transport:** Aldgate tube or Liverpool Street tube/rail.

Generally regarded as London's finest contemporary building, 30 St Mary Axe is a triumph of architecture-as-sculpture. It's sometimes called the Swiss Re Building (after its main occupier) but is better known by its nickname the Gherkin, although pine cone is probably more accurate and saucier epithets have also been suggested.

As visitors crane their necks to take in the 180m (591ft), 41-floor tower, they sometimes ignore the Gherkin's entrance. It's approached across a landscaped plaza which is bordered by the unusual Arcadian Garden, described as a 'poem and artwork'. On 20 granite benches are inscribed 20 lines of the poem *Arcadian Dream Garden* by the Bahamas-born Scottish poet, writer, gardener and conceptual artist Ian Hamilton Finlay (1925-2006).

It might seem inappropriate to have a work about gardens in conjunction with this towering building, but it's apt because Finlay was a sometime writer of so-called concrete poetry. This is poetry in which the layout and typography of the work contributes to the overall effect (sometimes called visual poetry). Further, the curves of the benches mirror those of the Gherkin and the poem itself has a number of architectural and structural references.

The Gherkin was designed by Norman Foster and Arup engineers, and won its creators the Stirling Prize in 2004.

22   THE GILT OF CAIN

> **Address:** Fen Court, EC3.
> **Transport:** Fenchurch Street tube/rail.

This sculpture is a collaboration between the sculptor Michael Visocchi and the poet Lemn Sissay. It commemorates the bicentenary, in 2007, of the abolition of the transatlantic slave trade and sits in a quiet passageway off Fenchurch Street. The work was unveiled in 2008 by Archbishop Desmond Tutu.

The granite sculpture comprises 17 cylindrical columns surrounding a podium, the latter recalling an ecclesiastical pulpit or slave auctioneer's block. The columns suggest either stylised stems of sugar cane (complete with segmented growth rings); a crowd gathered to hear a speaker, or a group of slaves standing before an auctioneer's podium. Extracts from Lemn Sissay's specially commissioned poem *The Gilt of Cain* are engraved into the granite, blending the language of the Stock Exchange's trading floor with Biblical Old Testament references.

> The Reverend Newton was an inspiration for (and also worked with) the politician and leading abolitionist William Wilberforce (1759-1833).

Fen Court is an apt site for the sculpture, as it's in the Parish of St Edmund the King and St Mary Woolnoth, which had a strong connection with the abolitionist movement. St Mary Woolnoth's rector from 1780-1807 was Reverend John Newton (1725-1807), a former sailor and slave trader who became a preacher.

CASH FLOW RUNS DEEP
BUT SPIRIT DEEPER
YOU ASK AM I MY
BROTHERS KEEPER?
I ANSWER BY NATURE
BY SPIRIT BY RIGHTFUL LAWS
MY NAME, MY BROTHER,
WILBERFORCE.

THE HANGING GIBBET   23

Address: The Prospect of Whitby, 57 Wapping Wall, E1W 3SH.
Transport: Wapping tube.

An eye-catching wooden gallows and dangling rope noose – a hanging gibbet – stand near the shoreline in the river by this ancient pub. The gibbet isn't for drinkers who fail to pay their bar tab but is a reminder of the long-gone Execution Dock (which was actually at Wapping Old Stairs by the Town of Ramsgate pub). The Dock was used for over 400 years to execute mutineers, pirates and smugglers, with the last executions taking place in 1830.

Execution Dock was for those who'd been sentenced to death by Admiralty Courts, whose jurisdiction was for all

The bodies of the most notorious offenders were sometimes tarred and hung in chains on the river as a warning to others about the penalty for piracy.

crimes committed at sea, either in home waters or abroad. The Dock symbolised this by being located just beyond the low-tide mark in the river. A particularly cruel death was reserved for those convicted of piracy: a slow, agonising strangulation from a shortened rope, the drop too short to break the prisoner's neck and kill him instantly. It was called the Marshall's Dance, because the prisoner's limbs often 'danced' during the slow asphyxiation.

Customarily, the bodies of those killed at Execution Dock were left hanging until at least three tides had washed over their heads.

24   THE LIBERTY OF NORTON FOLGATE

Address: Norton Folgate Street, E1.
Transport: Liverpool Street tube/rail.

A 'liberty' is one of the various legacies bequeathed to Britain by the long stretch of the Middle Ages (or medieval period, which lasted from the 5th to the 15th century). It refers to an area in which regalian rights are revoked and where land is held by a mesne lord (i.e. the land and its income are in private, not royal hands). The Liberty of Norton Folgate was situated between the Bishopsgate ward to the south, the parish of St Leonard, Shoreditch to the north and the parish of Spitalfields to the east.

The name is recorded as early as around 1110, as *Nortune* (north farmstead). Folgate might come from the manorial family name *Foliot*, or from *Foldweg*, the Saxon term for a highway, probably referring to Ermine Street, the Roman road that passed through the area. The liberty became part of

The existence of the Liberty of Norton Folgate became known to a much wider public when the ska/pop band Madness named their critically acclaimed 2009 concept album after it.

Whitechapel in 1855 and existed until 1900.

It's an atmospheric, historic area to wander around today, although the street called Norton Folgate, which connects Bishopsgate and Shoreditch High Street, comprises a rather less characterful stretch of the A10.

LIMEHOUSE'S PAGAN PYRAMID   25

Address: St Anne's Limehouse, 5 Newell Street, E14 7HP (stanneslimehouse.org).
Transport: Westferry DLR.

A 9ft high, four-sided, Grade II listed pyramid stands, mysterious and unexpected, in the graveyard of this Baroque church. St Anne's Limehouse, Grade I listed, was built by Sir Christopher Wren's pupil Nicholas Hawksmoor (c 1661-1736) in 1714-27. It was one of the dozen churches built as a result of the 1711 Act of Parliament, which set up a commission to build 50 churches in London (but fell well short). It was consecrated in 1730 and is one of Hawksmoor's six London churches.

The original purpose of the pyramid is unknown but it might have been intended to be installed on one of the corners of the east end of the building. The four pinnacles on the church's main west tower are capped with similar pyramids, albeit much smaller. Some commentators think the graveyard pyramid reflects Hawksmoor's interest in pagan and Masonic symbolism: the top of one of its faces is inscribed with

the words 'The Wisdom of Solomon' and under it is carved a raised coat of arms on which there's a unicorn.

The subject of Nicholas Hawksmoor's mystical interests is examined in Peter Ackroyd's Whitbread and *Guardian* prize-winning 1985 postmodern novel *Hawksmoor*, which describes the architect's churches as mysterious, with Masonic, occult and pagan links.

26   # THE LITTLE SHOP OF HORRORS

Address: 11 Mare Street, E8 4RP (020-7998 3617, viktorwyndofhackney.co.uk).
Opening hours: Sat, noon-7pm, or by appointment, for which there's a £10 charge.
Regular admission to the museum is £2 adults, £1 concessions.
Transport: Bethnal Green tube or London Fields rail.

Viktor Wynd

The interestingly-named Viktor Wynd is a multi-disciplinary artist and the Chancellor of the Last Tuesday Society. This dates from the 1870s and is devoted 'to exploring and furthering the esoteric, literary and artistic aspects of life in London and beyond' (thelasttuesdaysociety.org). The Little Shop of Horrors, which opened in 2009, is the Society's first permanent base and is a combination of art gallery, museum and shop.

It dubs itself 'Hackney's Leading Curiosity Shop' (although there probably aren't too many claimants to that crown) and describes itself as 'an attempt to recreate or reinterpret, within 21st-century sensibilities, a 17th-century *Wunderkabinett*; a collection of objects assembled at a whim on the basis of their aesthetic or historic appeal.' In short, it's an arbitrary display designed to give pleasure.

The venue is also available to hire for events, e.g. book launches, receptions, film and television shoots, and has a large selection of props for hire. There are also regular lectures on esoteric subjects (see website).

If you're looking for a gift for the man (or woman) who has everything, the Little Shop sells a wide variety of curiosities, including articulated skeletons, carnivorous plants, shrunken heads and taxidermy.

LLOYDS COFFEE HOUSE BLUE PLAQUE   27

Address: 18 Lombard Street, EC3.
Transport: Bank tube.

Coffee houses have a surprising and distinguished connection with the development of British high finance. Becoming popular in the 17th and 18th centuries, they became places not just to drink coffee, but also to hear the day's news and meet others to discuss matters of mutual concern. In that, they resembled ale houses and inns, but the absence of alcohol created an atmosphere more conducive to discussing serious matters, and they played a notable role in the development of financial markets and the newspaper industry.

Edward Lloyd's (c 1648-1713) coffee house was frequented by merchants, ship owners and ship's captains; it's where shipping industry deals, including insurance, began to be transacted. From these beginnings, it grew to become the world's most famous insurance market, Lloyd's of London.

Lloyds coffee house was founded in around 1688 and was originally on Tower Street, moving to Lombard Street in 1691. Edward Lloyd died in 1713, but merchants continued to discuss insurance at his coffee house until 1774, when a committee was formed and moved to the Royal Exchange on Cornhill as the Society of Lloyd's. The coffee house remained open on Lombard Street until 1785.

Lombard Street was an appropriate location for Lloyd's. The practice of marine insurance was introduced to England by the Lombard bankers who were leading lights in medieval London's financial sector.

28   LONDON'S LEAST PRIVATE HOUSE

Address: Wood Street, EC2V 7AF
Transport: St Paul's tube.

If you're looking for a curious and striking home, designed by Sir Christopher Wren, convenient for the City and you don't mind being overlooked, this is perfect. What was once the tower of St Alban's Church is now a private, six-storey house, which is unusually situated on a traffic island in the middle of a narrow City street. Large office buildings surround it, so it's overlooked by hundreds of people (certainly during office hours).

1685 and was built in a late Perpendicular Gothic style and extended by Sir George Gilbert Scott in 1858. The building was partially destroyed in the Blitz of 1940, leaving the 92ft tower. The ruins of the rest of the church were removed in 1955 and the tower converted into a private home.

The tower appears as the headquarters of the group AD1 in the 2009 film *St Trinian's II: The Legend of Fritton's Gold*.

There have been a number of churches on the site, perhaps as far back as the time of King Offa of Mercia (died 796AD), but it's been occupied for longer: the remains of two Roman buildings were discovered here in 1962, thought to be a 2nd-century barracks.

The current church (what remains of it) is a Sir Christopher Wren rebuild after the previous one was destroyed in the Great Fire of London. It dates from

LONDON'S MOST VULGAR STREET NAMES 29

Address: Around Cheapside, EC2.
Transport: Bank or St Paul's tube.

People who dislike spicy language should avoid this entry, which includes the ultimate four-letter word. During the Middle Ages, it was standard practice for street names to reflect the street's function or local economic speciality, however distasteful. Remarkable though it seems today, Gropecunt Lane was a not uncommon name in medieval England, denoting a street where prostitutes plied their trade. Its earliest known use is from around 1230 and it continued, with slight variations, until around 1560. Thereafter, the name was often softened to Grope Lane, Grape Lane or similar, as the Puritan streak of the new Protestantism made its mark.

London had several streets going by this delightful name, including one near

Cheapside, 19th century

Cheapside. It was part of a group of streets that comprised a small red light district outside the main one, which was Southwark. Its exact location is unknown, although a favourite as the former Gropecunt Lane is Milton Street near the Barbican, which was called Grub Street in the 19th century. A location near Cheapside was logical because an important market was held here and would have provided ready custom for the prostitutes.

There's a slightly gentler example of a robust street name near Cannon Street, EC4. In the 1270s, Sherborne Lane was Shitteborwelane Lane, later Shite-burn Lane and Shite-buruelane, probably because of nearby cesspits.

30   THE OLDEST HOUSE IN THE CITY

Address: 41/42 Cloth Fair, EC1A 7JQ.
Transport: Barbican tube.

Hidden down a small street and looking like something from a film set, 41/42 Cloth Fair is the City's oldest house, built 1597-1614, and the only one to survive 1666's Great Fire. Originally part of a larger group of houses with a courtyard in the middle, called The Square in Launders Green, the building escaped the worst of the fire because it was enclosed by a large set of priory walls.

It was nearly lost, however, when in 1929 it was put under review for demolition by the City of London Corporation; worse, it was served with a dangerous structure notice. Luckily the house was saved and today is Grade II* listed. It isn't open to the public but the impressive exterior can

be enjoyed, which is the safest option: there are rumoured to be skeletons in the foundations and stories of ghosts. A set of leaded windows carries the signatures (etched with a diamond pen) of some of the property's notable visitors, including the Queen Mother, Viscount Montgomery of Alamein and Sir Winston Churchill.

Appropriately the poet Sir John Betjeman, a great campaigner to save historic buildings, once lived close by at 43/4 Cloth Court.

It's worth exploring the narrow medieval streets around Cloth Fair, which was named after the Bartholomew Fair, held locally between 1133 and 1855.

THE PANYER ALLEY FRIEZE   31

Address: Panyer Alley, EC4.
Transport: St Paul's tube.

It's thought that the bas-relief used to be on the exterior wall of the Panyer Tavern (which was perhaps called the Panyer Boy), located around the corner on Paternoster Row until being destroyed in 1666 during the Great Fire of London.

An unusual bas-relief is set into the wall at the north end of this alley. It's of a naked boy astride what appears to be a panyer or bread basket (from the French *pannier*). The alley is so-called because manufacturers of panyers were once based here to supply the bakers in nearby Bread Street.

Below the relief is an inscription – 'When ye have sought, The Citty Round, Yet still this is, The Highest Ground' – and beneath it the date, 'August the 27th 1688'. The inscription's claim is incorrect, as Cornhill is the City's highest spot, being around 1ft higher than here. And it's thought that the bas-relief might predate the inscription under it; it certainly looks more weathered.

As to what the bas-relief signifies, it might simply have been a sign for the Panyer Tavern or to commemorate the boys who used to sell bread from baskets here. Or it might mark the site of an early medieval corn market. Some argue for a more general, vaguely pagan meaning, that of a general emblem of plenty.

32   A POETIC PLANE TREE

> **Address:** Corner of Wood Street and Cheapside, EC2.
> **Transport:** St Paul's tube.

A 70ft plane tree sits incongruously in the heart of London's financial district, on the corner of Wood Street and Cheapside. The tree has become emblematic of the area, having been here for a long time – nobody's sure how long, but various documents speculatively (and rather unhelpfully) refer to it as 'ancient' – and it has even inspired poetry

Where the tree is located was once within the churchyard of St Peter's, one of many churches destroyed by the Great Fire in 1666 and never rebuilt. In the late 1790s it inspired William Wordsworth to write a poem – *The Reverie of Poor Susan* – in which the natural world around Cheapside is reimagined by a girl hearing a thrush.

> Plane trees are hardy and can flourish in London's dust, grime, smoke and limited space. They are tolerant of both atmospheric pollution and the painful-sounding root compaction.

The Wood Street plane tree is protected. It rises above surrounding buildings, which aren't permitted to be built higher than the tree and so deprive it of light. Beneath it are a series of small shops, of a sort that have characterised this corner for several hundred years, a welcome change from the City's towering high-rises.

PRINCE ALBERT'S POLITE-BUT-DANGEROUS STATUE

Address: Holborn Circus, EC1N 2QX.
Transport: Chancery Lane tube.

Holborn Circus is a busy junction at the boundary between Holborn and Smithfield. In the centre is an elegant, equestrian statue of Prince Albert (1819-61), the much-missed, long-mourned husband of Queen Victoria.

The statue was unveiled in 1874 and is sometimes called the most polite in London, as the Prince is seen to be tipping his hat rather jauntily to pedestrians, when he might be expected to be saluting. However, saluting is a relatively recent development and until later in the Victorian era, officers doffed their hats rather than saluted; indeed, the latter would probably have been regarded as vulgar. The statue is the work of Charles Bacon and is the City of London's official monument to Prince Albert, whose tipped hat is intended to be directed towards the City.

Albert's statue has been cited as something of a hazard, partly to blame for Holborn Circus's high accident rate, as it obstructs drivers' sight lines. As a result, it's due to be moved, probably to a position on High Holborn.

Prince Albert died at the young age of 42. The cause is thought to have been typhoid, although recent theorists have mentioned Crohn's disease, renal failure and cancer as possible culprits.

34   SAFFRON HILL

Address: Saffron Hill, EC1.
Transport: Chancery Lane or Farringdon tube.

Names can be deceptive and the pretty, indeed fragrant, title of this street between Farringdon Road and Hatton Garden hides an unpleasant fact about the medieval diet. Saffron Hill is thus named because it was once part of an estate on which the spice was grown.

Twist, the Artful Dodger leads Oliver to Fagin's den in Field Lane, the southern extension of Saffron Hill: 'A dirty and more wretched place he had never seen. The street was narrow and muddy, and the air was impregnated with filthy odours'. So the fragrant hill has a mixed past.

Saffron has a bitter taste and hay-like fragrance, and these qualities meant it was widely used in the Middle Ages (when the labour to pick it was dirt cheap) to mask the taste of the rancid meat that many people had to eat. No wonder life expectancy was so short!

Saffron is derived from the crocus and because each flower's stigmas must be collected by hand, and there are only a few per flower, it's the world's most expensive spice.

Later, the area around Saffron Hill fell on hard times and became a squalid district, home to the poor and thieves. In Charles Dickens's 1837 novel *Oliver*

ST ANDREW'S BLUECOATS   35

Address: St Andrew's Church, St Andrew Street, EC4 (www.standrewholborn.org.uk).
Transport: Chancery Lane tube.

St Andrew's Church is ancient: it first appears in 951 and when the crypt was excavated in 2002, Roman pottery was discovered, so the site has been in use for much longer. A 15th-century tower is the oldest surviving part and the most curious aspect of the church is the two blue-coated figures – a boy and a girl – on the exterior wall by the west door. They were originally on the St Andrew's Parochial School, which was founded in Brook Market in 1696 (the date is displayed by the girl) and moved to Hatton Garden in 1721.

This attractive pair of figures was over the Cross Street entrance to the Hatton Garden School but was relocated here when the church was refurbished after World War II bomb damage. Such distinctive blue figures marked charity schools, with many dating from the mid-16th century.

The costumes were the usual school dress of the period. Blue was used for charity school children because it was the cheapest dye available for clothing. Socks were dyed in saffron because it was thought to stop rats from nibbling the pupils' ankles!

St Andrew's has another charity connection: it's the final resting place of Thomas Coram, who established the Foundling Hospital in 1741.

36   ST ETHELDREDA'S HAND

Address: St Etheldreda's Church, 14 Ely Place, EC1N 6RY (020-7405 1061, stetheldreda.com).
Opening hours: Mon-Sat, 8am-5pm; Sun, 8am-12.30pm.
Transport: Chancery Lane tube.

St Etheldreda's Church was built in 1290 and is a rare, surviving building from the reign of Edward I. It was once part of the Bishop of Ely's London headquarters – which resembled an independent state within the city – and is the proud possessor of a grisly and unlikely relic: the hand of St Etheldreda herself.

Etheldreda was a daughter of Anna, King (not Queen!) of East Anglia. Born in 630, she wanted to be a nun but agreed to a political marriage to King Egfrith from a nearby territory provided she could remain a virgin. When Egfrith later tried to break this agreement, she fled back to Ely and founded a religious community.

Etheldreda died in 679 and when her body was moved 15 years later, it was found to be in a perfect state of preservation. It was still intact when it was moved again, by the Normans, in 1106. A piece of her uncorrupted hand was given to St Etheldreda's church in the 19th century and now has pride of place in the church, displayed in a jewel case to the right of the high altar.

The saint's hand had been removed in Norman times and was later kept in a secret hiding place on the Duke of Norfolk's estate, at a time when all-things-Catholic were persecuted.

ST JOHN'S GATE   37

Address: Museum of the Order of St John, St John's Gate, EC1M 4DA (020-7324 4005, museumstjohn.org.uk).
Opening hours: Mon-Sat, 10am-5pm; Sun, closed.
Cost: Free, with a suggested £5 donation for guided tours.
Transport: Farringdon tube/rail.

This unexpected curiosity resembles a modern folly or the entrance to a medieval theme park. However, St John's Gate is much older and more distinguished, being one of the few physical reminders of trendy Clerkenwell's monastic past. Built in 1504, it was an entrance to the Priory of the Knights of St John, also known as the Knights Hospitallers, a Christian military order (and forerunners of the St John Ambulance).

The Knights' property was confiscated by Henry VIII and the buildings have subsequently had a varied history. During the 16th century they were the offices of the splendidly-named Master of the Revels, and 30 Shakespeare plays were licensed here.

The family of painter William Hogarth lived here from 1701-09, when the artist was a child, and from 1703 it was briefly a coffee house run by Richard Hogarth, William's father. He offered Latin lessons with the coffee, so it's hardly surprising that the enterprise wasn't a roaring commercial success! Later, Samuel Johnson got his first London job at St John's Gate, writing for *The Gentleman's Magazine*.

St John's Gate now houses the remarkable Museum of the Order of St John, which tells its story from its origins in 11th-century Jerusalem to the modern day.

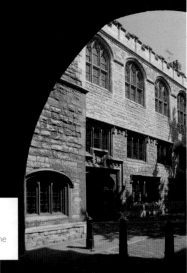

38   ST OLAVE'S SKULLS

Address: St Olave's Church, 8 Hart Street, EC3R 7NB (020-7488 4318, sanctuaryinthecity.net).
Opening hours: Mon-Fri, 9am-5pm for the church, although the skulls can be seen at any time atop the churchyard's entrance arch.
Transport: Aldgate tube or Fenchurch Street tube/rail.

St Olave's is on the corner of Hart Street and Seething Lane near Fenchurch Street Station. It was described by the poet and champion of old buildings Sir John Betjeman as 'a country church in the world of Seething Lane'. It's one of the few medieval churches to survive the ravages of the Great Fire in 1666, and also one of the City's smallest.

Charles Dickens was keen on this striking example of grisliness, including the church in his *Uncommercial Traveller* and naming it 'St Ghastly Grim'.

The church is first recorded in the 13th century and is dedicated to the patron saint of Norway, King Olaf II. The present building has a Perpendicular Gothic exterior, dates from around 1450 and was restored after World War II bomb damage. Its most striking and curious feature is the entrance arch to the churchyard, which dates from 1658. The arch is ghoulishly decorated with some splendid grinning skulls, three in the pediment and two more on the corners, as well as crossed bones and iron spikes.

Below the skulls is a quote from St Paul about happiness in death: *Christus vivere Mors mihi lucrum* (Christ is life to me, Death is my reward).

ST PAUL'S TOMBS 39

Address: St Paul's Cathedral, St Paul's Churchyard, EC4M 8AD (stpauls.co.uk).
Opening hours: Mon-Sat, 8.30am-4pm. Sundays open for worship only.
Cost: Adult, £16; concession, £14; age 6-17, £7; family (two adults and two children), £39.
Transport: St Paul's tube.

The tombs of two of those interred at St Paul's Cathedral have curious tales attached.

There are scorch marks at the base of the statue on the resting place of poet and preacher **John Donne**, who died in 1631. Donne's is one of very few effigies to survive the Great Fire of 1666 more or less intact. Donne was, of course, originally buried in the original St Paul's, not Sir Christopher Wren's cathedral.

Killed at the Battle of Trafalgar in 1805, **Lord Nelson** was buried at St Paul's after a state funeral. Strange to relate, his black marble sarcophagus is second-hand and some 300 years older than its occupant. It was originally made for Cardinal Wolsey (c 1473-1530), Lord Chancellor during Henry VIII's reign.

After Wolsey's fall from grace – which was partly the result of his failure to secure an annulment of Henry's marriage to Catherine of Aragon so that he could marry Anne Boleyn – the king confiscated the sarcophagus. It remained unused at Windsor until a suitable 'tenant' could be found. Nelson's viscount coronet now tops it.

John Donne's tomb

Nelson's sarcophagus contains his wooden coffin which was made from the mast of the *L'Orient*, a French ship salvaged after the Battle of the Nile in 1798.

Lord Nelson's tomb

40   A SHEPHERD & SHEEP IN THE CITY

Address: Paternoster Square, EC4M 7DX.
Transport: St Paul's tube.

Sleek Paternoster Square is the nicely anomalous location for a sculpture of a ram and four ewes walking ahead of a naked, androgynous shepherd. It sits at the north end of the square and is the work of Dame Elizabeth Frink (1930-93), made of bronze on a Portland stone plinth.

Dame Elizabeth Frink

The sculpture was commissioned in 1975, originally unveiled by Sir Yehudi Menhuin and installed in the refurbished square in 2003. It's thought that it was inspired by Frink's stay in the mountainous Cervennes region of France, where sheep and shepherds are an integral part of the landscape, and also by her admiration for Picasso's 1944 bronze *Man with Sheep*.

But the sculptor wouldn't have been entirely free to choose the subject matter, given the work's location, and the subject of a shepherd and sheep has obvious religious connotations, in keeping with its proximity to St Paul's Cathedral. Paternoster Square and nearby Paternoster Row are where the cathedral's clergy would walk in procession in medieval times, holding their rosary beads and reciting the Lord's Prayer.

Paternoster Square would have been full of sheep in the 17th century, when it was the site of the Newgate Meat Market (until 1889). Today, the square is home to another type of market: the London Stock Exchange.

THE STATUE WITH A REAL QUILL PEN

Address: St Andrew Undershaft, St Mary Axe, EC3A 8BN (020-7283 2231).
Opening hours: Viewing by appointment.
Transport: Aldgate tube or Liverpool Street tube/rail.

The church of St Andrew Undershaft is the setting for one of the City's more unusual rituals. Every three years, in early April, a service is held in memory of the historian and antiquarian John Stow (c 1525-1605), organised by the Worshipful Company of Merchant Taylors, of which he was a member.

Stow is best known for his *Survey of London*, published in 1598, which is

The next Stow memorial service is due to take place in April 2014, although the exact date hadn't been confirmed at the time of writing.

valued for its detailed account of the buildings, customs and social conditions of London during the reign of Elizabeth I. As a result, Stow's sometimes called the Father of London History, although he never made much money from his writing.

He was buried at St Andrew Undershaft and has a handsome terracotta monument which shows him, quill pen in hand, writing in a book. The quill is the only part of the monument that isn't made of stone, and during the service to give thanks for Stow's life and work it's replaced by a fresh one. The old quill and a copy of Stow's book are presented to a child who's written the best essay about London.

42   THE SWAN UPPING STATUE

Address: Garlick Hill, EC4V.
Transport: Mansion House tube.

Outside the curiously-named church St James Garlickythe is a statue that celebrates the strange ceremony of Swan Upping. Commissioned by the Vintners' Livery Company, the statue is by Vivien Mallock and called *The Barge Master and Swan Marker*. The barge master is shown in traditional costume and there's an attentive swan at his feet. It seems wary about the stick in his right hand, but it needn't be because the master has his swans' best interests at heart.

Swan Upping occurs in the third week of July each year and the ceremony dates back to the 12th century when the Crown claimed ownership of all mute swans, a valuable source of food for banquets and feasts. The Crown maintains ownership to this day, although the Queen generally exercises it only on the Thames and its tributaries. The ownership is shared with the Vintners' and Dyers' Livery Companies, which were granted this privilege in the 15th century.

The ceremony involves six traditional Thames skiffs making a five-day journey upstream to Abingdon in Berkshire. The swanherds count, weigh, measure and tag swans on the way, as well as checking their health, and then report the results. These days, of course, the swans are no longer eaten.

St James Garlickythe refers to the jetty, or 'hythe', at which garlic was landed in medieval times. It was probably then traded on Garlick Hill.

Swan upping

THE THOMAS BECKETT SCULPTURE   43

Address: St Paul's Cathedral gardens, EC4.
Transport: St Paul's tube.

A dramatic, expressive sculpture sits in the gardens by St Paul's Cathedral, capturing the final moments of a dying man. It's the work of Edward Bainbridge Copnall (1903-73) and was acquired by the Corporation of London in 1973. The sculpture depicts the death throes of Thomas Beckett (c 1118-70), who was born in Cheapside and rose from fairly humble origins to become Archbishop of Canterbury, from 1162 until his assassination in 1170.

Beckett had been involved in a conflict with Henry II over the Church's rights and privileges, and about Beckett excommunicating his opponents within the Church. There's a debate about whether Henry actually wanted the Archbishop dead and we have several competing versions of what he might have said. The most oft-quoted is 'Will no one rid me of this turbulent priest?', although its accuracy is disputed by some modern scholars.

But whatever Henry did or didn't say or wish for, four of his knights decided he wanted the Archbishop dead and they hacked him to death as he knelt praying in Canterbury Cathedral. A couple of years later, Beckett was canonised by Pope Alexander III and his shrine in Canterbury Cathedral became an important focus for pilgrims.

Murder of Beckett

The recumbent bronze sculpture at St Paul's graphically captures Becket's last moments and is regarded as one of Copnall's best works.

44   THE VIADUCT TAVERN

Address: 126 Newgate Street, EC1A 7AA (020-7600 1863, viaducttavern.co.uk).
Opening hours: Mon-Fri, 8.30am-11pm; Sat and Sun, closed.
Transport: St Paul's tube.

This attractive, showy Victorian gin palace was built in 1869 and is Grade II listed. As well as its range of ornate and gilded decorations, it has three interesting curiosities, two of them the result of human shortcomings, the third more other-worldly. First, at the rear of the bar is an unusual booth, from which the Victorian landlady would sell beer and gin tokens to customers. It had to be thus because her staff weren't always entirely trustworthy and weren't allowed to handle money.

Second, one of the paintings in the bar has a hole in it, made by the bayonet of a World War I soldier during a scuffle. Finally, the Viaduct Tavern is said to be one of London's more haunted pubs, where there have been bouts of poltergeist activity by a spectre known as Fred. Electricians working in one of the upstairs rooms have reported this but it's most common in the cellars, where several members of staff have experienced it.

The pub is built on the site of the now-demolished Giltspur Street Compter debtors' prison and its cellars are said to include five of the prison's cells. One or more of the former prisoners is thought to be the source of the supernatural activity.

A VULTURE IN THE CITY   45

Address: The George & Vulture, 3 Castle Court, EC3V 9DL.
Opening hours: Mon-Fri, noon-2.30pm. Sat-Sun, closed.
Transport: Bank tube.

The Grade II listed chop-house The George & Vulture is situated in a maze of narrow, atmospheric alleyways that hint at what the City used to look like. It has a number of interesting quirks, not least the origin of its name. Built in 1748 (although there's been an inn on the site since 1268), it was originally called The George. When a vintner occupied nearby premises, instead of putting up a sign to advertise his business, he tethered a live vulture outside. Subsequently, the vintner moved elsewhere and the chop-house adopted the bird and incorporated it into the name.

There's some confusion at the George & Vulture when it comes to spiritual matters: on the one hand, it sits on the boundary of two parishes – St Michael, Cornhill and St Edmund the King, Lombard Street – with the dividing line running through the middle of the restaurant. On the other, it's said to have been a regular haunt of the infamous, libertine Hellfire Club.

Charles Dickens was certainly a regular here (an unsubstantiated boast at many London hostelries) and the chop-house is immortalised in his first novel, *The Pickwick Papers* – Mr Pickwick buys Sam Weller lunch here.

Like a number of City establishments, the George & Vulture has a resident ghost: the upstairs dining room is said to be haunted by a grey lady.

46   THE WICKHAMS' GAP

Address: 69-89 Mile End Road, E1.
Transport: Mile End tube.

The ornately pillared frontage of the former Wickhams Department Store in Mile End had a notable gap, which was partially filled by a small shop. It somewhat resembled a broken tooth and appeared to be a botched or incomplete repair, perhaps following bomb damage. However, the 'gap' reflected a healthy, historic act of defiance by a family firm against a much larger opponent.

Salter's shop

The small shop filling the gap, at 81 Mile End Road, belonged to a family of German jewellers, the Spiegelhalters, who changed their name to Salter in 1919 due to anti-German sentiment following World War I. In the '20s, the rest of the row of shops was bought and demolished to facilitate the building of the sweeping Wickhams Department Store, subsequently dubbed the 'Harrods of the East End'.

The Salter family were offered a lot of money to sell their premises but refused, so the grand department store had to be built around their shop. When it opened in 1927, Wickhams' elegant classical façade with its Doric columns had a glaring gap, the jeweller being a sort of cuckoo in the nest.

Sadly, both the department and jewellery stores are now closed – the gap previously occupied by the jewellery shop is now a glass atrium – and the building is being redeveloped.

THE ALFRED HITCHCOCK MOSAICS   47

Address: Leytonstone Tube Station, Church Lane, E11 1HE.
Transport: As above.

The entrance corridors to Leytonstone tube station are decorated by 17 colourful, eye-catching mosaics which were installed to mark the centenary of the birth of the film director Alfred Hitchcock. Although associated with Hollywood, Hitchcock was British, born at 517 High Road, Leytonstone in 1899. He moved to Hollywood in 1939, became a US citizen in 1955 and died in 1980.

Unveiled in 2001 and made from 80,000 tiles (vitreous glass tessarae, to be more specific), 14 of the mosaics depict scenes from Hitchcock's films, while the other three show the great man himself: as a child outside his parents' shop; at work as a film director; and relaxing.

Each mosaic has an information plaque explaining what it depicts.

BRUNE STREET JEWISH SOUP KITCHEN   48

Address: Brune Street, E1.
Transport: Aldgate East tube.

It isn't surprising to find a soup kitchen in the deprived East End, but it's odd to find one as attractive and ornate as this, although the design was deliberate. Many Jewish immigrants to East London in the later 19th century struggled to survive, and in 1902 the Jewish community built this soup kitchen to help them.

Its impressive façade testifies to the wealth of some Jewish traders and was intended to show their less fortunate brothers that with hard work they, too, could succeed. It was also intended to reassure existing residents that Jewish incomers weren't going to be a drain on public funds. The lovely sandstone façade remains but the building has been converted into upmarket flats.

49   CABLE STREET MURAL

Address: 236 Cable Street, E1 0BL (battleofcablestreet.co.uk).
Transport: Shadwell tube.

This mural commemorates a 'victory' against fascism in 1936, when Oswald Mosley's British Union of Fascists was stopped from marching through Cable Street, then a Jewish area. The ensuing clash became known as the Battle of Cable Street, involving 250,000 anti-fascists and 10,000 police. After a series of running battles, Mosley abandoned the march, but the anti-fascists continued to riot, 150 people were arrested and over 100 injured.

The mural is painted on the side of St George's Town Hall, and was designed by Dave Binnington, who included many local characters in his work. He began it in 1980 but quit after it was vandalised, and the mural was completed by Ray Walker and Desmond Rochfort in 1982. It now has a coat of protective varnish.

DEAD DOGS IN THE CITY   50

Address: Houndsditch, EC3.
Transport: Aldgate tube.

Houndsditch follows the route of an ancient ditch that ran outside part of London's defensive wall. It became infamous as a place to dump rubbish, including dead dogs – obviously in some quantity, given the subsequent name. A ditch was first built here by the Romans, but it gradually became filled in. The Danes under Cnut the Great dug another one, which was re-dug again in 1211, this time around 75ft (23m) wide.

But its use as a rubbish dump became increasingly common and the name Houndsditch first appeared in the 13th century. Several dogs' skeletons were unearthed here in 1989,

perhaps because the City's kennels for hunting dogs were kept in the ditch, which some argue is the primary source of the name.

HOUNDSDITCH.
ONE OF THE BUSIEST STREETS OF LONDON

THE DRAGON'S GATE   51

Address: Mandarin Street and East India Dock Road, E14.
Transport: Westferry DLR.

An eye-catching sculpture of a pair of shiny metallic dragons marks the fact that Limehouse was the location of London's first Chinatown. The sculpture, by Peter Dunn, dates from 1997, while a plaque below reads, 'Biting each other's tails, they embody the power and unity of renewal'.

Limehouse was an obvious place for the Chinese to settle, as its docks stored opium and tea brought from their home country. The first immigrants arrived in the 1880s and consisted only of men as women weren't initially permitted. The Chinese community that developed seized the popular imagination – for example its opium dens appear in the *Sherlock Holmes* stories. Much of Limehouse's Chinatown was destroyed during the Blitz and a new one subsequently emerged in and around Soho's Gerrard Street.

52   ELIZABETH I'S SPYMASTER

Address: Walsingham House, 35 Seething Lane, EC3.
Transport: Tower Hill tube.

We think of spying as a modern, high-tech phenomenon, primarily the invention of the Cold War. However, it has a long history, as the unusual glass portrait above the entrance door to 35 Seething Lane reveals. It's of a bearded Elizabethan gent with an impressive neck ruff and depicts Sir Francis Walsingham (c 1532-90).

Sir Francis Walsingham

policy. Indeed, he was Principal Secretary to Elizabeth I from 1573-90 and became commonly known as her Spymaster, as he was particularly concerned with thwarting Catholic plots against her. He died at his Seething Lane mansion and Walsingham House is a Victorian office block built on the site.

He was born to a well-connected family and became one of a small group of people which directed Elizabethan England, deciding domestic, foreign and religious

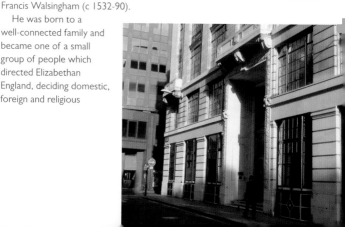

FACADISM   53

Address: Artillery Lane and Gun Street, E1.
Transport: Liverpool Street tube/rail.

Spitalfields has an example of the practice of 'facadism', i.e. leaving a historic façade in place when the building behind is replaced. If done well, the contrast between the old façade and new structure built behind it can look vibrant and interesting. But when done clumsily it can look odd or downright silly.

The historic façade on the corner of 18th-century Artillery Lane and Gun Street (so-called because the area was used for artillery practice until the end of the 17th century) is controversial, as the façade is slightly adrift of the new building behind, with large metal pins holding it at arm's length. Probably worse, its blank, empty windows are out of kilter with those behind. Not a great example then!

THE FIGHTING MICE   54

Address: 13 Philpot Lane, EC3.
Transport: Monument tube.

An unusual Italianate building on Philpot Lane has curious decorations of dogs' and pigs' faces. Less obviously, it also has a pair of brown mice fighting over a piece of cheese built into the fascia. They date from 1862 when the building was constructed for the spice merchants Messrs Hunt and Crombie.

Behind this seemingly innocent, even childlike addition to the building is a tragic tale. Builders were plagued by mice throughout the construction project and an argument apparently broke out when one workman accused another of eating some of his lunch. During the ensuing row, one of

them fell to his death. Later, it was discovered that mice had been the lunch culprits and two rodents were added to the building to mark this event.

55   'FILM SET' SHOP FRONTS

Address: 56-8 Artillery Lane, E1.
Transport: Liverpool Street tube/rail.

Numbers 56 and 58 Artillery Lane in Spitalfields are 'paired houses' – adjoining properties – and their elegant, historical frontages look like a Jane Austin film set. But they're actually original. These remarkable, welcome survivors were built in the early 18th century and remodelled in 1756-7. They were originally occupied by two prosperous Huguenot silk merchants, Nicholas Jourdain and Francis Rybot.

Number 56 is of particular note, as it's generally regarded as London's finest surviving mid-Georgian shop front, with varied, interesting detail that warrants close inspection. It's Grade I listed, while number 58 is the relatively poor relation, with an early 19th-century, plain Regency frontage and only Grade II listed.

A GLAMOROUS YOUTH HOSTEL   56

Address: 36-39 Carter Lane, EC4V 5AB.
Transport: St Paul's tube.

Winding, intimate Carter Lane is an appropriate location for one of London's most attractive youth hostels. Built in 1874-5 by F C Penrose as St Paul's Choir School, it opened in 1876 with 40 boys and is Grade II listed. It's a striking building of white brick, terracotta and plaster with unusual, important sgrafitto decoration. A Latin inscription on the frieze around the building is taken from St Paul's letter to the Galatians, 6:24.

Sgraffito is a technique of wall decoration produced by applying layers of plaster tinted in contrasting colours to a moistened surface. The word comes from the Italian *graffiare* – to scratch – and graffiti is a related term. It's been used in Europe since classical times and was common in 16th-century Italy.

THE GRAPES LADDER   57

Address: The Grapes, 76 Narrow Street, E14 8BP (020-7987 4396, thegrapes.co.uk).
Opening hours: Mon-Wed, noon-3pm and 5.30-11pm; Thu-Sat, noon-11pm; Sun, noon-10.30pm.
Transport: Westferry DLR.

This convivial, 500-year-old riverside pub in Limehouse is part-owned by the 'real Gandalf', Sir Ian McKellen. Charles Dickens knew the place well and is said to have used it as the model for The Six Jolly Fellowship Porters in *Our Mutual Friend*.

In addition to these pleasing filmic and literary associations, it has a grimmer side: at the back is a wooden ladder leading down to the shore, a reminder of the time when watermen (who ferried passengers across the Thames) would use it to leave the pub carrying drunks to the middle of the river, where they would drown them in order to sell their corpses to dissectors.

58   GRASSHOPPERS

> **Address:** Lombard Street, EC3V and Royal Exchange, EC3V 3LR.
> **Transport:** Bank tube.

Striking grasshoppers adorn both a building on Lombard Street and the top of the Royal Exchange. Their origin is the Elizabethan merchant, financial whizzkid and Royal Exchange founder Sir Thomas Gresham (c 1519-79), who worked for Edward VI and Queens Mary I and Elizabeth I.

The grasshopper is the crest above the Gresham coat of arms. According to family legend, the founder of the family, Roger de Gresham, was a foundling who'd been abandoned as a newborn baby in long grass in Norfolk in the 13th century. He was discovered by a woman whose attention was drawn to him by a grasshopper's chirruping. Less romantically, it's more likely that the grasshopper is a heraldic rebus on the name Gresham, with gres being Middle English for grass.

Thomas Gresham

THE HAGAN HOUSE 59

Address: 125 Golden Lane, EC1Y 0TJ.
Transport: Barbican tube.

An unusual, award-winning, seven-storey house by the architect Jo Hagan sits in Clerkenwell, north of the Barbican Centre. It's a tall, narrow property, of a type apparently called a 'slot-house' by architects. There's only one room per floor, but sufficient space for a lift and a roof garden at the top. The rooms can be seen quite easily from the lane, as the five main floors are glass-fronted.

Jo Hagan has managed to create a lot of space from a ground footprint which is little more than that of an average one-vehicle garage: the house covers 2,000ft², but the plot is a mere 11ft by 28ft. Such houses could be the way forward in London, where building land is scarce and expensive.

HODGE THE CAT 60

Address: Outside 17 Gough Square, EC4.
Transport: Chancery Lane tube.

The great man of letters Samuel Johnson (1709-84) was a cat lover. One of his felines, Hodge, is commemorated by a bronze statue outside the house that Johnson occupied for a dozen years and where he did much of the work for his *Dictionary of the English Language*.

The cat sits on a copy of this famous book, with a couple of oyster shells in front of him. Hodge was fond of oysters, which were a staple of the poor in Johnson's time rather than the luxury they are today. The statue, by Jon Bickley, was unveiled in 1997. Its inscription reads, 'But he is a very fine cat; a very fine cat indeed', after a remark Johnson made to his biographer James Boswell (1740-95).

61   JACK THE RIPPER'S PUB

Address: The Ten Bells, 84 Commercial Street, E1 6LY.
Opening hours: Sun-Wed, noon-midnight; Thu-Sat, noon-1am.
Transport: Liverpool Street tube/rail or Shoreditch High Street rail.

Nowadays Spitalfields is a gentrified part of London, peopled by creative types, so it's curious to learn that it's where Jack the Ripper committed some of his crimes. The Ten Bells, a Grade II listed pub, was at the heart of the Ripper's activities. At least two of his (prostitute) victims drank and solicited business here: Annie Chapman and Mary Kelly.

Mary was the Ripper's final recorded victim. She left the pub in the early hours of November 9th 1888, and her mutilated body was discovered the next morning in Millers Court, just across the road. The pub's grim past has apparently left a mark: a number of ghosts are said to haunt it.

JOHN WESLEY'S CHAPEL LAVATORIES   62

Address: 49 City Road, EC1Y 1AU (020-7253 2262, wesleyschapel.org.uk).
Opening hours: Mon-Sat, 10am-4pm; Sun, 12.30-1.45pm.
Transport: Old Street tube.

John Wesley was the co-founder of Methodism, with his brother Charles. In the year of his death, 1791 – at the grand age of 87 – he said, 'Slovenliness is no part of religion. Cleanliness is indeed close to Godliness'. So it's appropriate that his Chapel on City Road has an underground 'shrine' to that champion of the flushing lavatory and inventor of the ballcock, Thomas Crapper.

Installed in 1899, it's one of London's most decorative 'public' lavatories. Eight cedar cubicles face eight urinals, with eight marble washbasins at the end. The rest is an engaging blend of wooden surfaces, shining marble and mosaics. If only modern conveniences were this attractive.

THE KING'S WARDROBE   63

Address: Wardrobe Place, EC4.
Transport: St Paul's tube.

An alleyway off Carter Lane leads to a small, handsome square dating from 1720. A blue plaque marks it as the former site of the King's Wardrobe. In around 1359, Edward III moved his Royal Wardrobe from the Tower of London to this spot a stone's throw from St Paul's Cathedral. The Wardrobe consisted of a variety of royal possessions: arms, ceremonial clothing for state events and other personal items.

It was stored in a property the king purchased from a City burgher and was used until it was destroyed in the Great Fire of 1666. Today the square is a tranquil, historic haven, inhabited by the ghost of a lady who's seen dressed in white and drifting from door to door shortly after dusk.

64   LONDON'S BEGINNINGS?

Address: Number One Poultry, EC2.
Transport: Bank tube.

London was founded by the Romans, despite a desire among some people to prove that the city is older, in order to 'keep up' with Athens and Rome. Although the land that London covers had been occupied for thousands of years before, the first permanent settlement of any significance appeared shortly after the Roman invasion of Britain in 43AD.

When the distinctive, ocean liner-like building of Number One Poultry was erected, an extensive (and expensive) archaeological investigation preceded it. Among many interesting finds was a Roman wooden drain which was tree-ring dated to 47AD, making it the earliest London structure yet discovered. So this spot could mark the very beginning of the city. Opposite sit the remains of another early Roman landmark, the Temple of Mithras.

LONDON'S FLOATING CHURCH   65

Address: St Peter's Barge, West India Quay, Hertsmere Road, E14 4AL
(020-7093 1212, stpetersbarge.org).
Opening hours: There are regular events, meetings and services (see website).
Transport: West India Quay DLR.

If any of the 100,000 or so workers who toil at Canary Wharf need spiritual sustenance or just a break from the pressures of making money, this church is here to serve them. It's London's (and possibly Britain's) only floating church, although it isn't the capital's first waterborne place of worship: that was The Episcopal Floating Church, which operated from 1825-45 from the ship *Brazen*.

St Peter's is a Dutch freight barge that was purchased in 2003, refitted in the Netherlands and ferried across the North Sea. It opened in 2004 and is now permanently moored at West India Quay in the heart of Canary Wharf.

LONGPLAYER   66

Address: Trinity Buoy Wharf, 64 Orchard Place, E14 0JY (020-7515 7153,
http://longplayer.org).
Opening hours: Sat and Sun, 11am-5pm.
Transport: East India DLR.

Longplayer is an apt (perhaps understated) name for this 1,000-year-long musical composition. It began playing at midnight on 31st December 1999 and will continue to play, without repetition, until the end of 2999, when it will complete its cycle and begin again. The full technical details of how it avoids repetition are explained on the website.

The piece was conceived and written by Jem Finer, who is best known as a member of The Pogues. Longplayer was composed for singing bowls – an ancient type of standing bell – which can be played by humans or machines.

It can be heard at several listening posts around the world – including the lighthouse at Trinity Buoy Wharf, where it's been playing since it began – and on the internet.

67   THE MAYPOLE SITE

Address: By St Andrew Undershaft, St Mary Axe, EC3A.
Transport: Aldgate tube or Liverpool Street tube/rail.

In a splendid throwback to pagan times, a huge maypole (or shaft) used to be kept on iron hooks beneath the eaves of a row of houses on Shafts Court (now long gone). On May 1st it was erected outside St Andrew's Church on St Mary Axe. So long was the shaft that it was taller than the steeple of the church, which thus became known as under-the-shaft, later undershaft (see The Statue with a Real Quill Pen on page 171).

The practice was terminated in 1517 after rioting but the pole survived until 1547, when it was destroyed by a Puritan mob. They deemed it to be pagan and idolatrous, a sign of the times as Protestantism asserted its grip on the country.

THE NEWEST OLD PUB 68

Address: The Jerusalem Tavern, 55 Britton Street, EC1M 5UQ (020-7490 4281, stpetersbrewery.co.uk).
Opening hours: Mon-Fri, 11am-11pm.
Transport: Farringdon tube/rail.

Clerkenwell is home to what looks like one of London's oldest pubs, but appearances can be deceptive, as The Jerusalem Tavern didn't open its doors until the '90s. The premises qualify as vintage, however – they were built around 1720, although the current frontage is from 1810 – and the nicely wonky interior provides a civilised space in which to enjoy the fine beers from Suffolk's St Peter's Brewery, whose London outlet this is.

The pub was originally a merchant's house, then a workshop for clock and watchmakers. It's named after the venerable Priory of St John of Jerusalem, which was founded in 1140 and whose prominent remains are nearby (see St John's Gate on page 167).

THE ONCE WEEPING STATUE 69

Address: St Bartholomew-the-Great, West Smithfield, EC1A 7DQ (greatstbarts.com).
Opening hours: Mon-Fri, 8.30am-5pm (4pm, 11th November to 14th February); Sat, 10.30am-4pm; Sun, 8.30am-8pm.
Cost: Adult, £4; concession, £3.50; pre-booked groups, £3.50; family, £10 (two adults and up to three children).
Transport: Farringdon tube/rail.

This Grade I listed church dates from 1123 and has somehow escaped being burned down, bombed or substantially altered – a rare survivor. However, it's

acquired some oddities along the way, including a bust of Edward Cooke (1652), which used to 'weep'. Attributed to Thomas Burman (c 1617-74), the bust is made of marble, so moisture condensed easily on its surface and 'tears' would run from its stone eyes. The installation of a Victorian heating system put a stop to this 'miracle'.

70   THE QUACK'S PUB

Address: The Old Dr Butler's Head, 2 Mason's Avenue, EC2V 5BY.
Opening hours: Mon-Fri, 11am-11pm. Sat-Sun, closed.
Transport: Moorgate tube.

The Old Dr Butler's Head is an outlet of Kent's Shepherd Neame brewery and gets its curious name from a court physician to James I. However, Dr Butler was a fraud without any proper medical qualifications, who peddled a variety of absurd cures.

If a patient had epilepsy, for example, he would fire pistols near the poor, unsuspecting person. If somebody caught the plague, he plunged them into cold water. And another 'cure' involved dropping patients into the Thames through a trapdoor on London Bridge. Dr Butler also developed a popular medicinal ale (who knows what went into it), which was only available from taverns which displayed his head on their signs, as here.

THE ROA RABBIT 71

Address: 205-209 Hackney Road, E2 8JL.
Transport: Hoxton tube/rail.

An unexpected and striking rabbit adorns the side of The Premises Studios & Café in this robust part of town. The large – 3.5m/12ft tall – painting is the work of Roa, the pseudonym of a Belgian graffiti artist who's created artwork on the streets of various European and US cities. He generally paints wild animals, often in black and white, the idea being to 'reintroduce' wildlife to the world's cities.

Roa came to prominence in the UK in 2010 when Hackney Council threatened to paint over this impressive rabbit. However, a campaign was launched to save it – driven by the recording studio's owners and local people – and the council was forced to change its mind.

THE ROMAN REBURIAL 72

Address: 30 St Mary Axe, EC3A.
Transport: Aldgate tube or Liverpool Street tube/rail.

To the spirits of the dead the unknown young girl from Roman London lies buried here

DIS MANIBVS
PVELLA INCOGNITA
LONDINIENSIS
HIC SEPVLTA EST

In 1995, during the initial phase of the construction of the building nicknamed the Gherkin, the grave of a teenage Roman girl was unearthed. It seems to have been an isolated burial, as the location isn't part of a cemetery and would have been just outside an early boundary ditch marking the edge of the Roman city. Aged between 13 and 17, the girl died in AD350-400, as dated from pottery associated with the burial.

Her remains were kept in the Museum of London while building work was completed. In 2007, the girl was reburied at the skyscraper's base, which is marked with a memorial. The reburial was carried out in traditional Roman manner, with a procession and dedication ceremony, involving music and libations.

73 SAXON RECYCLING

Address: All Hallows-by-the-Tower, Byward Street, EC3 R 5BJ (ahbtt.org.uk).
Opening hours: Mon-Fri, 8am-6pm; Sat, 10am-5pm; Sun, 10am-1pm.
Transport: Tower Hill tube.

Crypt Museum

London's oldest church contains what might be the capital's oldest example of recycling. Founded in 675 and now Grade I listed, the church has an intact, 7th-century Saxon arch, which includes a number of clearly visible Roman tiles.

These might have been taken from the nearby Roman wall, an extensive section of which can still be seen just outside Tower Hill underground station. Or the tiles might have been recycled from the Roman building that stood on the site before the church was built. Traces of this structure remain in the crypt (which now houses a small museum), as does a section of Roman pavement.

THE TOBACCO DOCK SCULPTURE   74

Address: Tobacco Dock, E1W 2SF.
Transport: Shadwell tube.

Built in 1811, Tobacco Dock is a Grade I listed warehouse, once used as a store for imported tobacco. Oddly, at its north entrance is a 7ft bronze sculpture of a boy standing in front of a tiger which commemorates a dramatic incident in 1857.

Charles Jamrach (1815-91) was a wild animal dealer who owned the world's largest exotic pet shop on Radcliffe Highway near Tobacco Dock. A Bengal tiger escaped from the shop and a young boy, unaware of what it was, tried to pet it. He was picked up in the tiger's jaws but was saved by Jamrach, who prised its teeth apart with his bare hands. Despite this, the boy sued him and was awarded £300 in damages.

75   WHITECHAPEL'S ORIGIN

Address: Altab Ali Park, Adler Street, E1.
Transport: Aldgate East tube.

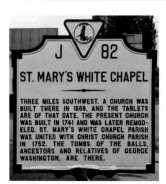

A ltab Ali Park in Whitechapel is the site of the 14th-century St Mary Matfelon Church. St Mary's was the original white chapel after which this part of East London is named, so-called because it was painted with a whitewash made of lime and chalk. Matfelon is the name of the family responsible for the church's construction.

The last of the series of churches on the site was destroyed in the Blitz in 1940 and all that remains of it in the park is the floor plan and some graves. What was formerly St Mary's Park was renamed Altab Ali Park in memory of a Bangladeshi clothing worker who was the victim of a racially-motivated murder in Adler St in 1978.

Mortuary Chapel, Kensal Green Cemetery

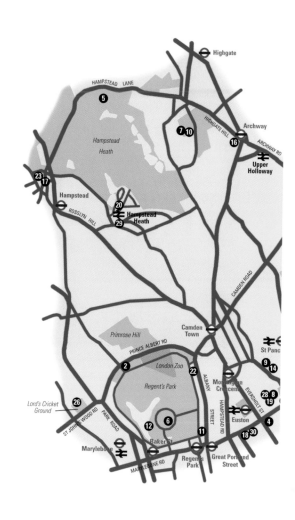

CHAPTER 3

NORTH LONDON

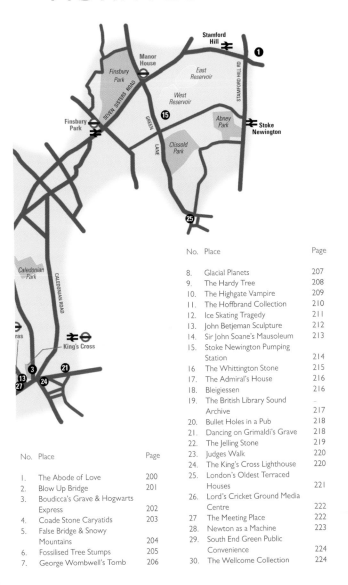

THE ABODE OF LOVE

Address: The Church of the Good Shepherd, Rookwood Road, N16.
Transport: Stamford Hill rail.

The conventionally-named Church of the Good Shepherd in Upper Clapton was built by the decidedly unconventional Agapemonite cult in 1892. The cult's name was derived from the Greek *Agapemone* – 'abode of love' – and members had some unusual ideas about women and sex. These are partly reflected in the building itself: a fine stained glass window depicts woman's submission to man, while the handsome church exterior is rich in statuary and symbolism.

The cult's leader, Henry James Prince, had convinced his followers that he was a manifestation of the Holy Ghost and surrounded himself with

The Church of the Good Shepherd is now a Georgian Orthodox church and is Grade II listed, mainly for its 'curiosity value'.

'soul brides' to indulge his sexual desires. In one memorable stunt, he sought to prove his infallibility by deflowering a 16-year-old virgin before a compliant (if flabbergasted) congregation.

Prince told his followers that he was immortal, so it must have been an unexpected disappointment to them when he died in 1899. John Hugh Smyth-Pigott took over as leader of the cult and carried on Prince's good 'work': he even went a step further than his predecessor by declaring himself The Messiah. After Smyth-Pigott died in 1927, the cult gradually declined, with the last member dying in 1956.

BLOW UP BRIDGE 2

Address: The Regent's Canal, Regent's Park, NW1 4NR.
Opening hours: During daylight hours.
Transport: Camden Town or St John's Wood tube.

The Regent's (or North Metropolitan) Canal was built in 1812-20 and opened in two stages. Before the construction of the railway network, it was an important part of London's industrial transport system, carrying all sorts of cargo. Horse-drawn traffic used the canal up until 1956 and commercial traffic travelled along here as recently as the '60s. On a section running along the northern edge of Regent's Park, one of its bridges, the Macclesfield Bridge, is better known as the Blow Up Bridge following a tragic accident.

The first bridge here was destroyed in October 1874 by a huge explosion, which killed three men and a horse. It was caused by a blast on a barge as it travelled directly underneath. The barge was carrying an inflammable and volatile cargo of petroleum and sacks of gunpowder (the latter weighing around five tons).

Such was the force of the explosion that some surrounding houses were badly damaged; a few had walls and roofs blown away. Windows were broken and other damage experienced for around a mile to the east and west of the explosion. And the noise woke people throughout London.

The Regent's Canal was closed for four days after the explosion. The ensuing chaos is difficult to imagine today at what has become a tranquil leisure spot.

3   BOUDICCA'S GRAVE & HOGWARTS EXPRESS

Address: King's Cross Station, N1C 9AP.
Opening hours: Mon-Fri, 5-1.36am; Sat, 5-12.40am; Sun, 5.30-1.36am.
Transport: King's Cross St Pancras tube/rail.

Much nonsense has been spouted about the resting place of Boudicca, Queen of the Iceni tribe who led an uprising against the Romans. We've also struggled with her name: until recently, she was known as Boadicea, the result of a mis-transcription of Tacitus, the Roman historian who's the main source of her story.

Various places are cited as her place of burial. A specific and curiously popular one is under a platform at King's Cross Station (10 is the favourite, although 8 and 9 have their supporters). The supposed 'evidence' is that a former name of King's Cross is Battle Bridge, regarded as a possible site of the Battle of Watling Street with the Romans; so it's tenuous at best. The 'theory' was bolstered by Lewis Spence's 1937 book *Boadicea – Warrior Queen of the Britons*. Spence wrote about folklore, the occult and 'alternative' history, and wasn't renowned as the most academic or accurate writer.

Boudicca

Other 'authorities' state that Boudicca is buried in Parliament Hill Fields or in a mound on Hampstead Heath traditionally known as 'Boadicea's tomb', although it's probably a Roman boundary mark. There's no credible evidence for either site.

The Boudicca-King's Cross link is now overshadowed by the 'fact' that Harry Potter catches the Hogwarts Express from a King's Cross platform, which is marked by a trolley partially lodged in a wall.

COADE STONE CARYATIDS

Address: St Pancras New Church, Euston Road and Upper Woburn Place, NW1 2BA
(020-7388 1461, stpancraschurch.org).
Transport: Euston tube/rail.

Charles Rossi

The St Pancras caryatids are made from Coade stone, an unusual artificial stone. It's a special kind of terracotta, said to be the most waterproof ever made. Coade stone was popular in the 18th and early 19th centuries, but the factory making it closed in 1840 and the secret of its manufacture was lost for many years.

St Pancras New Church is a beautiful Greek revival building, and was the most expensive church of its day when consecrated in 1822. However, a curiously and appealingly schoolboy-like error of measurement has detracted from the perfection of one of its most notable features.

At the east end, guarding the entrance to the crypt, are two caryatid porticos – a caryatid is a sculpted female figure serving as an architectural support, replacing a column or pillar. The caryatids are by Charles Rossi, a sculptor of Italian descent. When they arrived at the church, however, they were found to be too tall to fit their allotted space, and so a section had to be cut out of their midriffs.

As a result, the caryatids are rather dumpy and lack the elegance of the Greek originals from which they're copied, which are on the Erechtheion, a 5th century BC temple on the north side of the Acropolis.

5   FALSE BRIDGE & SNOWY MOUNTAINS

Address: Kenwood House, Hampstead Heath, NW3.
Transport: Highgate tube.

The northern section of verdant Hampstead Heath is graced by Kenwood House, a white, stucco building which was once a stately home. This elegant 17th-century house is set in an artfully-designed landscape with gardens and a lake. It's all very picturesque, but part of the effect is false, as the attractive 'stone' bridge at one end of the lake is actually a wooden cut out. It was placed here to improve the view and does so very effectively, despite being a folly with just one proper side. It's painted white, which helps to cast a striking reflection in the lake and adds to the decorative effect.

An earlier example of an optical illusion in Hampstead – though not a deliberate one – occurred in the 16th century, when the area was where many of London's washerwomen worked. So great were the swathes of white linen laundry put out to dry on the heath that workers on the Thames used to think there were snow-capped mountains in Hampstead!

The laundry business took off in Hampstead, partly because its water was thought to be pure and also because its elevated position was breezy and well away from the city's grime.

Kenwood House

FOSSILISED TREE STUMPS   6

Address: Inner Circle, Regent's Park, NW1 4NR (020-7486 7905, royalparks.org.uk/parks/the-regents-park).
Transport: 5am to between 4.30 and 9.30pm, depending on the month – see the website for exact details.
Transport: Baker Street or Regent's Park tube.

Regent's Park boasts many majestic, aged trees in its 410 acres. The oldest living trees were planted after 1818, when John Nash's plans for the park were enacted, but there are also some that date back much further, to between 20 and 100 million years ago.

They're a small group of fossilised tree trunks that lie within the Inner Circle. They are located near the waterfall in Queen Mary's Gardens and are easy to overlook in the midst of the floral splendour.

The fossils were probably brought here by the Royal Botanical Society, which leased land in Regent's Park from the 1840s to the 1930s. It's thought that they were coniferous trees, which were laid down in sedimentary rock in Lower Purbeck in Dorset, an area famous for its fossilised reptiles and early mammals. One of the trees appears to be a relative of the *araucaria*, or monkey puzzle tree, from South America. Appropriately, the monkey puzzle itself is a primitive tree, sometimes called a 'living fossil'.

Queen Mary's Gardens boast London's largest collection of roses, around 12,000 plants, which are at their best in the first two weeks of June.

7   GEORGE WOMBWELL'S TOMB

> **Address:** Highgate Cemetery, Swain's Lane, N6 6PJ (tour bookings 020-8340 1834, highgate-cemetery.org).
>
> **Opening hours:** Visits to the West Cemetery are by tour only. Mon-Fri, one tour per day, at 1.45pm; Sat and Sun, tours are hourly, from 11am-3pm. Tickets are sold on a first-come-first-served basis, so arrive early.
>
> **Cost:** Adult, £12; children 8-16, £6. Includes free entry to the East Cemetery within a month
>
> **Transport:** Archway tube.

Highgate Cemetery isn't a sculpture park or a burial ground for animals, so why is there a majestic statue of a lion atop one of the tombs in the West Cemetery? The big cat is called Nero and once belonged to the man whose grave he now guards – an interesting character called George Wombwell (1777-1850).

One of 170,000 who now 'rest' in this famous cemetery (see also The Highgate Vampire on page 209), Wombwell was an exhibitor of exotic animals in Regency and early Victorian Britain. He was the founder of Wombwell's Travelling Menagerie, which included elephants, a gorilla, giraffes, a kangaroo, lions, monkeys, ostriches, a rhino, tigers and zebras. By 1839, the menagerie had grown so large that it required 15 wagons to move all the animals and was accompanied by a brass band.

Many of the animals were from warmer countries and didn't survive for long in the British climate. However, George Wombwell made the best of this unfortunate situation, sometimes selling their bodies to taxidermists or medical schools, or even exhibiting the dead animals as curiosities.

> Wombwell was the first person to breed a lion in captivity in Britain. He named it William in honour of Scots freedom fighter William Wallace.

GLACIAL PLANETS   8

Address: The British Library, 96 Euston Road, NW1 2DB.
Transport: Euston or King's Cross St Pancras tube/rail.

Anthony Gormley

Eight large stones in the British Library forecourt resemble oversized brains. They actually depict the planets in our solar system and comprise a work of art called *Planets*. The stones are glacial erratics – stones moved and deposited by glaciers – and each is inscribed with a different body silhouette. They were selected and sculpted by Anthony Gormley.

Gormley sourced the stones – chosen for their colour and texture – from a glacial area in Sweden (now a quarry). He apparently asked family and friends to drape themselves over the stones to give him ideas and templates for the human forms he subsequently carved into them. In this way, human bodies are used to represent celestial bodies (and vice versa).

And to those who claim that there are nine rather than eight planets in our solar system, you're sadly out of date. There used to be nine, but Pluto, the last of the planets to be discovered, was downgraded to the status of dwarf planet or plutoid in 2006. Gormley's

work was completed in 2002 so predates this celestial downgrade, suggesting that the sculptor knew something the astronomers didn't; or that his arithmetic was sloppy.

Anthony Gormley is probably best known for the vast, metallic statue *Angel of the North*, located at Gateshead, Tyne and Wear.

9   THE HARDY TREE

Address: St Pancras Old Church, Pancras Road, NW1 1UL.
Opening horus: 9am-dusk.
Transport: King's Cross St Pancras tube/rail.

A carefully arranged collection of old gravestones sits around the base of an ash tree in the graveyard of St Pancras Old Church. They're in the form of a wheel and the tree has grown among them since they were placed here over 150 years ago. This growth has broken and cracked some of the stones, but the whole remains an elegant memorial to those whose graves were disturbed in the 19th century.

Thomas Hardy

It's so-called because the graves were moved under the instruction of the novelist and poet Thomas Hardy (1840-1928). Before turning to writing full time, Hardy studied architecture in London under Arthur Blomfield. The Midland Railway was built over part of the original St Pancras churchyard in the 1860s and Blomfield was commissioned by the Bishop of London to supervise the dismantling of tombs and exhumation of human remains.

He passed this tricky job to Hardy in 1865 – rather unfairly – and as part of the process, a number of headstones were placed back to back around the base of this ash tree, arranged like the spokes of a wheel.

It's a clever way of displaying the headstones, which form an interesting conjunction with the ash growing around them – hopefully the tree won't fall prey to ash dieback disease, which is currently spreading.

THE HIGHGATE VAMPIRE

Address: Highgate Cemetery, Swain's Lane, N6 6PJ (tour booking 020-8340 1834, highgate-cemetery.org).
Opening hours: East Cemetery: Mon-Fri, 10am-4pm; weekends and Bank Holidays, 11am-4pm. West Cemetery: tours only, Mon-Fri, 1.45pm; Sat and Sun, tours hourly, 11am-3pm. Tickets sold on a first-come-first-served basis, so arrive early.
Cost: East Cemetery: adult, £3; student, £2. West Cemetery tours: adult, £12; age 8-16, £6; includes free entry to the East Cemetery within a month.
Transport: Archway tube.

Highgate Cemetery is a Victorian burial ground and *de facto* nature reserve. It covers over 37 acres and boasts some impressive monuments (see George Wombwell's Tomb on page 206). It's also associated with bizarre tales of supernatural activity.

Established in 1839, the cemetery had become neglected by the 1960s and it seems likely that occult ceremonies were held here. Tales emerged in the early '70s that the cemetery was stalked by a vampire. It was claimed that the bloodsucker was a medieval Romanian noble who'd been brought to England in the 18th century and buried on land that later became the cemetery; he was apparently 'raised' by Satanists.

A fair amount of publicity was generated by these supposed events, including newspaper articles and books, and a couple of competing 'experts' claimed to know the truth (their dispute is thought to continue to this day). The cemetery was restored to its past glory in the '80s, although there are still reports of supernatural activity.

Highgate Cemetery catacombs

The Highgate Vampire has been cited by academics as an example of modern legend-building and how public perception can be shaped into a story by exaggeration, rumour, selection and stereotyping.

11 THE HOFFBRAND COLLECTION

Address: The Royal College of Physicians, 11 St Andrews Place, NW1 4LE (rcplondon.ac.uk).
Opening hours: Mon-Fri, 9am-5pm.
Transport: Regent's Park tube.

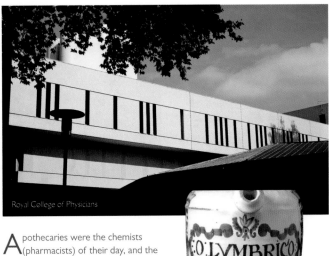

Royal College of Physicians

Apothecaries were the chemists (pharmacists) of their day, and the Hoffbrand Collection of apothecary jars in the Royal College of Physicians' museum demonstrates how very bizarre (and dangerous) were some of the 'cures' administered to the sick in previous centuries.

There are 183 jars in total, dating from the 1640s to 1745, used to store medicines and their ingredients. They were assembled by Professor Victor Hoffbrand and comprised the country's largest privately-owned collection of English delftware apothecary jars.

Apothecaries stored their goods in these attractive, fashionable and functional jars to impress both customers and other medical professionals. Decorative Latin labels revealed the contents and what contents they were! Foxes' lungs, for example, were thought to be good for strengthening human lungs. Just as oddly, they were taken in the form of a 'lohoch', i.e. sucked from the end of a liquorice stick. Oil of swallows apparently cleared the sight, and eating the birds' burnt ashes helped to protect against drunkenness, as well as soothing sore throats and inflammations.

Delftware is the name given to a type of tin-glazed earthenware first made in the Netherlands. It was brought to England around 1567 when Dutch potters started arriving from Antwerp to escape religious persecution.

ICE SKATING TRAGEDY   12

> **Address:** Regent's Park, NW1 4NR (020-7486 7905,
> royalparks.org.uk/parks/the-regents-park).
> **Opening hours:** 5am to between 4.30 and 9.30pm, depending on the month
> (see website).
> **Transport:** Baker Street or Regent's Park tube.

quickly began to refreeze. It was over a week before it was certain that all the victims had been found and it could be confirmed that 40 people had died.

As a result of the disaster, the lake's depth was reduced from 12ft to 4-5ft, using soil and concrete. This safety measure worked, as when a similar incident occurred later in the Victorian period, none of the 100 or so people who fell into the water died.

Ice skating was popular with well-to-do Victorian Londoners and frozen lakes and ponds were often advertised in the press. Hundreds of skaters came to Regent's Park on 15th January 1867 to take advantage of the frozen lake in its southwest corner. And despite warnings that the ice was thin – there had been a minor break the previous day – many took to the lake.

Unfortunately, a light fall of snow had disguised cracks in the ice, which began to give way near the banks of the lake. Hundreds of skaters (estimates vary between 200 and 500) were pitched into the icy water, ill-prepared to cope. The coldness, heavy Victorian clothing and skates, as well as limited swimming ability, combined to add to the subsequent scale of the tragedy.

Recovering the bodies proved difficult because the ice

THE ILLUSTRATED LONDON NEWS. SKATING IN THE REGENT'S-PARK. [JAN. 26, 1850.

13   JOHN BETJEMAN SCULPTURE

Address: St Pancras International Station, Euston Road, N1C 4QP (020-7843 7688, stpancras.com).
Opening hours: Daily, 24 hours.
Transport: King's Cross St Pancras tube/rail.

An oversized bronze sculpture of a chubby, badly-dressed man stands in the impressive space of the renovated St Pancras International railway station. The subject is the poet laureate Sir John Betjeman (1906-84), who had a passion for both Victorian architecture and railways. He was the driving force behind the campaign to save this site when it was threatened by developers in the '60s.

The sculpture is by Martin Jennings and stands nearly 7ft tall, i.e. much larger than life (Betjeman was actually rather short). It's on the station's main concourse, next to where the Eurostar trains arrive. Quotations from Betjeman's poetry are set in Cumbrian slate discs at the base of the sculpture.

The statue depicts Betjeman walking into the station for the first time and looking up at the huge arc of the train shed, something that he apparently always used to do, never tiring of the view. The poet is portrayed as a plump man carrying a bag and holding onto his hat, his coat billowing out behind him as if caught by the wind from a passing train.

Jennings' likeness of Betjeman perfectly captures his famously shabby dress sense. His collar is undone and one of his shoelaces consists of knotted string.

SIR JOHN SOANE'S MAUSOLEUM   14

Address: St Pancras Old Church, Pancras Road, NW1 1UL (020-7424 0724, posp.co.uk/old-st-pancras).
Opening hours: 9am-dusk.
Transport: King's Cross St Pancras tube/rail.

Sir John Soane

The Soane tomb is Grade I listed and comprises a central marble cube enclosed by a marble canopy, supported by four Ionic columns. Surrounding it is a Portland limestone balustrade, while a flight of steps leads down into the vault itself.

Sir John Soane (1753-1837) is most famous as the architect of the Bank of England and Dulwich Picture Gallery, and his house on Lincoln's Inn Fields is one of London's quirkiest museums, exhibiting the fruits of his obsessive collecting (see page 62). Soane's approach to death was also curious, as it's unusual to design your own tomb.

Sir John built this distinctive, elegant mausoleum in 1816 to house the body of his wife Elizabeth, who'd died the year before. He joined her in 1837 and their son also rests here. The tomb sits in the large, leafy graveyard of St Pancras Old Church, one of Britain's oldest Christian sites – there's thought to have been a church here since the 4th century.

The architect Sir Giles Gilbert Scott based his design for the roof of K2 – the first of Britain's emblematic red telephone kiosks – on the stone canopy of Soane's tomb. The invitation to submit a kiosk design came soon after Scott had been made a trustee of Sir John Soane's Museum.

15 STOKE NEWINGTON PUMPING STATION

Address: Castle Climbing Centre, 218 Green Lanes, N4 2HA (020-8211 7000).
Opening hours: The exterior can be viewed anytime. The centre is open Mon-Fri, noon-10pm; Sat and Sun, 10am-7pm; Bank Holidays, 10am-10pm.
Transport: Manor House tube.

This impressive, Grade II listed Victorian water pumping station was built 1852-56 in the style of a baronial Scottish castle. It was designed by William Chadwell Mylne for the New River Company and is a throwback to an era when even practical service buildings often had flamboyant designs. This was partly a reflection of Victorian confidence and their love of dramatic decoration, but was also an attempt to 'disguise' the building. When its construction was first proposed, local people had objected to the idea of an industrial building in their green, leafy area.

A variety of towers and turrets rise from the battlements, while tall, narrow windows add a further medieval touch. The towers and turrets appear random but were designed to house elements with particular functions: a chimney shaft, water tank and spiral staircase.

The building ceased operating as a pumping station in 1942 and was saved from demolition in 1971 following a campaign by local residents. The interior has been given a new lease of life as a climbing centre and the building remains a popular local landmark.

It's thought that the design of the pumping station was inspired by Stirling Castle and by nearby Holloway Prison. The building's impressive position comes from being built on an artificial mound.

THE WHITTINGTON STONE   16

Address: Highgate Hill, N6.
Transport: Archway tube.

On the west side of the road near the foot of Highgate Hill sits the curious arrangement of a stone with a sculpted cat on top, surrounded by a railing. Legend has it that the stone marks the spot where Dick Whittington (c 1354-1423, a legendary Lord Mayor of London) heard the Bow bells ring out.

Legend has it that this made him change his mind about leaving London, where he'd thus far enjoyed little success. And if it seems unlikely that the sound of the bells could have carried to Highgate from St Mary-le-Bow in the City, scientists confirm that it would have been possible in the days before the obscuring noise of modern traffic and industry.

There's a belief that if the stone is ever removed, great change and disaster will befall the surrounding area. However, it's uncertain quite how long it's been here and the current stone is thought to be at least the third on the site. It was restored, a railing fixed and a lamp put up in 1821; the sculpture of the cat that Dick Whittington was supposed to have owned was added in 1964.

The Whittington stone's inscription has two rather obvious mistakes: Whittington was Lord Mayor of London four times, not thrice, and while he also became Sheriff, he was never knighted.

17 THE ADMIRAL'S HOUSE

Address: Admiral's Walk, The Grove, Hampstead, NW3.
Transport: Hampstead tube.

This quirky, Grade II listed Hampstead house was built in the early 18th century and occupied by an eccentric former naval lieutenant called Fountain North. He built two decks on the roof – a main deck and a quarter deck – and mounted cannons on them, with which he fired salutes to mark the King's birthday and notable naval victories.

Apparently, it was the inspiration for the home of Admiral Boom in Disney's film version of *Mary Poppins*; Boom's behaviour has obvious similarities with Fountain North's. In the 19th century, Sir George Gilbert Scott lived here (the architect responsible for St Pancras Station and the Albert Memorial) and local resident John Constable painted the house a number of times.

18 BLEIGIESSEN

Address: The Wellcome Trust, Gibbs Building, 215 Euston Road, NW1 2BE (020-7611 8888, wellcome.ac.uk).
Opening hours: Public tours on the last Friday of the month at 2pm. Book in advance.
Transport: Euston Square tube.

The Wellcome Trust is a biomedical research charity (see The Wellcome Collection on page 224), while *Bleigiessen* is a striking work of art. The latter was commissioned from the noted Thomas Heatherwick Studio to fill the eight-storey vertical space in the northwest corner of the Trust's headquarters. It's constructed of around 150,000 specially-made glass spheres, suspended on almost 1m metres of stainless steel wire. The whole weighs a total of 15 tonnes.

The term *Bleigiessen* means 'lead-guessing' and is a New Year's Eve tradition in central Europe: lead is poured into water to produce weird and wonderful shapes from which your fortune in the coming year is predicted. Appropriately, this monumental artwork glows with a shifting range of colours.

THE BRITISH LIBRARY SOUND ARCHIVE   19

Address: 96 Euston Road, NW1 2DB (020-7412 7332, bl.uk and sounds.bl.uk).
Opening hours: Library: Mon, Wed, Thu and Fri, 9.30am-6pm; Tue, 9.30am-8pm; Sat, 9.30am-5pm; Sun, 11am-5pm. The Reading Rooms are closed on Sundays.
Transport: Euston or King's Cross St Pancras tube/rail.

The British Library contains much that's curious and fascinating, including one of the world's largest collections of recorded sound. It has over 3.5m recordings, with specialist collections that include: classical music; drama and literature; moving images; oral history; popular music and jazz; radio recordings, spoken language and dialects; wildlife and other nature sounds; and world and traditional music.

Recordings may be listened to in the Reading Rooms, by appointment, and copies can be purchased, subject to copyright restrictions. To use the Reading Rooms, you must register for a Reader Pass before your first visit; see the website for details. You should apply at least ten days before the first visit and you can pre-register online. For full Reader Registration information, call 020-7412 7676.

20   BULLET HOLES IN A PUB

Address: The Magdala Pub, 2A South Hill Park, NW3 2SB (020-7435 2503, http://the-magdala.com).
Opening hours: The holes are on the pub's exterior and are best viewed during daylight. The pub opens Mon-Thu, 11am-11pm; Fri and Sat, 11am-midnight; Sun, noon-10.30pm.
Transport: Hampstead Heath rail.

and took responsibility for what she'd done, saying on 20th June 1955: 'It's obvious when I shot him I intended to kill him'. Whisper it, but there are suggestions that a former landlord enlarged or even created the holes in the pub's exterior tiles to cash in on the incident.

David Blakely & Ruth Ellis

The bullet holes in the wall of this Hampstead pub indicate where Ruth Ellis (1926-55) shot and killed her lover, racing driver David Blakely, on Easter Sunday 1955. When she was found guilty of his murder, Ellis became famous as the last woman to be executed in the UK.

After the shooting she immediately gave herself up to the police. At her trial she was composed and courteous,

21   DANCING ON GRIMALDI'S GRAVE

Address: Joseph Grimaldi Park, Pentonville Road, N1.
Opening hours: 8am-dusk.
Transport: King's Cross St Pancras tube/rail.

Joseph Grimaldi Park is built on a former burial ground and is so-called because it contains the grave of the 'Clerkenwell Clown'. Grimaldi (1778-1837) was born locally and became the most popular English entertainer of the Regency era, credited with inventing the modern clown. On and around his

grave is an unusual memorial by Henry Krokatsis, consisting of two coffin-shaped caskets set into the ground.

One is on Grimaldi's grave, the other on the grave alongside it. The surfaces of the caskets are made of phosphor bronze tiles. These respond to pressure by playing musical notes, so you can make music by dancing on them. The old clown would surely approve.

THE JELLING STONE   22

Address: 4 St Katherine's Precinct, NW1.
Transport: Camden Town or Great Portland Street tube.

The grounds of the Danish Church in Regent's Park have an unusual plaster cast of a Jelling stone. This is a large, carved, memorial runestone from the 10th century, from the town of Jelling in Denmark. The original stones represent a transitional time between Norse paganism and the spread of Christianity in Denmark.

The larger of the stones at Jelling was raised by Harald Bluetooth, grandfather of King Canute (Cnut), in memory of his parents and as a celebration of his conquest of Denmark and Norway, and his conversion of the Danes to

Christianity. The replica cast in Regent's Park was made for an exhibition and is painted, like the original used to be – enough small flakes of paint remain to show which colours were used.

23 JUDGES WALK

Address: Judges Walk, NW3.
Transport: Hampstead tube.

Great Fire a year later. Lawyers and judges apparently transacted business here in makeshift tents until it was safe and practical to return to London. Local resident John Constable painted Judges Walk in around 1820.

This thoroughfare's name reflects the time when Hampstead was a place that Londoners escaped to, rather than being an upmarket suburb of the capital. Hampstead sits 440ft (135m) above sea level and was once a refuge away from the hot, polluted and sometimes unhealthy city. Visitors came for fresh air, clean water and to avoid the plague, which regularly swept through London.

Judges Walk is said to be named after the justices who came here following the Great Plague of 1665 and/or the

24 THE KING'S CROSS LIGHTHOUSE

Address: The corner of Gray's Inn Road and Pentonville Road, N1.
Transport: King's Cross St Pancras tube/rail.

On top of a building near King's Cross station is what resembles a lighthouse, complete with cast-iron observation balcony. Its exact date and original purpose are unknown, but it's thought to have been built around 1875. It's thought that the building was originally an oyster house – at a time when oysters were

a popular type of 'fast food' – and such establishments were often advertised by lighthouses, their equivalent of McDonalds' golden arches.

Despite being Grade II listed, it's long been neglected and is falling to pieces in places. However, there are plans to renovate

it and the building has recently been put under wraps and scaffolding erected. It seems that there will be a branch of the Co-op on the ground floor.

LONDON'S OLDEST TERRACED HOUSES   25

Address: 52-55 Newington Green, N16 9PX.
Transport: Highbury & Islington tube or Canonbury rail.

London's oldest surviving terraced houses are situated on the west side of Newington Green, a slightly off-the-beaten-track location on the borders of Islington and Hackney. They date from 1658 and are rare and welcome survivors of the Great Fire of London of 1666 which wrought so much destruction on the capital's historic building stock.

Grade I listed, the houses are strikingly attractive, with gabled fronts, brick pilasters on the upper storeys and recessed blank arches to the first floor windows. Shop fronts were (rather sacrilegiously) added in the 1880s, but have since been removed from three of the properties, which now look much as they did originally.

Newington Green

26 LORD'S CRICKET GROUND MEDIA CENTRE

> **Address:** Lord's Cricket Ground, NW8 8QN (020-7616 8500, lords.org).
> **Opening hours:** Tours are available throughout the year but times vary widely (see website for details).
> **Cost:** Tour prices: adult, £15; concession, £9; family, £40.
> **Transport:** St John's Wood or Warwick Avenue tube.

The curious, elegant Lord's Media Centre is in the form of a futuristic, giant pod. It sits above the stands at the ground that's regarded as the home of cricket, an example of modernity and tradition happily coexisting. Completed in 1999, it cost around £5.8m, was designed by Future Systems and won the prestigious RIBA Stirling Prize for design that year.

It rises 15m above the ground and is supported only by the structure around its two lift shafts. The lower tier accommodates over 100 journalists, while the top tier contains radio and television commentary boxes, providing a fine view of the action.

27 THE MEETING PLACE

> **Address:** St Pancras International Station, Euston Road, N1C 4QP (020-7843 7688, stpancras.com).
> **Opening hours:** Daily, 24 hours.
> **Transport:** King's Cross St Pancras tube/rail.

The Meeting Place (2007) is a 9m-tall bronze sculpture of a couple locked in an intimate embrace. It's an unusually demonstrative display of affection for the supposedly reserved British and is often known as 'The Lovers'. The work of Paul Day (born 1967), it's supposedly modelled on an embrace between the sculptor and his wife, and it stands under the St Pancras clock.

Around the base is a sculpted frieze, depicting people in different stages of travel by tube or train. It's designed to

be a tapestry about travellers parting, meeting and reuniting. The work isn't loved by everybody, however: the sculptor Anthony Gormley singled out *The Meeting Place* when he described a lot of the UK's recent public art as 'crap'.

Frieze detail

NEWTON AS A MACHINE   28

Address: The British Library, 96 Euston Road, NW1 2DB.
Transport: Euston or King's Cross St Pancras tube/rail.

Eduardo Paolozzi's (1924-2005) unusual bronze sculpture of the scientist Sir Isaac Newton (1642-1727) sits in the forecourt of the British Library. It was installed in 1995 and is based on a 1795 print of Newton by the painter, poet and printmaker William Blake (1757-1827). In the print, Newton crouches naked on a rock covered with algae, apparently on the seabed – an interesting setting for a physicist and mathematician who's regarded as one of the most influential scientists of all time.

In Paolozzi's large sculpture, Newton's hunched-over body is depicted making mathematical

measurements and appears to have been partly bolted together; it seems to suggest that a scientist who investigated the laws of nature was himself a machine.

29   SOUTH END GREEN PUBLIC CONVENIENCE

Address: South End Green, NW3 2PT.
Opening hours: Daily, 9am-9pm.
Transport: Belsize Park tube or Hampstead Heath rail.

South End Green is a fine, now-rare example of the impressive decoration lavished on their public conveniences by the Victorians. It dates from 1897, is Grade II listed and sits between the Royal Free Hospital and Hampstead Heath railway station.

Decorative cast iron arches mark it above ground, while there's ample space in the convenience below. Wall-to-ceiling white tiling makes the facility gleam and the lightness of the tiles contrasts effectively with the adjacent black pediments, giving a Gothic feel. There are also generously sized wooden cubicles, which were apparently part of the attraction for the gay playwright Joe Orton, who frequented South End Green; it featured in the film about Orton's life, *Prick Up Your Ears*. Nearby Hampstead Heath remains a popular gay haunt.

30   THE WELLCOME COLLECTION

Address: 183 Euston Road, NW1 2BE (020-7611 2222, wellcomecollection.org).
Opening hours: Tue, Wed, Fri and Sat, 10am-6pm; Thu, 10am-10pm; Sun, 11am-6pm.
Transport: Euston tube/rail or Euston Square tube.

The collection belonging to the Wellcome Trust (see Bleigiessen on page 216) runs to over 100,000 items of medical and related exhibits, a number of them unusual or bizarre. There's much here to draw the eye, including items as diverse as Napoleon's toothbrush, shrunken heads, used guillotine blades and ancient sex aids.

The so-called 'Merman' is an example of the fakes that were quite common from the mid-medieval period onwards, often displayed in travelling shows to relieve people of their money. It's stitched together from parts of 'fish, fowl and monkey'. And as is usually the case with London museums, there are some strange erotic exhibits, including a series of hinged porcelain fruit which open to reveal depictions of a couple having sex in various positions.

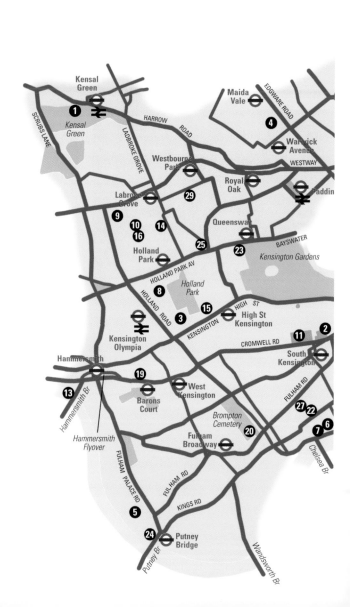

CHAPTER 4

WEST LONDON

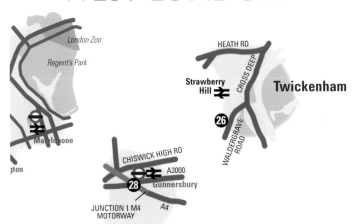

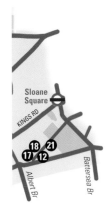

KENSAL GREEN CEMETERY

Address: Harrow Road, W10 (020-8969 0152, kensalgreencemetery.com).
Opening hours: Apr-Oct: Mon-Sat, 9am-6pm; Sun, 10am-6pm. Oct-Mar: Mon-Sat,
9am-5pm; Sun, 10am-5pm. Bank Holidays, 10am-1pm.
Transport: Kensal Green tube/rail.

Kensal Green Cemetery dates from 1833, making it the oldest of the so-called Magnificent Seven burial grounds built by the Victorians to alleviate overcrowding in London's church cemeteries. Inspired by Père Lachaise Cemetery in Paris (said to be the world's most-visited burial ground), it has a number of Grade I and II listed buildings, tombs, memorials and mausoleums, and covers 72 acres in Kensington and Chelsea. Kensal Green is still used as a burial ground and has a number of curious features, including:

column running down to the coffin. At the top of the column, which was a couple of feet above the ground, was a small covered bell. This could be rung by pulling on a chain that ran down the column, thus the 'corpse' could alert passers-by that it wasn't their time just yet!

Buried Alive: During the late Victorian period, many people lived in mortal fear of being buried alive. This stemmed from their lack of confidence in doctors' ability to accurately pronounce death. Their fears were fuelled by tales of bodies rising from slabs in the morgue slabs, not yet ready for the grave and lucky to avoid the grizzly fate of waking up in a coffin six foot under.

More advanced versions of the so-called safety coffin were equipped with an electric alarm. However, there's no record of anyone ever ringing for help.

To solve the problem of premature burial and put elderly Victorian minds at rest, an ingenious new type of tomb was invented, of which several examples can be seen in Kensal Green. They were built with a hollow stone

Henry Russell's Tombstone: Kensal Green Cemetery contains the remains of many people who were much more famous and distinguished than Henry Russell, but none has such an eye-catching or, indeed, comfortable memorial. Russell (1812-1900) was a composer, pianist and baritone singer, best known for

his composition *A Life on the Ocean Wave*. He was laid to rest beneath a rather elegant gravestone in the shape of a chair, a reference to one of his songs, *My Old Armchair*. Russell was a prolific composer responsible for some 800 popular songs, including the amusingly-titled *Woodman! Spare That Tree!* and *Cheer, Boys, Cheer!*

The list of notable 'residents' at Kensal Green numbers some 700 and includes characters as diverse as author William Makepeace Thackeray, playwright Harold Pinter, novelist Anthony Trollope, and engineers Marc and Isambard Kingdom Brunel.

2 THE VICTORIA & ALBERT MUSEUM

Address: Cromwell Road, SW7 2RL (020-7942 2000, vam.ac.uk).
Opening hours: Daily, 10am-5.45pm (Fri until 10pm).
Transport: South Kensington tube.

Copy of Michelangelo's 'David'

The world's leading museum of art and design is a happy hunting ground for those in search of the bizarre and the curious. Prominent examples include the following:

The Cast Court Collection: Museums are expected to display original exhibits. Curiously, however, the Victoria and Albert (or V&A) also has copies of exhibits from other museums. The Cast Collection is the name of two large galleries of the museum's most important plaster cast and electrotype reproductions.

They're close copies of works of art and architectural details which were taken throughout Europe, mainly in the 19th century, when collecting casts was at its most popular. Casts allowed people who couldn't travel abroad to admire some of Europe's major monuments and works of art, and they retain great visual impact even today.

Famous casts range from the incredibly detailed, such as Giovanni Pisano's pulpit from Pisa Cathedral, to the simply immense. The cast of Trajan's Column – the original is 30m high – was split into two sections to fit it into the museum.

The Rotunda Chandelier:

An enormous, colourful chandelier hangs under the dome of the V&A's main entrance, a striking and unusual introduction to the museum. Installed in 1999 and enlarged in 2001, it was designed by Dale Chihuly and is one of a number of works from his 'Chandelier' series which he began in 1992. It's as much a sculpture as a light fitting.

Chihuly draws on the historic techniques of Venice's Murano glassworks and the Rotunda Chandelier reflects this. It's made up of different types of blown glass, formed into free-flowing tendrils and curlicues, in glorious hues of blue, green and yellow. Not surprisingly, the 11m-tall chandelier presents a notable challenge to the V&A's cleaners.

Tipu's Tiger: This visually-striking exhibit manages to be innocent, jolly and sinister all at the same time. It's a painted wooden carving of a life-sized tiger crouched on top of (and eating) the prostrate figure of a European dressed in late 18th-century attire. It's named after its original owner Tipu, Sultan of Mysore, India, from 1782 to 1799.

Tipu Sultan was an enemy of the East India Company, which was extending British dominion in his part of India. The two came into armed conflict on several occasions, and Tipu died defending Mysore during a battle in 1799. Many of his possessions were seized by the British, including this carving. It was displayed at the East India Company's museum and when the Company was dissolved in the mid-19th century, it was given to the Indian Section of what is now the V&A.

What makes Tipu's Tiger especially macabre are its sound effects. Hidden inside is a mechanical pipe-organ, operated by a handle that protrudes from the tiger's shoulder, which produces the growls of the tiger and the cries of its victim.

3   THE ARAB HALL

Address: Leighton House, 12 Holland Park Road, W14 8LZ (020-7602 3316, rbkc.gov.uk/subsites/museums/leightonhousemuseum1.aspx).
Opening hours: Daily, except Tue, 10am-5.30pm.
Cost: Adult, £5; concession, £3.
Transport: High Street Kensington tube.

The Arab Hall is one of London's most ornate and unusual interiors, resembling a film set for *The Arabian Nights*. The hall is part of the former home of painter Frederic, Lord Leighton (1830-96), which has been open to the public since 1929. Leighton House (Grade II listed) was built for the artist in 1863 by George Aitchison (1825-1910), and in the late 1870s they added the two-storey Arab Hall, an ambitious and expensive extension.

Lord Leighton

The stunning tiles that line the walls are a combination of those collected by Leighton during an 1873 trip to Damascus and those bought for him in Cairo, Damascus and Rhodes by Sir Caspar Purdon Clarke and the explorer and diplomat Sir Richard Burton (see Sir Richard Burton's Bedouin Mausoleum on page 267). Most of the tiles are

from the late 15th and early 16th centuries and comprise an important collection; they are complemented by carved latticework windows of a similar period.

The capitals of the Hall's large columns are gilded and carved in the shape of birds, there's a fountain in the centre of the floor and the domed ceiling has elaborate paintwork. The whole is a riot of colour and pattern, and belies the building's plain, almost austere, red-brick exterior.

The Arab Hall is modelled on the interior of a 12th-century Sicilio-Norman palace called La Zisa in Palermo, Sicily.

THE ART NOUVEAU PUB

4

Address: The Warrington, 93 Warrington Crescent, W9 1EH (020-7286 8282, www.faucetinn.com/warrington).
Opening hours: Mon-Thu, 11am-11pm; Fri and Sat, 11am-midnight; Sun, 11am-10.30pm.
Transport: Maida Vale tube.

At one stage the hotel was rumoured to have been an upmarket brothel; interestingly, this was at a time when it was owned by the Church of England.

Art Nouveau is quite rare in London – Glasgow is regarded as its British heartland, mainly thanks to Charles Rennie Mackintosh and his colleagues – and Art Nouveau pubs are even rarer, so this Maida Vale hostelry certainly has curiosity value. Its styling is unusually colourful and decorative for a British pub, and it retains a number of beautiful original features, both outside and inside. These include Art Nouveau friezes, a marble fireplace, mosaic floors, a pillared portico and stained glass windows; the pub is Grade II listed accordingly.

It was built in 1857, originally as a hotel, and is currently a pub with a dining room attached. Potty-mouthed chef Gordon Ramsay owned it for a while, although it's now part of the Faucet Inn group.

The Warrington is striking even before you enter: two large, rare lamps sit in the entrance porch, while the porch columns and walls are covered in colourful glazed tiles. Inside, the huge bar is dominated by a marble-topped, semi-circular bar counter, with a carved mahogany base. Above it, cherubs gaze down on customers, while the rest of the bar boasts Art Nouveau glass, mahogany and ornate plasterwork.

5   THE BISHOP'S TREE

Address: Fulham Palace garden, Bishop's Avenue, SW6 6EA.
Opening hours: Dawn to dusk.
Transport: Putney Bridge tube.

Grade I listed Fulham Palace was home to the Bishops of London from the 11th century (perhaps earlier) until 1975. It boasts important, historic gardens in a prime location by the river, 13 acres of which remain from the original 36. They contain many rare trees and were significant in the development of horticulture, driven by a number of so-called 'gardening bishops'.

The most celebrated was Henry Compton (1632-1713), who established a noted collection of plants and gave the gardens global significance, importing specimens from all over the world. Other bishops

also did important horticultural work here and in homage to these green-fingered clerics, a recent addition to the gardens is the unusual, slightly child-like Bishop's Tree. It's by Andrew Frost, an 'environmental sculptor', and shows some of the bishops and their animals, rendered on the stump of a Cedar of Lebanon (*Cedrus libani*) on the north side of the Palace.

The bishop standing on top of the tree is Bishop Porteus (bishop 1787-1809) and others are shown half way up and at the foot of the trunk. On a carved oak bench near the tree is a napping Bishop Compton, presumably taking a well-earned rest after his important work on the gardens.

Among the rare and unusual plants which Bishop Compton managed to cultivate was the first coffee tree to be grown in England.

CHAINED BOOKS   6

Address: Chelsea Old Church, 64 Cheyne Walk, SW3 5LT (020-7795 1019, chelseaoldchurch.org.uk).
Opening hours: Tue-Thu, 2-4pm.
Transport: South Kensington tube.

This handsome church in upmarket Chelsea is the only one in London to retain a chained library (albeit a small one), a curious throwback to medieval times. The current Chelsea Old Church is mainly a rebuild following substantial bomb damage during World War II, but there's thought to have been a place of worship on the site since Christianity arrived in England.

Sir Hans Sloane

A 'chained library' is one where the books are attached to their bookcase by a chain. It's long enough to allow the books to be removed from the shelves and read, but stops them being taken from the library. This was the usual practice in reference libraries (i.e. the vast majority of libraries) from medieval times until around the 18th century, as books were so valuable.

This small library of chained books was presented to the church by Sir Hans Sloane (1661-1753), whose collections provided the foundation of the British Museum, British Library, Natural History Museum and Chelsea Physic Garden. The books in the church consist of the Vinegar Bible (1717), two volumes of Foxe's *Book of Martyrs* (1684), a Prayer Book (1723) and Homilies (1683).

Chelsea Old Church also boasts what's said to be London's second-finest collection of church monuments, after Westminster Abbey.

7   CROSBY HALL

Address: Cheyne Walk, SW3 5AZ.
Transport: Earl's Court or Fulham Broadway tube.

This impressive, Grade II listed medieval survivor can make a strong claim to be London's ultimate architectural moveable feast: it once stood across the capital, on Bishopsgate in the City, and was moved to Chelsea stone by stone in 1910 to save it from demolition.

It was built in 1466-75 by wealthy wool merchant Sir John Crosby, and was occupied by Richard III in 1483 when he was Duke of Gloucester (it's mentioned in Shakespeare's play as the location of Gloucester's plotting). Sir Thomas More owned the hall from 1532-4 and Sir Walter Raleigh lodged here in 1601, and it housed the headquarters of the East India Company between 1621 and 1638. After a fire in 1672, only the Great Hall and Parlour wing of the mansion survived, and it's these that make up the version that now stands in Chelsea.

Crosby Hall is now a private house and closed to the public. It was purchased in 1989 by the controversial City businessman Christopher Moran, who has undertaken a long-running, expensive restoration project, whose completion date keeps being extended.

Crosby Hall's site on upmarket Cheyne Walk, overlooking the river, is suitably impressive for a house that's been described by English Heritage as 'London's most important surviving secular domestic medieval building'.

DEBENHAM HOUSE   8

Address: 8 Addison Road, W14.
Transport: Holland Park or Kensington (Olympia) tube.

Debenham House is one of London's odder, more eye-catching residences, sometimes called the Peacock House due to its colourful exterior. It's a large, Grade I listed private property in Holland Park, built 1905-8 by the architect Halsey Ricardo (1854-1928). The building is in the Arts & Crafts style, which stood for traditional craftsmanship using simple forms and often applied folk, medieval or romantic decorative styles.

It was built for the shopping magnate Ernest Debenham, who'd previously lived in another house designed by Ricardo at nearby 57 Melbury Road. The interior has tiles by William de Morgan (a friend of William Morris), a mosaic dome painted by Gaetano Meo (an associate of the Pre-Raphaelites) and ceilings painted by Ernest Gimson, who was described by the art critic Nikolaus Pevsner as 'the greatest of the English architect-designers'.

The exterior uses tiles, pale terracotta and coloured glazed bricks; its bottom section is green, the higher section blue with green roof pantiles. The idea was for the house to merge with the sky and surrounding trees. The use of glazed bricks was partly decorative, but it also helped to make the exterior impervious to London's damp climate and air pollution.

This striking property has featured in a number of films and television series, most recently the enjoyably over-the-top BBC spy drama *Spooks*.

9   FRESTONIA

Address: Freston Road, W10.
Transport: Latimer Road tube.

Frestonia
125-135 Freston Road
London
W10 6TH

Frestonia was the name used by the residents of a small area of North Kensington when they tried to secede from the UK in 1977. It covered a mere 1.8 acres of land – the triangle formed by Freston Road, Bramley Road and Shalfleet Drive. Many of the people who lived here were squatters and when the Greater London Council (GLC) planned to develop the area, the 120 residents adopted the surname of Bramley, the aim being to make the council re-house them collectively.

The GLC threatened formal eviction so, taking inspiration from the Ealing comedy film *Passport to Pimlico*, the residents decided to declare independence, which they did on 31st October 1977. The late actor David Rappaport was the Foreign Minister, while playwright Heathcote Williams was Ambassador to Great Britain. Frestonia had its own newspaper, National Theatre, stamps and there were plans to introduce a currency.

On Frestonia's fifth anniversary in 1982, the population was 97 people, occupying 23 houses. The 'experiment' went into decline soon after, partly because some of its 'citizens' had drink and drug problems, and a more conventional community developed in the area.

The People's Hall, Frestonia

Frestonia even considered applying to join the United Nations, in case its troops were needed to keep the GLC at bay!

THE GRASS-FREE LAWN

Address: Avondale Park, Walmer Road, W11 4PQ.
Opening hours: 7.30am-dusk.
Transport: Latimer Road tube.

In summer 2013, the Royal Borough of Kensington and Chelsea became the first in Britain to lay a grass-free lawn, if that's not a contradiction in terms. It's instead made up of herbs and flowers, which seems appropriate in the part of London that hosts the world's leading flower show.

The lawn is in Notting Hill's Avondale Park and replaces a floral meadow which was on the same site. The meadow was a success from the biodiversity perspective but dogs and children tended to flatten it and the plants didn't recover well; the new lawn is lower growing and more trample-tolerant.

The herb and flower lawn is the result of four years of research at Reading University and is scented to provide an attractive habitat for pollinating insects. It attracts 25 per cent more insect life than a grass lawn and incorporates around 75 different

Avondale Park was created in 1892, built on what had been a huge, filthy pool nicknamed 'The Ocean', part of the notorious Piggeries slum (see The Old Pottery Kiln on page 245).

species of plant, including chamomile, Corsican mint, daisies, pennyroyal, red-flowering clover and thyme. And it's less labour-intensive than grass – it only needs mowing up to nine times per year, compared with 20 to 30 times for a grass lawn.

HAIR-SPLITTING GARGOYLES, RELIEFS & STATUES

> **Address:** The Natural History Museum, Cromwell Road, SW7 5BD (020-7942 5000, nhm.ac.uk).
> **Opening hours:** Daily, 10am-5.30pm.
> **Transport:** South Kensington tube.

The Natural History Museum mimics a medieval cathedral, both in its impressive bulk and because of its exterior decoration. The building is adorned with weird and wonderful gargoyles, reliefs and statues, which tend to go unnoticed, alas. Work began on the museum in 1873 and it opened in 1881. The architect was Alfred Waterhouse, who sketched each of the hundreds of external decorations before they were cast in terracotta, mostly very faithfully to his drawings.

Those on the east side of the museum represent animals and plants which are now extinct, while those on the west side portray those still living. This division of species is said to be the result of an odd, seemingly hair-splitting disagreement between two prominent scientists. The strict separation was a statement by the museum's Superintendent Richard Owen against Charles Darwin's attempt to link present species with past ones through his theory of evolution by natural selection.

Owen was no religious fundamentalist, however. He was an anatomist, biologist and palaeontologist who agreed with Darwin that evolution had occurred, but thought it more complex than Darwin's viewpoint as expressed in *On the Origin of Species*. Maybe Owen had too much time on his hands.

> It was Richard Owen who first coined the classification *Dinosauria*, meaning 'Terrible Reptile' or 'Fearfully Great Reptile'.

THE LAVA & TOWER OF LONDON ROCKERY

12

Address: The Chelsea Physic Garden, 66 Royal Hospital Road, SW3 4HS
(020-7352 5646, chelseaphysicgarden.co.uk).
Opening hours: Summer (end of Mar to end of Oct), Tue-Fri and Sun, 11am-6pm;
open until 10pm on Wed from early Jul to early Sep. See website for winter opening
times.
Cost: Adult, £9; concessions and 5-15s, £6.
Transport: Sloane Square tube.

The Chelsea Physic Garden is Britain's second-oldest botanical garden, after one at Oxford, which was founded in 1621. Its riverside location provided an equable microclimate and ready transport link.

Founded in 1673 as the Apothecaries Garden, the Chelsea Physic Garden's initial purpose was to train apprentices in identifying plants – 'physic' is the science of healing. It later became an important international seed exchange, a role which continues to this day.

Various types of environment were built at Chelsea to support different plants. The most unusual is the pond

rock garden, which was made from a strange variety of rock types – the website describes it (aptly) as 'a curious structure'. Finished in 1773 and now Grade II listed, it's the oldest rock garden in England on view to the public. It consists of a stony oval mound, and is made from fused bricks and flint, plus around 40 tons of stones from the Tower of London, very white and often ornately carved.

The rockery also includes Icelandic lava which was brought to Britain by Sir Joseph Banks in 1772 in the ballast tank of the *St Lawrence*. The mound was decorated with oddities collected over the years, including unusual minerals, brain coral and giant clamshells brought back from the South Seas by Captain Cook. One of these still remains.

13 LONDON'S MOST BOMBED BRIDGE

Address: Hammersmith Bridge, W6.
Transport: Hammersmith tube.

This impressive suspension bridge (London's first) is Grade II listed and carries traffic between Hammersmith and Barnes. It's the second permanent bridge on the site, opened in 1887 and designed by the noted civil engineer Sir Joseph Bazalgette, who's most famous for building London's sewer system and embanking the Thames.

Hammersmith also has the odd and more dubious distinction of being London's most bombed bridge. The IRA first attacked it in March 1939: a pedestrian crossing the bridge noticed

It was rumoured (facetiously) that Barnes' residents planted the 2000 bomb in order to close the bridge and keep their area free from its traffic.

smoke and sparks coming from a suitcase on the walkway. When he opened it, he found a bomb and promptly threw it into the river where the resulting explosion caused a 60ft column of water. (The passer-by was later awarded an MBE for his quick-thinking bravery). Soon after, a second device exploded, damaging some girders on the west side of the bridge.

In 1996, the Provisional IRA bombed the bridge with the largest Semtex bombs ever used on the British mainland, while in June 2000 the bridge was damaged by a bomb underneath the Barnes span. The Real IRA was suspected, although nobody was caught.

MAGNIFICENT PICTURES OF THE ROYAL FAMILY MIDDLE PAGES

You'll feel fitter on HOVIS

DAILY SKETCH

SPECIAL LATE EDITION

No. 9,529   WEDNESDAY, MARCH 29, 1939   ONE PENNY   RADIO: PAGE 20

HAMMERSMITH BRIDGE DAMAGED BY EXPLOSIONS THIS MORNING: BACK PAGE

Jack's The Lad, When The World Is Sad, To Drive Its Cares Away

LONDON'S RACECOURSE   14

Address: Notting Hill, W11.
Transport: Holland Park tube.

Strange as it seems today, upmarket, heavily residential Notting Hill was once the site of a racecourse. The Kensington Hippodrome was built by local entrepreneur John Whyte in 1837 on around 150 acres of land that he leased from the Ladbroke Estate. It was an ambitious project, as Whyte hoped to rival established courses such as Ascot and Epsom.

Notting Hill's grassy knoll was enclosed by railngs to form a natural grandstand for spectators, while the stables and paddocks were sited along Pottery Lane. Unfortunately Whyte had built his racetrack near the notorious Potteries and Piggeries slum (see The Old Pottery Kiln on page 245), so it was easily accessed by the area's notoriously rough inhabitants, which didn't square with the sort of stylish operation he was aiming for.

An equally big problem was the heavy clay soil, which meant poor drainage. The ground was often too waterlogged to use and during the racecourse's relatively short life (from 1837 to 1841 or 42) only around 13 meetings were held. A lot of jockeys refused to participate, claiming the heavy clay was too dangerous to ride on. When Whyte gave up and the operation folded, the land was used for building.

Look at a map of Notting Hill and you'll see there's still evidence of Whyte's racecourse – a number of the district's elegant crescents follow the route of the circular racetrack.

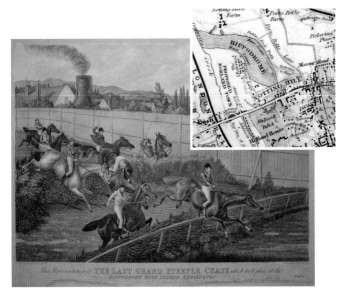

This Representation of THE LAST GRAND STEEPLE CEASE which took place at the HIPPODROME RACE COURSE, KENSINGTON.

15

NUDE PHOTOS AT LINLEY SAMBOURNE HOUSE

Address: 18 Stafford Terrace, W8 7BH (020-7602 3316,
rbkc.gov.uk/subsites/museums/18staffordterrace).
Opening hours: Visits are by guided tours, which run from mid-Sep to mid-Jun, Wed,
Sat and Sun, 11.15am, 1pm, 2.15pm and 3.30pm.
Cost: For public guided tours: adult, £8; concession, £6; age 5-16; £3. Private tours are
also available (see website).
Transport: High Street Kensington tube.

The veneer of Victorian respectability hid many a secret urge and vice, as a visit to 18 Stafford Terrace, Kensington subtly reveals. It was the home of Linley Sambourne, a cartoonist for the now-defunct satirical magazine *Punch*. He bought the five-storey house in 1875 and it remains beautifully preserved today, almost exactly as it was when the respectable, middle-class Sambournes occupied it.

Linley Sambourne was a keen photographer and used to have his family and servants pose as models. There's a striking picture of his coachman dressed as the mad Roman Emperor Nero and plucking a lyre (actually a firescreen). Moving into darker territory, Sambourne also had a taste for taking pictures of his maid – while she was asleep in bed. And hidden among the period furniture, fixtures and fittings is evidence of an impressive number of nudes photographed by the cartoonist.

Many are stored in the attic, but some are more obviously displayed for public consumption, in the bathroom. No sniggering, please.

Sambourne took most of his more risqué photos when his wife and children were on one of their regular seaside holidays, although Mrs Sambourne obviously knew of this 'interest', as she refers to it in her correspondence.

THE OLD POTTERY KILN   16

Address: Walmer Road, W11.
Transport: Latimer Road tube.

This kiln is a curious, unusual feature on a Notting Hill road mainly composed of neutral modern accommodation. The rectangular blue plaque on the front states that it's one of London's few remaining examples of a bottle kiln. It's a simple, strong, sculptural structure and harks back to the early 19th century when the area's soft clay was fired into bricks, drainpipes, pots and tiles. Appropriately, Walmer Road is just north of the infamous Pottery Lane.

Today, Notting Hill is one of London's more fashionable and expensive areas, but in the mid-19th century it was a notorious slum known as the Potteries and Piggeries. Pig farmers had moved in after being forced out of the Marble Arch area, while potters were drawn by its clay. The pig keepers were thought to be a respectable lot, but the brickmakers were described as 'notorious types' known for 'riotous living'.

It was also a filthy place to live. Extraction of the clay left holes, which over time became pools filled with stagnant water, pig slurry and sewage. One of these pools grew so large that it was known as 'The Ocean' – it was filled in 1892 and is now the site of Avondale Park.

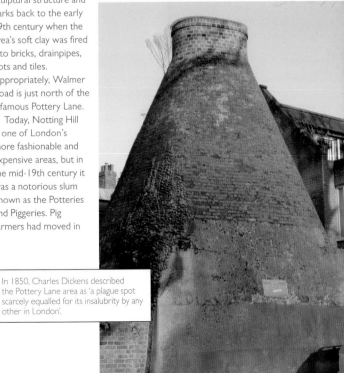

In 1850, Charles Dickens described the Pottery Lane area as 'a plague spot scarcely equalled for its insalubrity by any other in London'.

17   PEACOCKS BANNED HERE

Address: Cheyne Walk, SW3.
Transport: South Kensington tube.

The Aesthetic Movement left its mark on Chelsea's Cheyne Walk, not so much in design terms as in regard to which pets could be kept here. The Aesthetic Movement was a group of artists – including Frederic

Leighton, Dante Gabriel Rossetti and James Whistler – which embraced bold, rich colours, painted unusual subjects and venerated naturally beautiful items, including sunflowers and peacocks (of which more later). It also influenced architecture, design and fashion, with William Morris and others applying its ideas.

In short, these aesthetes wanted to escape the ugliness of contemporary life and thought all art should focus on the creation of beauty. Dante Gabriel Rossetti expressed his aesthetic ideals by keeping a remarkable menagerie of animals at his home at 16 Cheyne Walk, where he lived 1862-82. It included a wide range of creatures – not all of them beautiful – including armadillos, bulls, kangaroos, salamanders and wombats.

Stars of the show were abovementioned peacocks. However, they demonstrated that weaving beauty into everyday life isn't always practical, as they made a huge amount of noise and disturbed the road's other residents. So troublesome were they that peacocks were banned from Cheyne Walk, a rule that exists to this day: every lease is specific on this.

Frederic Leighton loved peacocks, too, but had a more pragmatic way of enjoying them: he kept a stuffed one in his house.

TRACES OF HENRY VIII'S MANOR HOUSE   18

> **Address:** 19-26 Cheyne Walk, SW3 5HH.
> **Transport:** Sloane Square tube.

These Grade II listed houses on Cheyne Walk occupy the exact frontage that was once the site of Henry VIII's Manor House, and retain intriguing, evocative traces of the former buildings. It's thought that Henry decided to buy a property here following visits to Sir Thomas More, who lived in Chelsea for over 20 years. Henry moved to the Old Manor House, located behind the Old Church, in around 1510, and had the New Manor built soon after 1536.

It was home to Elizabeth I when she was a child and to Catherine Parr after the King's death. The last royal resident was Anne of Cleves. The Manor was pulled down in the 1750s and numbers 19-26 were built 1759-65. There's been a fair amount of alteration since, but suggestions of the original survive.

There are several courses of two-inch Tudor brickwork in the base of number 20's front wall. Number 21 has a large share of the former Manor House's garden, with an old Tudor boundary wall to the north and a number of aged trees. The garden of number 26 also retains remnants of Chelsea's Tudor past and number 24's basement is part of the Manor House's original vaults.

> The last occupant of Henry's Manor House was physician and collector Sir Hans Sloane (1660-1753) whose name is now synonymous with Chelsea.

ROYAL BOROUGH OF KENSINGTON AND CHELSEA
KING HENRY VIII'S MANOR HOUSE
STOOD HERE UNTIL 1753 WHEN IT WAS DEMOLISHED AFTER THE DEATH OF ITS LAST OCCUPANT, SIR HANS SLOANE. NOS. 19 TO 26 CHEYNE WALK WERE BUILT ON ITS SITE IN 1759-65. THE OLD MANOR HOUSE GARDEN STILL LIES BEYOND THE END WALL OF CHEYNE MEWS AND CONTAINS SOME MULBERRY TREES SAID TO HAVE BEEN PLANTED BY QUEEN ELIZABETH I.

19   THE ARK

> **Address:** 201 Talgarth Road, W6 8BJ (thelondonark.co.uk).
> **Transport:** Hammersmith tube.

This prominent, iconic office building in Hammersmith is one of London's more singular, visually interesting structures. It derives the name from its hull-like shape and has the added characteristic of looking different depending on the angle you view it from. It was designed by the noted architect Ralph Erskine for the Swedish developers Ake Larson and Pronator.

Building began in 1989 and finished in 1992. The concept behind the design was 'the office as a community', i.e. a self-contained building with an interior which encourages teamwork and open communication. However, it's struggled to live up to this ideal and find long-term owners or tenants, and in mid-2013 it was for sale.

20   BEATRIX POTTER NAMES IN BROMPTON CEMETERY

> **Address:** Old Brompton Road, SW10 (020-7352 1201, royalparks.org.uk/parks/brompton-cemetery).
> **Opening hours:** 8am to between 5 and 8pm, depending on the time of the year (see website).
> **Transport:** West Brompton tube.

Brompton Cemetery is a 41-acre burial ground, one of the so-called Magnificent Seven cemeteries built in the 19th century to alleviate overcrowding in

THE TALE OF PETER RABBIT *by* BEATRIX POTTER

existing church burial sites. For much of her life, the author, conservationist, illustrator and natural scientist Beatrix Potter (1866-1943) lived nearby in

The Boltons. She often walked in the cemetery and apparently took the names of many of her animal characters from its tombstones.

Names on headstones include Mr Nutkins, Jeremiah Fisher, Tommy Brock and there's even a Peter Rabbett. It's also thought that Mr McGregor's walled vegetable garden was based on the cemetery's colonnades.

BERLIN WALL   21

Address: National Army Museum, Royal Hospital Road, SW3 4HT (020-7730 0717, nam.ac.uk).
Opening hours: Daily, 10am-5.30pm.
Transport: Sloane Square tube.

The National Army Museum tells the story of the British Army, so it's curious to find it displaying a number of sections of the Berlin Wall. Three sections can be seen behind the front railings – they weigh nine tonnes and were moved here by the Royal Logistical Corps – and there's another, smaller piece inside the museum.

The Berlin Wall fell on November 9th 1989, having been the great symbol of the Cold War. It was erected in 1961 on the orders of East Germany's then leader, Walter Ulbricht, to stop people leaving for the West. Despite this, around 5,000 people successfully crossed the wall into West Berlin, although over 200 were killed while doing so.

22   BLUEBIRD CHELSEA

Address: 330-350 King's Road, SW3 5UU (020-7559 1000,
www.bluebird-restaurant.co.uk).
Transport: Sloane Square or South Kensington tube.

This elegant, Grade II listed Art Deco building has undergone one of London's more unusual transformations: from garage to restaurant. It was built for the Bluebird Motor Company in 1923, the design of architect Robert Sharp. Strangely for such a central London location, it was reputedly Europe's largest garage at the time. It covered 50,000ft² (4,600m²), with room for around 300 cars in the main garage, and a further 7,000 ft² (650m²) was given over to workshops and other use.

Despite its connections with Sir Malcolm Campbell, holder of the land speed record in the '20s, the Bluebird garage didn't last long, going out of business in 1927. It later became an ambulance station and Sir Terence Conran's team converted it into its present use in 1997.

23   THE ELFIN OAK

Address: Kensington Gardens, W2 2UH.
Opening hours: 6am-dusk.
Transport: Queensway tube.

The quaintly-named Elfin Oak sits next to the Diana Princess of Wales Memorial Playground. Designed in 1930 by the illustrator Ivor Jones, it's a sculpture carved with animals, elves and fairies out of the hollow stump of an oak tree – the tree was originally in Richmond Park and is said to have lived for 900 years.

The Elfin Oak was exposed to a much wider audience when it appeared on the inside cover of the 1969 Pink Floyd album *Ummagumma*, with guitarist David Gilmour. In 1996 the late comedian Spike Milligan raised money for its restoration and it was Grade II listed a year later. It's set within a cage – albeit an attractive one – to protect it.

MR & MRS MURR'S HEADSTONE 24

Address: All Saints Church, Bishops Park, SW6 3LA (020-7736 3264, allsaints-fulham.org.uk).
Opening hours: Graveyard, 7.30am-dusk.
Transport: Putney Bridge tube.

Joseph and Isabella Murr's headstone might be London's oddest and most dismissive memorial. Its upper half praises Isabella at some length, while the lower half, which was presumably reserved for Joseph, has a mere three words.

Isabella's memorial reads: 'Sacred to the memory of Isabella Murr of this parish who departed this life on the 29th November 1829 in the 52nd year of her age. Ye who possess the brightest charms of life. A tender friend – a kind indulgent wife. Oh learn their worth. In her beneath this stone, these pleasant attributes together shone. Was not true happiness with them combin'd? Ask the spoil'd being she has left behind'.

In short, sharp contrast, Joseph's memorial reads: 'He's gone too'.

25   POETIC MANHOLE COVERS

Address: Notting Hill, W11.
Transport: Notting Hill Gate tube.

Together, the manhole cover poets comprise an impressive list of talent. Margaret Drabble has a cover on Notting Hill Gate outside the Coronet Cinema, which she describes as a place of 'diamonds, tears and dreams'. On Holland Park Avenue, PD James writes about Roman soldiers filling the streets, while other authors include Sebastian Faulks, Michael Holroyd (who's married to Margaret Drabble) and Colin Thubron.

The combination of manhole covers and poetry is a curious one, but sprinkled around smart and arty Notting Hill are seven specially-designed manhole covers that were installed in 2008. Each is engraved with a poem and all the authors – or Pavement Poets – are local residents.

26   THE ROCOCO SEA SHELL

Address: Garden of Strawberry Hill House, 268 Waldegrave Road, TW1 4ST (020-8744 1241, strawberryhillhouse.org.uk).
Opening hours: 10am-6pm, early Apr to early Nov (see website for exact dates).
Cost: The gardens are free but there's a fee to visit the house.
Transport: Strawberry Hill rail.

Strawberry Hill is an impressive example of Georgian Gothic architecture, built at Twickenham in stages by Horace Walpole, between 1749 and 1776. Its enjoyably over-the-top decorative style was extended to

some of the garden fixtures and fittings, notably a large seat in the shape of a sea shell. The original was recreated during a 2012 restoration and is nicely camp and blowsy, resembling a large ashtray on its side, with the creamy curves and scrolls of Rococo design.

Rococo was an 18th-century artistic movement that was a reaction against the grandeur and strict regulations of the Baroque. It's more florid and jocular, noted for creamy colours and curves, as illustrated by this splendidly showy garden chair.

THE RUSSIAN HOUSE   27

Address: The Vale, SW3.
Transport: South Kensington tube.

Wealthy Russians continue to buy property in London's upmarket postcodes, so this quiet street off Chelsea's King's Road is an appropriate

location for a cottage built in the style of a traditional Cossack *izba*, or peasant dwelling. It isn't completely authentic, as it has a tiled roof rather than one of rough thatch, and it should probably be whitewashed rather than having its boards painted black. Some of the windows are also rather fancy.

It was designed and built by Russians as part of their country's pavilion for an early 20th-century international exposition. It was subsequently purchased from them, transported to London in sections and reassembled here, a quietly quirky addition to the area.

28 THE RUSSIAN ORTHODOX CATHEDRAL OF THE DORMITION

Address: 57 Harvard Road, W4 4ED (020-3642 6459, russianchurchlondon.org).
Opening hours: Under review – see website.
Transport: Gunnersbury tube.

This attention-grabbing cathedral is unexpectedly situated just north of the Great West Road in the area between Kew and Chiswick. It's a small, beautiful structure, built by the Russian Orthodox Church Abroad (ROCA). The square, white building has some impressive external woodwork and a striking, blue, onion-shaped dome painted with gold stars and topped with a large, decorative, gold cross.

The cathedral is a recent arrival in London; the first stone was laid in 1997 and it opened in 1999. Work is ongoing inside, and in 2013 the interior was around 80 per cent complete. It boasts a number of old icons and paintings, which were smuggled out of Russia during the Revolution. There are few seats, however, as Orthodox Christians traditionally worship standing up.

29 THE TABERNACLE

Address: 35 Powys Square, W11 2AY (020-7221 9700, tabernaclew11.com).
Opening hours: 9.30am-10pm.
Transport: Westbourne Park tube.

Adele at the Tabernacle

This unusual, striking building in Notting Hill was built in 1887 as an evangelical church. It has an attractive Curved Romanesque façade of red brick and terracotta, and towers with broach spires on both sides. Today it's an arts, cultural and entertainment venue, with a theatre, art gallery, bar and kitchen, among other facilities.

It has a distinguished history as a rock venue and still hosts gigs. In the past some of the greats performed here: the Rolling Stones and Pink Floyd rehearsed at The Tabernacle, while The Clash played gigs. As such, it vies with Chalk Farm's Roundhouse and North Greenwich's O2 to be London's most visually interesting and unusual rock venue.

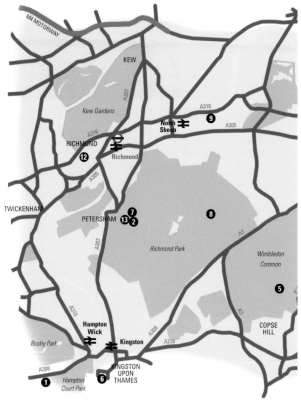

CHAPTER 5

SOUTHWEST LONDON

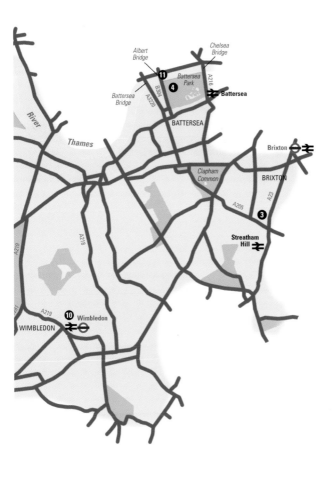

HAMPTON COURT PALACE

Address: East Molesey, KT8 9AU (hrp.org.uk/HamptonCourtPalace).
Opening hours: Daily, 10am-6pm.
Cost: Palace, gardens and maze (see website for other ticket variations): adult, £17.60 (£16.50 online); concession, £14.85 (£13.65); under-16, £8.80 (£8.25); family (two adults and up to three children), £45.10 (£41.80).
Transport: Hampton Court rail.

This magnificent palace was built in around 1514 by Cardinal Wolsey and later appropriated by Henry VIII. It has a number of curiosities and quirks, including the following three must-see items:

The Astronomical Clock: This unusual, decorative timepiece is of impressive size and is one of Europe's most important late-medieval clocks. It's on a tower overlooking Clock Court in the centre of the palace and was constructed in 1540-42 when Henry VIII was rebuilding Wolsey's original Hampton Court. Made by the French clockmaker Nicholas Oursian, it was designed before the game-changing discoveries of Copernicus and Galileo, so it shows the earth being orbited by the sun (rather than vice versa).

The face is 15ft in diameter and consists of three copper dials of different sizes which perform a wide range of functions. As well as telling the hour, day and month, they also show the 12 zodiac signs; the position of the sun in the ecliptic; the number of days

to have elapsed since the start of the year; and the moon's phases, including the hour when the moon crosses the meridian and, therefore, the time of high (and low) water at London Bridge.

Astronomical clock

Monarchs needed to know the tide times when leaving Hampton Court for London. A Thames barge was the preferred method of transport – certainly by Henry VIII and his entourage – and dangerous rapids developed at London Bridge at low water, so these times were best avoided.

The Great Vine: The English have long been keen consumers of wine and during warmer periods in history have produced it in some quantity. So it isn't so surprising that Hampton Court boasts what the 2005 *Guinness Book of World Records* lists as the world's largest grape vine. Planted in 1769 under the direction of the noted garden designer and landscaper Lancelot 'Capability' Brown, it was grown from a cutting taken not in Bordeaux or Burgundy, but in Essex.

Great Vine

It produces black dessert grapes, and its dimensions vary seasonally – grape vines are heavily pruned in late autumn. The vine's average annual crop is an impressively hefty 600lb (272kg) of grapes, while its record yield was 845lb (383kg) in 2001.

The Hammerbeam Roof: We usually think of roofs and ceilings as functional items, but that wasn't always the case. Flying high over Hampton Court's Great Hall, this is a wonderful example of the English Gothic-style,

decorative, open timber roof truss – a style that's been called 'the most spectacular endeavour of the English medieval carpenter'. Its splendour is offset by the walls of the Great Hall which are hung with Henry VIII's most impressive tapestries, illustrating *The Story of Abraham*.

> The Great Hall was the palace's most important room during the Tudor period. It was where the monarch dined in state, seated at a table on a raised dais.

Hammerbeam roof

2   THE ALTERNATIVE SEAT OF GOVERNMENT

Address: Pembroke Lodge, Richmond Park, TW10 5HX (020-8940 8207, pembroke-lodge.co.uk).
Opening hours: Park opens 7am (7.30am in winter) to dusk. Tea rooms at the Lodge open 9am-5.30pm or 30 minutes before the park closes, if earlier.
Transport: Richmond tube/rail.

Pembroke Lodge is an impressive Georgian mansion, enjoying splendid views from its lofty location in Richmond Park. It grew from small beginnings – in terms of its size and significance – to become an alternative (if unofficial) seat of government for a time in the 19th century.

The building dates from the 1750s, when it was a one-room cottage occupied by a mole catcher, whose job was to control the moles whose 'hills' were a danger to riders in the park. The lodge was subsequently enlarged, and in 1787 it was granted to the Countess of Pembroke, a 'close friend' of George III. She extended it further and in 1847, Queen Victoria gave it to Lord John Russell, who was then the Prime Minister.

Lord Russell disliked London society, so he conducted much government business here, including hosting cabinet meetings and entertaining an impressive list of distinguished visitors, from home and abroad. Earl Russell (as he'd become) died at the Lodge in 1878. However, perhaps he should have spent more time at Westminster, as neither of his two periods of office ran very smoothly or achieved a great deal.

Pembroke Lodge is now a venue for weddings and corporate events, but you can get a peek inside by visiting the excellent tea rooms.

THE BRIXTON WINDMILL 3

Address: Windmill Gardens, off Brixton Hill, SW2 5EU (020-7926 6213, brixtonwindmill.org).
Opening hours: Easter to Oct. See website for exact times and details of 'open access' visits and to book guided tours.
Transport: Brixton tube.

Brixton is urban, lively and multicultural, and the last place you'd expect to find a windmill. This 19th-century mill off Brixton Hill is the nearest surviving example to central London and is the last of a dozen or more working windmills that once operated in Lambeth. It was built in 1816 when the area was part of Surrey: a rural idyll of open fields and few houses. The windmill became known as Ashby's Mill, after local miller John Ashby and his family leased it and produced ground wholemeal flour.

In 1862 Ashby moved his business to water mills at Mitcham because new housing being built near the Brixton windmill was restricting the winds required to drive it. The sails were removed in 1864 and the windmill was used for storage for some decades. It resumed working after a new set of stones and a steam engine to drive them were installed in 1902, the latter subsequently replaced by a gas engine.

The windmill continued working until 1934, the year before John Ashby (grandson of the first miller) died, and was Grade II* listed in 1951. After extensive restoration, it reopened in 2011.

> The restored windmill has new sails which have allowed it to begin production again, grinding locally grown barley and wheat.

4   THE BROWN DOG STATUE

Address: Battersea Park, SW11 (020-8871 7530, batterseapark.org).
Opening hours: 8am-dusk.
Transport: Battersea Park rail.

This expressive, understated statue of a terrier sits in a tranquil spot north of Battersea Park's English Garden. The statue commemorates the dogs used in vivisection experiments in the early 20th century and is a reminder of a bitter, often forgotten controversy that raged in Edwardian England from 1903-10, which became known as the Brown Dog affair.

The current statue replaced the original, which portrayed a dog on top of a drinking fountain (with a dog trough, of course) and was erected near the Latchmere Pub in 1906. The statue became something of a lightning rod and was attacked a number of times by pro-vivisectionists who objected to its message. Local residents sometimes fought back, as they'd grown fond of their brown dog.

The statue was removed in 1910 to avoid further trouble, which by then had escalated to include pitched battles between medical students and the police. The current memorial dates from 1985 and is a simpler affair, on a plain plinth, with no fountain or drinking trough. It was moved to its present site in 1992 and the brown dog, a terrier, is based on one owned by its sculptor, Nicola Hicks.

Vivisection – an early form of live animal testing – was popular in the early 1900s, a time of experimental medicine.

CAESAR'S CAMP 5

Address: Wimbledon Common, SW19.
Transport: Wimbledon tube/rail.

This corner of the Common has been called Caesar's Camp since the 1830s, but there's little evidence that the Romans ever occupied Wimbledon. It's actually an Iron Age hill fort that covers around seven acres in an area that's now part of the Royal Wimbledon Golf Club. And it's the location of a shocking act of vandalism.

The fort was initially thought to have been built around 250BC, after pottery found on the site was dated to that time, but further studies indicate that it might date back to 700BC or before. It would have been a significant archaeological site but was destroyed in the 1870s by a builder, who almost levelled it in preparation for construction work that in the end didn't take place.

Before this needless act of destruction, the site comprised a fort surrounded by a circular earthwork around 300 yards in diameter, with two ramparts separated by a ditch. The ramparts were between 10 and 20ft in height, while the ditch averaged 12ft in depth and 30ft in width. Today, all that remains are undulations on an upmarket golf course, to which there's limited access – signs on the Common indicate the way.

Caesar's Camp is a name also appended to a number of Iron Age forts outside London, including forts in Bracknell Forest, Berkshire and Farnham, Surrey.

6   THE CORONATION STONE

> **Address:** Guildhall, High Street, Kingston-upon-Thames, KT1 1EU.
> **Transport:** Kingston rail.

A large, intriguing lump of ancient, weathered sarsen stone sits next to the Guildhall in suburban Kingston-upon-Thames. Sarsen is also called Greywether sandstone and has been used in Britain for thousands of years, including in the building of megalithic monuments such as Stonehenge. The Kingston sarsen is thought to have been the coronation stone for up to seven Anglo-Saxon kings.

It's known that Aethelstan was consecrated at Kingston in 925, Eadred in 946 and Aethelred the Unready in 979. There's also evidence that another four kings were consecrated in the town: Edward the Elder, Edmund I, Eadwig and Edward the Martyr.

The sarsen block was recovered from the ruins of Kingston's Saxon church of St Mary, which collapsed in 1730, having been undermined by grave digging. The Anglo-Saxon kings were believed to have been crowned in the church at the coronation block. For a while the stone was used as an a mounting block, until in 1850 it was moved to a more dignified setting and mounted on a plinth, with the names of the seven kings written around the base. It was moved to its current location in 1935.

> In Old English, *tun*, *ton* or *don* means farmstead or settlement, so Kingston would have been the farmstead or manor or estate of the kings (and was called *cyninges* tun in 838).

KING HENRY'S MOUND   7

Address: Gardens of Pembroke Lodge, Richmond Park, TW10 5HS
(royalparks.org.uk/parks/richmond-park).
Opening hours: 7am (7.30am in winter) to dusk.
Transport: Richmond tube/rail.

were later used as a viewpoint for hunting and falconry. (Being a keen hunter, Henry VIII might have graced it with his bulk on another occasion.) It's still a popular viewpoint and you can see St Paul's Cathedral over 10 miles (16km) to the east.

This mound is another of London's curious misnomers. It sits at the highest point in Richmond Park, Richmond being the largest of the capital's eight Royal Parks and the largest enclosed space in London, covering 2,360 acres. The mound is located in the public gardens of Pembroke Lodge and is said to be where Henry VIII stood on 15th May 1536 to watch for a rocket fired from the Tower of London.

This was the signal that his second wife, Anne Boleyn, had been executed for treason, meaning that he was free to marry Lady Jane Seymour. However, it's highly unlikely he was here that night as it's on record that Henry spent the evening in Wiltshire.

The mound is thought to be a prehistoric burial chamber – possibly Bronze Age – the remains of which

The view from the mound to St Paul's is protected to a 'dome and a half' width of sky on either side. Nothing can be built to obscure the view, although there's talk that this 'protected width' might be reduced in the near future.

8   PARAKEETS

Address: Around southwest London, including Barnes Common, Battersea Park and Richmond Park.

Parakeets are tough, adaptable birds and have colonised parts of the UK – especially areas of outer London – adding an unusual touch of eye-catching colour and glamour. There are a number of species of the bird and currently the rose-ringed parakeet – which is native to parts of Africa and Asia – is the most common.

UK parakeet numbers are estimated at anywhere between 30,000 and 50,000; most are concentrated in the south and west of the capital. London's parakeet population explosion dates from the mid-'90s – numbers were very low until then – although 'wild' parakeets were first spotted as long ago as 1855.

Their origin is unknown but some creative ideas have been advanced and popular stories – almost certainly inaccurate, if interesting – include that they escaped from Ealing Studios during the filming of *The African Queen* in 1951 (it was actually made at Isleworth Studios). Another cites Jimi Hendrix as the culprit: he's said to have released a pair of parakeets in Carnaby Street in the '60s to inject some psychedelic colour into London.

More realistically, though, it's thought that the birds from whom the current large numbers have descended escaped from an aviary during the Great Storm of 1987.

Whatever their origin, London's parakeets are becoming a problem, threatening native species and building nests on electricity cables. There's even talk of culling them.

SIR RICHARD BURTON'S BEDOUIN MAUSOLEUM

Address: St Mary Magdalen Church, 61 North Worple Way, SW14 8PR (020-8876 1326, stmarymags.org.uk).
Opening hours: Mon-Sat, excluding Thu, 9am-5pm; Sun, 9am-7.30pm.
Transport: Mortlake rail.

Sir Richard Burton

from his death – and the couple's coffins can be seen through a window at the back. She also paid for a stained glass memorial window to Sir Richard in the church. By the early '70s, the mausoleum had fallen into a bad state of repair, but it was restored in 1975 and today is a striking, unexpected sight.

Burton was an Arabist – a non-Arab specialist in Arabic language and culture – and a master of disguise. These skills allowed him to secretly visit Mecca, Medina and other holy sites that were barred to non-Muslims.

A Catholic cemetery in Mortlake is the site of one of London's most curious and singular tombs. It's a large, rectangular stone reproduction of an Arab tent, set on a base and measuring 12ft by 11ft. Made of stone from the Forest of Dean, it's carved to represent the natural folds and irregularities of a fabric tent.

It's the final resting place of Sir Richard Burton (1821-90) and his wife Isabel (1831-96). Burton was something of a renaissance man, being, among other things, an explorer, linguist (it's claimed that he spoke 29 languages), translator, travel writer and spy. He was also a British consul in various locations, from Damascus to Trieste.

The tomb was designed by Isabel – it's said she never quite recovered

10   THE STAG LODGE

Address: St Mary's Road, SW19.
Transport: Wimbledon Park tube.

Stag Lodge sits at the entrance to St Mary's Church in Wimbledon and draws the eye because of the large, seated stag perched on its roof. The decorative lodge was originally the gatehouse to the last of Wimbledon's four manor houses, Wimbledon Park House, which stood near here from 1588 to 1949. Stag Lodge was a late addition, built in 1850 by a property developer called John Augustus Beaumont, who'd purchased the manor house and adjacent park in 1846; it became home to one of the estate's gardeners.

Beaumont sold the manor in 1872 and Stag Lodge was sold separately as a private house. It's unclear exactly when and why the stag was installed on the roof, although there's a suggestion that it dates from 1881 and represents the long history of deer in Wimbledon Park.

The stag that gazes down inquisitively from the lodge's parapet today is a '80s replacement. The original was accidentally broken during its removal for safekeeping during World War II, when it was dropped by the butler!

Renowned huntsman Henry VIII once owned a property just behind St Mary's Church (there's been a church on the site since 1086) and almost certainly hunted in Wimbledon.

THE TREMBLING LADY WITH A CANINE PROBLEM

11

Address: Albert Bridge, SW11.
Transport: Sloane Square tube.

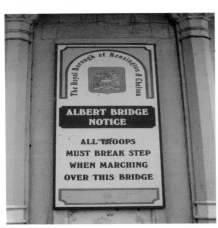

If the bridge struggles with pedestrian traffic, things are even worse with vehicles. Its roadway is only 27ft (8.2m) wide, and ill-equipped to cope with modern road traffic. Despite this, it staggers on in its elegant way, remaining open to vehicles, although strict traffic controls have limited its use.

In the '90s, the bridge was rewired and painted an unusual colour scheme of pink, blue and green to increase its visibility in fog and reduce the risk of shipping hitting the fragile structure during the day. At night it's a striking sight, when it's illuminated by some 4,000 bulbs.

The curiously-designed, Grade II* listed Albert Bridge is a remarkable survivor, as it has never really been fit for the purpose for which it was designed. It was built in 1873 to connect Chelsea and Battersea but proved structurally unsound from the start and has needed strengthening work on and off ever since. The bridge soon became nicknamed 'The Trembling Lady' due to its worrying tendency to vibrate when large groups of people walk over it. Signs at either end warn troops from the nearby Chelsea Barracks to break step (i.e. stop marching) while crossing.

Albert Bridge has another, more unusual problem: its timber deck structure is being badly damaged by the urine of the many dogs which cross it on their way to Battersea Park.

12   HAMMERTON'S FERRY

Address: Orleans Road, TW1 2NL (020-8892 9620).
Opening hours: At weekends, year round except Nov, 10am-dusk; Feb-Oct, Mon-Fri, 10am-6pm.
Cost: Adult, £1; adult's bicycle or child, 50p; child's bicycle, pushchair and dog, free.
Transport: Richmond tube/rail.

This pedestrian and cycle ferry service across the Thames is one of the few surviving ferry routes in the capital not to have been replaced by a bridge or tunnel. It links the northern bank of the river near Marble Hill House with the southern bank near Ham House.

Such services date back several hundred years – there's known to have been one at nearby Richmond from 1459 – but this service dates only from the early 20th century. A local resident called Walter Hammerton began to operate a regular ferry service across the river in 1909, using a 12-passenger clinker-built skiff and charging a penny per trip. The original boat is now displayed in the Docklands Museum.

13   THE IAN DURY MEMORIAL BENCH

Address: Poet's Corner, Pembroke Lodge, Richmond Park, TW10.
Opening hours: Park opens summer: 7am-dusk; winter: 7.30am-dusk.
Transport: Richmond tube/rail.

The life of late singer and actor Ian Dury (1942-2000) is celebrated by a solar-powered, interactive bench – what else? It's an unusual item, allowing you to plug in a set of headphones and listen to his music while enjoying his favourite views of Richmond Park. Designed by Mil Stricevic as part of his

Sonic Vista project, it plays eight of Dury's songs and an interview from his 1996 appearance on *Desert Island Discs*.

Richmond Park was special to Ian Dury and he was a frequent visitor. The bench has had a few 'technical' problems and doesn't always work – due to vandalism or the elements – but in 2013 plans were afoot for new technology to restore it to its former glory.

Ian Dury

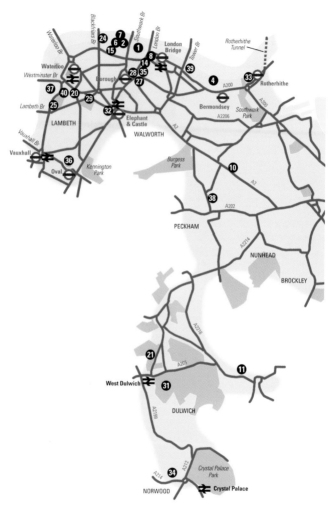

CHAPTER 6

SOUTHEAST LONDON

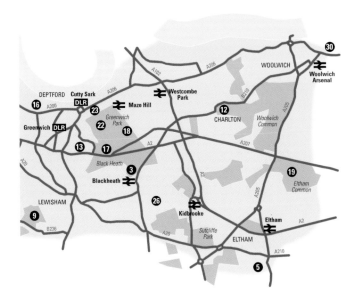

THE CLINK PRISON MUSEUM

Address: 1 Clink Street, SE1 9DG (020-7403 0900, clink.co.uk).
Opening hours: Jul-Sep, daily, 10am-9pm; Oct-Jun, Mon-Fri, 10am-6pm; Sat and Sun, 10am-7.30pm.
Cost: Adult, £7.50; concession and under-16, £5.50; family (2 adults and 2 under-16s), £18.
Transport: London Bridge tube/rail.

This enjoyably grisly museum is on the site of what was a notorious prison in the Bishop of Winchester's park for around 650 years. It has a number of unusual, curious and disturbing exhibits and features, including those listed below.

The Boot: This oversized metal boot looks benign enough – comical even – but was actually a torture device, designed to crush human feet. After a victim's foot was put in

the boot, wood was packed on and around the foot, filling the boot. It was subsequently doused with oil or water, causing the wood to swell and crush the foot within. However, the torture could get even worse: a fire was sometimes lit under the boot, boiling the contents, which apparently often resulted in the foot eventually dropping off!

Ghosts: The Clink was a prison from 1144 to 1780 (it was burned down during the anti-Catholic Gordon Riots) and it's said that the long centuries of neglect, pain and torture inflicted on inmates have left some ghostly reminders. A number of visitors claim to have seen and heard strange

The Clink is a popular venue with ghost hunters, and séances and other paranormal investigations take place here. See the website for information.

consists of a restraining tool at the end of the pole and was used to grab criminals around the throat, while the pole's length protected its user against those who were dangerous and/or armed. It's said to be the origin of the expression 'the long arm of the law'.

things, including spectral dogs running through the museum, people walking through walls, doors opening and closing, glasses smashing, lights turning on and off, and other oddities. And there have apparently been over 50 reports of a lady sitting and playing with her chains in a corner of the museum.

The Scold's Bridle: In some ways, this is the most shocking and unpleasant exhibit in the museum, because it was designed to punish a 'crime' that no one would consider unlawful these days. It's a metal skull cap which goes over the head and inserts an iron gag (which was sometimes sharpened) into the mouth, the idea being to prevent wives scolding (or nagging) their husbands. At best, the gag prevented the wearer from speaking, at worst it was a form of torture that crushed and cut the tongue.

The Thief Catcher: This long, metal device for retrieving prisoners

'The Clink' developed into general slang for a prison but may have been an onomatopoeic reference either to the sound of the prisoners' chains rattling or the metallic clink of prison doors being bolted.

2   BEAR GARDENS

Address: Bankside, SE1.
Transport: London Bridge tube/rail.

BEAR-BAITING.—SEE PAGE 276.

B ear Gardens is a street that runs off the riverside path at Bankside. The name sounds cute and cuddly, but is a reminder of a much more brutal London. In the 16th and 17th centuries, it was the site of the Bear Garden, a round or polygonal open structure that was used for bear-baiting, bull-baiting and other animal 'sports', which were popular during much of the Tudor period.

Contemporary drawings show a substantial three-storey building that resembles nearby theatres, including the Globe and the Rose. The Bear Garden's Bankside position might have been changed once or twice and its exact building date is unknown, but it certainly existed by 1550. It drew the good and the great,

including Henry VIII and Elizabeth I, and foreign ambassadors and visitors were often brought here to be 'entertained'.

Bear-baiting involved trained bulldogs or mastiffs attacking a bear that was tethered to a long chain – bears often, though not always, had their teeth filed down. Bull-baiting was more common in Britain, due to the scarcity and cost of bears, and the bulls sometimes tossed the attacking dogs so far and high that they landed on spectators' laps.

The last animal baiting recorded at Bankside was in 1682. Oliver Cromwell attempted to suppress it, but the 'sport' wasn't made illegal in Britain until 1835.

BEAR GARDENS st
LONDON BOROUGH OF SOUTHWARK

BLACKHEATH'S TROUBLED PAST 3

Address: Blackheath, SE3.
Transport: Blackheath rail.

Genteel Blackheath is a London 'village' named after a wide swathe of grassland that divides Lewisham and Greenwich. There's a long-standing idea that it's so-called because of an association with the Black Death in the mid-14th century. It's claimed that Blackheath was a mass burial ground,

Wat Tyler

but while it was indeed used to dispose of bodies, so were many places, such was the scale of the pandemic.

Despite being an elegant place to live – sometimes called the Hampstead of south London – Blackheath has a surprising history as a gathering place for revolutionaries. It was a rallying point in 1381 for the Peasants' Revolt; Wat Tyler's Kentish rebels were met here by representatives of the royalist government, who tried (unsuccessfully) to persuade them to return home. This event is remembered in the name of Wat Tyler Road on the heath.

In 1450, Blackheath was a gathering place for Jack Cade's rebellion, again fomented in Kent. Later, in 1497, Cornish rebels pitched camp here before being defeated in the Battle of Deptford Bridge. And in the 17th and 18th centuries, Blackheath was the haunt of highwaymen.

So it has only relatively recently become a desirable place to live.

Blackheath is one of the largest areas of public grassland in Greater London. Its name dates back to at least 1166 when it was called *Blachehedfeld* – 'dark coloured heathland' – in Old English.

4   EDWARD III'S MANOR HOUSE

Address: Bermondsey Wall East, SE16 4QH.
Transport: Bermondsey tube.

Overlooked by a row of bland, modern townhouses near the river in Rotherhithe, the low remains of a number of walls rise intriguingly from an area of neat turf. They're part of the remnants of a modestly sized royal manor house, which had two courtyards surrounded by a moat.

It was built c1349-1353 when the land was a marshy island in the Thames. By the 16th century, land reclamation had caused the small island to become merged with the mainland and river water was used to create a moat. The manor was built for Edward III (1312-77), who was crowned in 1327 when he was just 14.

It's thought that Edward used the manor as a rural retreat and somewhere to indulge his love of falconry. His grandson, Henry IV (1366-1413) may also have spent a lot of time here, invariably bandage-draped, as he suffered from a skin disease, thought to be leprosy or, possibly, psoriasis. The manor became a pottery works

Edward III

Edward III reigned for 50 years and is noted for his military successes and for restoring royal authority after the disastrous reign of his father, Edward II.

in the 17th century and was excavated in 1985, although much of what was found was subsequently reburied to protect the remains from vandalism.

ELTHAM PALACE   5

Address: Court Yard, SE9 5QE
(english-heritage.org.uk/daysout/properties/eltham-palace-and-gardens).
Opening hours: Late Mar to the end of Nov (see website for exact dates); Sun-Wed,
10am-5pm.
Cost: Adult, £9.90; concession, £8.90; age 5-15, £5.90; family (two adults plus up to
three children), £25.70.
Transport: Eltham or Mottingham rail.

This Grade II listed property is an intriguing blend of medieval castle and Art Deco mansion. A royal castle since the early 1300s, the lease was acquired by Stephen and Virginia Courtauld in 1933. They restored the Tudor Great Hall and incorporated it into a new and stylish Art Deco home.

Their house was ahead of its time when it came to mod cons and was equipped with concealed electric lighting, under-floor heating, a centralised vacuum cleaning system with built-in pipes and sockets in the skirting of each room. There was even an internal telephone system, although the couple also installed a pay phone so guests could make external calls at their own expense.

Eltham Palace is now managed by English Heritage and is on its list of most haunted places. One of its spirit residents is said to be a former member of staff who died a week after retiring. A man looking and sounding just like him is said to have invited visitors for a tour when the site was supposedly empty.

The Courtaulds had a pampered pet, a ring-tailed lemur called Mah-Jongg, which had a room on the upper floor of the house but also had the run of the property – one can only hope that it was scrupulously toilet-trained.

6   THE FERRYMAN'S SEAT

Address: Bear Gardens, SE1.
Transport: London Bridge tube/rail or Southwark tube.

The plain, elegant, flint-like seat which today is incongruously built into the side of what is now a Greek restaurant is a curious anachronism. Nobody knows exactly how old it is, but it's a throwback to when these seats were common along the banks of the Thames. They were resting places for the ferrymen (or wherrymen, as water taxis were also known as wherries) in the days when there was a thriving water taxi service across the river.

It was an important and busy trade, certainly until 1750, before which London Bridge was the only other means of carrying people and goods across the river. Many of the patrons using the ferries to and from Bankside (the location of this particular ferryman's seat) would have been rowdy, as this part of the south bank was a notoriously filthy, lawless place. It was known for its drinking dens and pleasure houses, including brothels (or 'stews', as they doubled up as steam baths), theatres and a bear-baiting arena; the seat's present location is a reminder of the last (see Bear Gardens on page 276).

> The ferrymen seem to have verged on the undernourished (presumably because of all the exercise involved in their work), as this ferryman's seat is a very tight squeeze indeed for better-padded modern posteriors.

The Ferryman's Seat

The Ferryman's seat, located on previous buildings at this site, was constructed for the convenience of Bankside watermen, who operated ferrying services across the river. The seat's age is unknown, but it is thought to have ancient origins.

Historic Southwark

A FORTUNATE LABELLING ERROR   7

Address: Cardinal's Wharf, 49 Bankside, SE1 9JE.
Transport: London Bridge tube/rail.

This is the oldest house on recently-renewed Bankside and its frontage bears an elegant, antique-style plaque that makes two impressive claims: 'Here lived Sir Christopher Wren during the building of St Paul's Cathedral. Here also, in 1502, Catherine Infanta of Castile and Aragon, afterwards first queen of Henry VIII, took shelter on her first landing in London'.

Unfortunately, the first claim is almost certainly untrue, while the second definitely is. The house wasn't erected until some 200 years after Catherine of Aragon arrived in England. It was built around 1710, the same year that St Paul's (situated directly across the river) was completed, so it's highly unlikely that Wren stayed here while working on his grand design.

But the 'deception' may well have saved the house from the destruction that befell so many of the area's old properties. It's thought that the plaque may have originally been on a nearby house, long demolished, and was placed on this one around 1945 by its owner, Malcolm Munthe, who was apparently something of a fantasist and dreamer.

Next to the house is a narrow passageway called Cardinal Cap Alley which dates back to 1579. It's said to have derived its name from a cleric who lost his hat while legging it away from a house of ill repute!

8   GARGOYLES

> **Address:** On the exterior of Southwark Cathedral, London Bridge, SE1 (cathedral.southwark.anglican.org).
> **Transport:** London Bridge tube/rail.

Southwark Cathedral

The 1,000-year-old Southwark Cathedral has a curious and extensive collection of gargoyles. Medieval architects often used them on large buildings to divert the flow of rainwater off the roof and reduce the potential damage from heavy rain. Gargoyles are usually designed as elongated fantastic animals, such as dragons, or animal-human hybrids. The length of the gargoyle determines how far the water is taken away from the wall.

As well as this practical function, gargoyles were also intended to convey

> The term gargoyle comes from the French *gargouille*, meaning throat or gullet.

A gargoyle is a type of grotesque (a carved stone figure) that contains a water spout. They are usually made of granite and the spout is designed to carry water away from the roof and sides of a building, to stop it from running down the walls and eroding the mortar – a bit like modern-day guttering and drainpipes. A trough is cut in the gargoyle's back to direct the flow of water, which usually exits through the open mouth.

a warning: they were representations of evil and a reminder that judgement was imminent, and thus designed to scare people into going to church! Their physical position also suggested that evil is kept outside the walls of a church or cathedral.

HILLY FIELDS STONE CIRCLE   9

Address: Hilly Fields, SE4 (hilly.org.uk).
Transport: Brockley rail.

London retains traces of its prehistoric past, with a number of damaged or partially flattened tumuli, burial mounds and forts. There are also thought to have been at least a couple of stone circles, including where St Paul's Cathedral and Westminster Abbey now sit – cathedrals were often built on earlier places of worship – but evidence of these has disappeared.

The lack of a London Stonehenge was made up for in 2000 when a modern stone circle was erected in Brockley by local artists to mark the millennium. Hilly Fields is a suitably elevated setting for the project – our ancestors often built their monuments on high land – as it stands 160ft above sea level and has views towards Canary Wharf, Crystal Palace and the North Downs in Kent. It's also been the site of an annual midsummer fair for around 30 years – another connection with pagan beliefs.

To build the modern stone circle, boulders were brought from Scotland and erected on the spring equinox

(March 21st). The stones act as a sundial and as well as marking the spring and autumn equinoxes and summer and winter solstices, they can also be used to tell the time of day.

Some people claim that the London Stone on Cannon Street is a fragment of a standing stone, but it's more likely to be the top of a Roman distance marker.

10   THE HISTORY OF THE OLD KENT ROAD

> **Address:** North Peckham Civic Centre, 600-608 Old Kent Road, SE15.
> **Transport:** Queens Road Peckham or South Bermondsey rail.

This striking mural is made from 2,000 ceramic tiles and depicts the history of the Old Kent Road, from Roman times until the '60s. It was installed in 1964 on the exterior of the former North Peckham Civic Centre.

Its many scenes and subjects include two carved heads of the Roman god Janus, similar to examples discovered near here in 1865. It also shows Chaucer with characters from his *Canterbury Tales* – a nearby spot called St Thomas a Watering (on the corner of Albany Road and Old Kent Road) was the first resting spot for pilgrims on their way to Canterbury. Among scenes, we see Henry V returning from victory at Agincourt, Jack Cade's rebellion and Charles II's return from exile. More recent times are represented by Pearly Kings and Queens, Belisha beacons and aeroplanes flying overhead.

The mural is the work of Polish artist Adam Kossowski (1905-86), who came to Britain in 1943 as a refugee from the Russian labour camps. He was noted for his works for the Catholic Church, and in 1953-70 he completed many large murals and reliefs. *The History of the Old Kent Road* is probably the largest and is his major secular work.

> The Old Kent Road follows the route of Roman Watling Street which ran all the way from Dover to Wroxeter (Viroconium) in Shropshire.

THE HORNIMAN MUSEUM

Address: 100 London Road, SE23 3PQ (horniman.ac.uk).
Opening hours: 10.30am-5.30pm.
Transport: Forest Hill rail.

This quirky museum reflects FJ Horniman's passion for collecting. There's much to enjoy, notably anthropological and cultural objects, natural history items and musical instruments. Curious exhibits abound and include the following:

Bone Clappers: This is a type of ancient Egyptian musical instrument, designed in the form of a pair of human hands. It was collected by the Egyptologist Flinders Petrie (see The Petrie Museum of Archaeology on page 57) in the late 19th century and is around 3,500 years old, the oldest of the Horniman's collection of over 8,000 musical instruments.

Torture Chair: This disturbing object was reputedly used by the Spanish Inquisition during the 17th century. The back of the chair is an upright iron bar which functions as a garrotte, used to execute victims by strangulation. On top of the garrotte is a device designed to encircle the head with bands and tension screws to break jawbones and penetrate ears.

Totem Pole: A 20ft (6.1m) red cedar totem pole stands outside the museum's main entrance. It was carved in 1985 as part of the American Arts Festival by Nathan Jackson, a Tlingit from Alaska. The carvings depict figures of legend, including a girl who married a bear.

For all its 17th-century claims, the torture chair might be a 19th-century reconstruction, embellished to feed the Victorians' fascination for gruesome display.

12   A HUGE HORTICULTURAL ERROR

Address: Charlton House, Charlton Road, SE7 8RE (charlton-house.org).
Transport: Charlton rail.

The splendid, Grade I listed Charlton House is one of England's finest Jacobean mansions and a living reminder of a right royal mistake. Charlton House was built 1607-12 for Sir Adam Newton, tutor to James I's eldest son. A mulberry tree next to the house dates from 1608 and was planted on the king's orders; it's a long-standing testament to a curious tale of horticultural incompetence and wishful thinking.

James I wanted England to become part of the silk industry then booming in Europe, notably Italy. The caterpillars that produce silk eat mulberry leaves, so James imported 10,000 saplings from Virginia and encouraged his courtiers

to plant them on their property. Unfortunately, the project hadn't been researched properly: the king's trees were Morus Nigra, the black mulberry, whereas silkworms eat the leaves of Morus Alba, the white mulberry, which originates in China. So James I left an inheritance of a great many mulberries but, alas, no silk industry.

Mulberries can be very long-lived, and a number of the original saplings still survive, including the example at Charlton House. It's claimed to be the country's oldest, although 'supporters' of a mulberry tree in Suffolk dispute this.

There's even a black mulberry cultivar called 'Charlton House' available to buy from some seed and plant retailers.

JACK CADE'S CAVERN   13

Address: Maidenstone Hill and surrounds, SE10.
Transport: Greenwich rail and DLR.

A series of caverns extends for several hundred feet under land known as The Point between Blackheath and Greenwich. Nobody knows how old they are. Some claim they were cut by prehistoric people using antler picks, citing ancient remains in the area, including tumuli to the southwest of Flamsteed House in Greenwich Park. These are thought to be early Bronze Age barrows, later re-used for burials by 6th-century Anglo Saxons.

Others point to Druids or Romans, and the latter were certainly in this area: to the east, at Maze Hill, is the site of a Roman temple or villa. The majority view, however, is that the caverns are the work of 17th-century miners burrowing into a chalk escarpment. Apparently a miner called William Steers was fined £40 in 1677 for overenthusiastic mining which undermined the King's Highway, causing carriages to overturn.

In 1780, an entrepreneurial builder carved 40 steps into the caverns and opened them to paying visitors. Later, a bar was installed, parties were held and there were tales of licentiousness; the bar was closed in 1854 and the entrance filled in. The Jack Cade association comes from the fact that the rebel who led his Kentish forces against Henry VI in 1450 gathered his men on Blackheath.

The caverns continue to cause road problems today: in 2002, part of the A2 on Blackheath Hill fell into a crater.

14   THE MAHOMET WEYONOMON MEMORIAL

Address: Southwark Cathedral, London Bridge, SE1 9DA.
Transport: London Bridge tube/rail.

Mahomet Weyonomon was a Native American, the chief of the Mohegan tribe from Connecticut. He travelled to England in 1735 to petition George II for better treatment of his people, who had lost much of their agricultural and hunting land to English colonists.

The chief travelled with his three companions – including two colonists, John and Samuel Mason, who supported his cause – and the group rented accommodation at St Mary Aldermanbury in the City while they prepared to petition the king. Alas, Mahomet and one of his party died from smallpox in 1736, before they could present their case; the chief was aged just 36.

As a foreigner, Mahomet couldn't be buried in the City, so he was interred in an unmarked grave in Southwark Cathedral, the exact location unknown. In 2006, the Queen and Duke of Edinburgh dedicated a distinctive, eye-catching, stone memorial to him, accompanied by a traditional funeral ceremony conducted by members of the Mohegan tribe. So Mahomet did get to 'meet' a British monarch, albeit 270 years after his original appointment.

The memorial, which sits in the cathedral's south churchyard, is the work of the sculptor Peter Randall-Page. It's made from a five-tonne pink granite block which came from the Mohegan tribal reserve in New England, where it's traditional to name a boulder after a chief who has died.

THE MONUMENT TO THE UNKNOWN ARTIST

Address: Sumner Street, SE1.
Transport: Southwark tube.

An appealingly odd combination of art and animatronic technology sits behind the Tate Modern gallery. It's a detailed bronze sculpture of a man wearing a loose-fitting suit, shoes and a scarf knotted around his neck, and holding a paintbrush in his right hand. The sculpture is an impressive size; over 3m tall and standing on a 3m-high granite plinth. It's called the *Monument to the Unknown Artist* and was designed by the art collective Greyworld and installed in 2007.

What makes it curious and unique is that the figure changes position every few minutes. It's programmed to be influenced by its surroundings and can mimic the movements of passers-by, so that people can create their own dialogue with it. If you stand close enough and make an arm movement, the statue might do the same – but be patient, as it can take a little time to catch up with you.

There's a Latin inscription on the statue's plinth, which changes every few months. Captions have included

Quidquid Latine dictum sit altum videtur (anything said in Latin sounds profound) and *Non plaudite modo pecuniam jacite* (don't applaud, just throw money).

Proof that life does indeed imitate art is illustrated at nearby Southbank, where there are often a number of real people dressed as various characters, keeping still and pretending to be statues… for money, of course!

16   THE ORIGINAL SKULL & CROSSBONES

Address: St Nicholas Church, Deptford Green, SE8 3DQ (020-8692 2749, deptfordchurch.org).
Transport: Deptford rail.

The striking design of the pirate flag the Jolly Roger is said to have been based on the skulls and crossbones which adorn the gate posts of this Deptford church. There's been a church on the site for around 800 years and the flag dates back to the long years of conflict between Britain, France, Spain, Holland and others over the lucrative trade routes between Europe and Africa, the Americas and India. Much of this conflict was carried out 'unofficially' by privateers, i.e. ships that were privately owned, and whose activities were tacitly endorsed by their countries.

British privateers wanted a flag that would hide their origin and induce fear when they approached potential targets to loot, e.g. Spanish galleons loaded with gold bullion. Because many of these pirate ships sailed from Dartford, there's a belief that the local church was the inspiration for the skull and crossed bone design on their flags.

Ironically, the laurel that wreathes the skulls on the church's gate post is a symbol of everlasting life, although this would have been of little comfort to the pirates' victims.

There are other skulls on display inside the church, including on a carved panel called *The Valley of the Dry Bones*, which is attributed to the master wood sculptor Grinling Gibbons.

PRINCESS CAROLINE'S SUNKEN BATH   17

Address: Greenwich Park, SE10.
Opening hours: 6am-dusk (between 6 and 9.30pm, depending on the month).
Transport: Blackheath rail.

Caroline of Brunswick

Montague House was once the home of Princess Caroline of Brunswick (1768-1821) and its last vestige can be seen at the southern end of Greenwich Park, near the Charlton Way entrance. Caroline was the cousin and wife of the Prince Regent, later George IV (1762-1830). It's an amusingly ironic remnant, as we shall see.

Unfortunately, Caroline and George's match wasn't made in heaven. She was stocky, plain, coarsely spoken and less than scrupulous about personal hygiene. He was no great catch himself, being overweight and in debt – the latter was the reason for the marriage. They're said to have slept together only three times, but did manage to produce a child, Princess Charlotte.

Keen to return to his philandering, George effectively banished Caroline to Greenwich. She fought back from this snub by living it up at Montague House, where she resided from c1797-1814, holding wild parties and developing quite a salacious reputation. Furious George had the place razed to the ground when Caroline left and moved to Italy.

Given her reputation for body odour, it's a splendid irony that all that remains of the property is the sunken bath that was originally the central part of an elaborate bath house.

It's said that Prince George called for a shot of brandy when he first met his betrothed, so shocked was he by her appearance and smell.

18   QUEEN ELIZABETH'S OAK

Address: Greenwich Park, south end of Lover's Walk, near Maze Hill Gate, SE10.
Opening hours: 6am-dusk (between 6 and 9.30pm, depending on the month).
Transport: Maze Hill rail.

Greenwich Park is one of London's eight Royal Parks and boasts an aged, now-faded piece of regal history. It's the fallen trunk of a large oak tree dating back to around the 12th century, which is said to have strong links with the Tudor line. Henry VIII (1491-1547), who was born at Greenwich, is supposed to have wooed his second wife Anne Boleyn (c 1501-36) here by dancing around the tree with her. And their daughter Elizabeth I (1533-1603) apparently enjoyed taking refreshments in its shade and even within its massive, hollow trunk.

The trunk is said to have been so large (20ft in girth) that its hollow was turned into a room measuring 6ft in diameter, and was sometimes used as a lock-up for people who had misbehaved in the park. The tree died sometime in the 19th century, but the surrounding soil and the thick ivy which covered it combined to hold it upright until 1991, when a heavy rainstorm washed away much of the soil and the tree toppled over.

The Duke of Edinburgh planted a small oak next to the fallen giant in 1992 and there's a plaque detailing the ancient tree's history.

QUEEN ELIZABETH'S OAK

This ancient tree known as Queen Elizabeth's Oak is thought to have been planted in the 12th Century and it has been hollow for many hundreds of years.

It has traditions linking it with Queen Elizabeth I, King Henry VIII and his Queen Anne Boleyn, it may also have been a lock-up for offenders against park rules.

It died in the late 19th Century and a strong growth of Ivy supported it until it collapsed in June 1991.

The English Oak alongside was planted by
His Royal Highness
The Prince Philip, Duke of Edinburgh, KG, KT
Baron Greenwich on 3rd December 1992

The tree was donated by Greenwich Historical Society to mark the 40 years of the reign of Queen Elizabeth II.

Oaks are seen as symbolic of England, as they were used to build the ships that spread England's and, later, Britain's power around the world.

SEVERNDROOG CASTLE   19

Address: Castle Wood, off Shooter's Hill, SE18 3RT (severndroogcastle.org.uk).
Transport: Welling or Woolwich rail.

Jupp (1728-99), who was surveyor to the British East India Company for around 45 years. It's a memorial to Commodore Sir William James (c 1721-83), naval commander and former chairman of the East India Company, and was commissioned by his widow, Lady James of Eltham. The unusual name recalls the island fortress of Severndroog on the west coast of India which was attacked and destroyed by Sir William's forces in 1755.

Although the name Severndroog sounds like something from a children's book, it comes from an 18th-century military victory. And it isn't a real castle but a Grade II* listed folly. A folly is a building designed for aesthetic pleasure rather than any practical purpose, often incorporating elements of fakery or eccentricity – many are so extravagant that they outdo the building they're supposed to represent. Follies first appeared in the late 16th and early 17th centuries, and flourished in the following two centuries.

Severndroog Castle was designed in 1784 by the architect Richard

His Gothic-style tower is 63ft (19m) high and triangular in section, with a hexagonal turret at each corner. Its elevated position commands fine views across London and beyond.

A restoration project began at Severndroog Castle in 2013 and there are plans to open it to the public in the future. Check progress via the website.

20   THE STARS & STRIPES SPIRE

Address: Christchurch and Upton Chapel, corner of Westminster Bridge Road and Kennington Park Road, SE1.
Transport: Lambeth North tube.

This landmark spire is notable for its unusual Stars and Stripes brickwork – an architectural version of the US flag, using a polychromatic colour scheme of red and white Kentish ragstone. The spire was donated by Abraham Lincoln's family as a thank you to Christ Church, Lambeth for its support in the fight to free America's slaves, and it later became known as the Lincoln Tower.

The church had been completed in 1873, while the spire was added in 1876. Christ Church became the base for a number of social movements, including the Bible Society (dedicated to translating, publishing and distributing the Bible at affordable prices), Shaftesbury Society (the 7th Earl of Shaftesbury was one of Britain's greatest social reformers), Ragged School Movement (which provided free education for destitute children) and several others. It was also the central London headquarters of William Wilberforce's movement to put an end to slavery in the British Empire.

The church was bombed during World War II and only the spire remains. An office block and the Christ Church and Upton Chapel were built onto it in the '60s – and they make an interesting contrast with the Gothic-style tower.

The Lincoln Tower was opened on 4th July 1876, the centenary of the American Declaration of Independence.

THE TAKEAWAY REMBRANDT   21

Address: The Dulwich Picture Gallery, Gallery Road, SE21 7AD
(dulwichpicturegallery.org.uk).
Opening hours: Tue-Fri, 10am-5pm; Sat and Sun, 11am-5pm; Mon, closed.
Cost: Adult, £6; senior, £5; concession and under-18, free.
Transport: North or West Dulwich rail.

Jacob de Gheyn III, Rembrandt

The ground-breaking, historically-important Dulwich Picture Gallery boasts many attractions. One of the more unusual is a portrait that's become known as the 'Takeaway Rembrandt' because it's been stolen so frequently. Dating from 1632, it's a painting of Jacob de Gheyn III (1596-1641), a Dutch engraver. One half of a pair of pendant portraits, it depicts him with a rather unfortunate bowl-like hairstyle.

The picture is small – it measures just 11.8 by 9.8in (29.9 by 24.9cm) – and very portable, which partly explains why it's been nicked so often. The Takeaway Rembrandt has been stolen four times since 1966. In one of the incidents, it went missing for three years and was eventually found in 1986 in a luggage rack at the train station of a British army garrison in Münster, Germany.

At other times the missing painting has been retrieved from underneath a bench in a Streatham graveyard and from the basket of an abandoned bicycle. Security around the Rembrandt has been tightened in recent years, which might put a stop to the thefts.

Despite its reputation, the Takeaway Rembrandt is only the world's second-most stolen artwork. In first place is *The Ghent Altarpiece* by Jan van Eyck (currently on display in St Bavo Cathedral, Ghent), which has been stolen six or seven times.

Dulwich Picture Gallery

22   THE TIME BALL

> **Address:** Flamsteed House, Royal Observatory, Blackheath Avenue, SE10 8XJ
> (rmg.co.uk/royal-observatory/flamsteed-house-and-meridian/flamsteed-house).
> **Opening hours:** Greenwich Park is open from 6am to dusk (between 6 and 9.30 pm).
> **Transport:** Cutty Sark DLR.

Flamsteed House was the original Royal Observatory building, designed by Sir Christopher Wren in 1675. The striking red ball on the top is a throwback to the days when very few people could afford to own a clock or watch. It's one of the world's earliest time signals, communicating time to ships on the nearby Thames, as well as to Londoners.

At 12.55 each day the time ball rises half way up its mast; at 12.58 it rises to the top; and at 1pm it falls, providing a time signal to anybody who happens to be looking. It drops at 13.00 GMT during the winter and at 13.00 BST during the summer, providing the weather isn't too windy.

In the days before time balls, time was an inexact science. Only the richest could afford clocks and watches, and the vast majority of people relied on public sundials. This led to different times across the country, with readings on the east side of the country around half an hour ahead of those in the west. The difficulties created by everyone using their own local time led to the countrywide adoption of Greenwich Meridian Time (GMT).

> The Greenwich time ball was first used in 1833 and still operates to this day.

THE TULIP STAIRCASE GHOST   23

Address: The Queen's House, Romney Road, SE10 9NF (rmg.co.uk/queens-house).
Opening hours: Daily, 10am-5pm.
Transport: Cutty Sark DLR or Maze Hill rail.

Queen's House, Greenwich

One of Britain's most notable 'ghost' photographs was taken at the architecturally-important Queen's House in Greenwich. The property, which dates back to 1638, was designed by Inigo Jones. It was England's first classical building, based on Jones' studies of Roman and Renaissance architecture in Italy, and was commissioned by Charles I for his queen, Henrietta Maria.

The intriguing 'ghost' photograph was taken in 1966 by the Reverend R W Hardy on the elegant tulip staircase. He waited for the staircase to be free of people before taking his shot, but when developed it showed what appear to be two or three shrouded figures on the stairs. The negative was examined by experts – including representatives of Kodak – who concluded that it hadn't been tampered with.

Other unexplained figures have been seen on or near the staircase and footsteps are sometimes heard, as well as doors slamming and children chanting. Some visitors have described being pinched by unseen fingers. The source of this activity is thought to date back 300 years to when a maid was thrown from the highest banister, falling 50ft to her death.

The tulip staircase is Britain's first geometric, self-supporting spiral staircase, although the term 'tulip' is misleading. The stylised flowers in the wrought-iron balustrade are fleurs-de-lis, the emblem of the Bourbon family, of which Queen Henrietta Maria was a member.

24   UNUSED BRIDGE COLUMNS & AN UNEXPLAINED HANGING

Address: Blackfriars Bridge, SE1.
Transport: Blackfriars tube/rail.

There have been three bridges at Blackfriars and two of them currently co-exist (sort of), presenting a curious sight. The original bridge, which opened in 1769, was replaced by one designed by Joseph Cubitt in the 1860s. Cubitt's bridge was built for the London, Chatham and Dover railway and the company's insignia was displayed on the massive abutments (supports) at each end of the bridge. It eventually became too weak to carry modern trains and was removed in 1985, but the striking, Grade II listed abutments were left standing at the southern end, and are visible from the modern bridge.

Roberto Calvi

On 18th June 1982 Blackfriars Bridge was in the news for a more macabre reason, when the body of banker Roberto Calvi was found hanging beneath the bridge. His clothing was stuffed with bricks and he was carrying around $15,000 of cash in three currencies. The death was subject to two coroner's inquests: the first recorded a verdict of suicide, the second an open verdict.

According to a later, independent forensic report, Calvi's injuries and the circumstances of his death indicated that he'd been murdered. It's claimed that his murder was linked to the Vatican Bank, the Mafia and the Freemasons.

Calvi – or 'God's Banker' as he was dubbed – was a mason and had been chairman of Banco Ambrosiano, which was alleged to have laundered money for the Mafia.

Blackfriars Bridge

WILLIAM BLIGH'S BREADFRUIT TOMB   25

Address: The Garden Museum, 5 Lambeth Palace Road, SE1 7LB (020-7401 8865, gardenmuseum.org.uk).
Opening hours: Sun-Fri, 10.30am-5pm; Sat, 10.30am-4pm.
Transport: Lambeth North or Westminster tube.

William Bligh (1754-1817) was a British Royal Navy officer whose tomb, curiously, is topped with a breadfruit. He's most famous because of the mutiny that occurred during his command of HMS *Bounty* in 1789 on a voyage to Tahiti and the Caribbean.

Captain William Bligh

Shortly after the ship left Tahiti, Bligh and his supporters were set adrift in the *Bounty*'s launch by the mutineers and made a seemingly-impossible journey to Timor, which was testimony to Bligh's remarkable skills of seamanship.

The purpose of the journey to Tahiti had been to obtain breadfruit trees to take to the Caribbean, where it was hoped they would become a viable food crop for slaves. The mutiny put paid to this, but on a subsequent voyage in 1791-93, as commander of the HMS *Providence*, Bligh successfully carried breadfruit to the West Indies, where it remains a popular foodstuff today.

After his death in 1817, Bligh was buried in the family plot in St Mary's Lambeth (the church is now deconsecrated and houses the Garden Museum). His simple, elegant tomb is made of Coade stone (see Coade Stone Caryatids on page 203) and is topped by a breadfruit in a bowl.

Breadfruit is one of the highest-yielding food plants, so-called because its cooked fruit has a texture similar to freshly baked bread.

HMS Bounty

26   THE ARCHITECT & SOCIETY SCULPTURE

Address: Hallgate, Foxes Dale, Blackheath Park, SE3.
Transport: Blackheath rail.

A sculpture of a male figure is set within a wall in front of the smart Hallgate block of 26 Span flats in Blackheath. He's of black granite, naked and stylised, lying on his back and with his legs bent up. The sculpture seems to support the weight of the slab above with its head, shoulders and knees.

Hallgate is a private housing scheme built by Span Developments Ltd, whose ethos was to build sensitively designed housing in well-considered landscaping. The sculpture dates from 1958 and is by Keith Godwin. It represents the development's architect Eric Lyons (1912-80) being crushed by public opinion, difficult bye-laws and planning restrictions. It was sculpted to celebrate Lyons's planning victory here, although the design suggests that this didn't come easily.

27   THE BLACK-FACED CLOCK

Address: St George the Martyr Church, Borough High Street, SE1 1JH.
Transport: Borough tube.

There's been a church on this site since at least 1122, with the current one dating from 1736. It's of red brick with Portland stone dressings and is the church where Little Dorrit was married in the Charles Dickens novel of the same

name.

The steeple's clock has four dials and was made by George Clarke of Whitechapel in 1738, for £90. However, whereas three of the faces are painted white and illuminated at night, the other is black.

It's the face that points towards Bermondsey and this is allegedly because parishioners there refused to donate money to the church when it was being built – the black dial of the clock facing in their direction is a decisive snub for their parsimony.

THE BLUE MEN   28

Address: Maya House, 134-138 Borough High Street, SE1 1LB.
Transport: Borough tube.

Three blue musicians unexpectedly clamber up and brighten the front of this rather ordinary building on historic Borough High Street. The figures carry different musical instruments, strike various poses and thereby draw the eye. They comprise a quirky art installation from 2007 by the Israeli artist Ofra Zimbalista (born 1939), who often uses realistic figures as the basis for her sculptures, usually family members or friends.

Such deep blue figures have become the artist's signature pieces and this example of her work is probably best seen in sunshine, which throws interesting shadows from the figures onto the building behind.

29   THE BRASS CROSBY MILESTONE

Address: St George's Road, SE1 6HZ.
Transport: Lambeth North tube.

Crosby was locked in the Tower but released after a public outcry. Later, he won a campaign to allow the free reporting of Parliament. This large milestone was erected on St George's Circus as a memorial to him, but moved to its present site in 1905, thereby rendering its very precise measurements incorrect.

The Brass Crosby Milestone stands outside the Imperial War Museum, but it isn't made of brass and also isn't accurate, despite the distances on it being indicated to the last foot. It's named after Brass Crosby (1725-93), a Lord Mayor of London who became something of a national celebrity in 1771 when he refused Parliament's order to jail a printer who'd had the impertinence to report their proceedings in the press.

Brass Crosby

30   BRONZE FOR VICTORIA CROSSES

Address: Firepower – The Royal Artillery Museum, Royal Arsenal, SE18 6ST (020-8855 7755, firepower.org.uk).
Opening hours: Tue-Sat, 10am-5pm.
Cost: Adult, £5.30; concession, £4.60; child, £2.50.
Transport: Woolwich Arsenal rail.

This well-named museum houses two of the most famous guns in Britain. They're Chinese and were probably captured by the British during the Second Anglo-Chinese War

of 1860. Their fame comes from the curious fact that they supply the bronze from which Victoria Cross medals are made. The guns are accordingly known as the Victoria Cross

Guns, although the first of the medals were probably made from Russian guns captured at Sevastopol during the Crimean War.

The Victoria Cross is the highest military decoration awarded for valour 'in the face of the enemy' to members of the armed forces of British Commonwealth countries. Hancock's Jewellers has manufactured Victoria Crosses from gunmetal since 1856 and over 800 of the medals have been made.

Corporal Johnson Beharry VC, with a 'Victoria Cross gun'

THE DULWICH TOLLGATE   31

Address: College Road, SE21 (thedulwichestate.com/tollgate).
Transport: West Dulwich rail.

This is London's last remaining tollgate, a throwback to former times. It was established in 1789 and manages to survive, despite other tollgates having been abolished by legislation in 1864. It's on the Dulwich Estate's private section of College Road and all motor vehicles except motorbikes must pay the toll.

The original tolls can be seen on display by Tollgate Cottage near the gate. These days, the standard fee is £1 for each single journey through the tollgate, although regular users can reduce the cost by buying a pass (called a Tag). The gate currently operates Mon-Fri, 7am-9.30pm; Sat, 8am-6pm; Sun and public holidays, 9am-5pm. On Christmas Day, passage is free.

32   THE FARADAY MONUMENT

Address: Elephant & Castle, SE1.
Transport: Elephant & Castle tube.

Michael Faraday

A large, enigmatic cube of polished steel sits at the heart of the hectic Elephant and Castle roundabout system, adding style and interest to this slightly unkempt part of London. It's a memorial to the scientist Michael Faraday (1791-1867), a pioneer in various fields, notably electricity. It was designed by Brutalist architect Rodney Gordon (1933-2008) and built in 1961.

The memorial is sited here because Faraday was born nearby, in the delightfully named Newington Butts. Inside it contains an electricity substation for the tube, which is appropriate given Faraday's scientific speciality. The monument was Grade II listed in 1996 and is especially impressive on a sunny day, with light gleaming off it.

33   THE FIRST UNDERWATER DINNER PARTY

Address: The Thames Tunnel, Brunel Museum, Railway Avenue, SE16 4LF (020-7231 3840, brunel-museum.org.uk).
Opening hours: 10am-5pm. There's also a wide variety of special events (see website for details).
Cost: Adult, £3; concession, £1.50; under-16, free.
Transport: Canada Water tube/rail or Rotherhithe rail.

Built 1825-43 by the noted Brunel family of engineers, the Thames Tunnel was the first channel to have been successfully built under a navigable river. On 10th November 1827 it was the venue of the world's first underwater dinner party to celebrate the tunnel's repair after a flood. Later, this stunning feat of Victorian engineering – which is the oldest section of the world's oldest underground railway – became, for a short time, one of the country's biggest tourist attractions.

After its completion in 1843, it drew an estimated two million visitors in its first year, an astonishing figure. Attractions included an underwater fair and fairground, and it was even described as the Eighth Wonder of the World.

THE GIPSY TOWER   34

Address: Gipsy Hill, SE19 1QG.
Transport: Gipsy Hill rail.

This splendidly eccentric house is at the Dulwich end of Crystal Palace and consists mainly of a church tower converted into a home. Christ Church was a Victorian Gothic pile, completed in 1861 and designed by John Giles, who also built the Langham Hotel in Portland Place opposite the BBC. The church was largely destroyed by arsonists in the '80s, with only the 120ft tower remaining.

This tower and some additions now form the house, which has four floors and covers around 3,500ft². It's Grade II listed and because the tower's base is built on land 300ft above sea level, it enjoys panoramic views of the City and beyond.

35   THE GUY'S HOSPITAL LUNATICK CHAIR

> **Address:** Guy's Hospital, Great Maze Pond, SE1 9RT.
> **Transport:** London Bridge tube/rail.

A large, sculptural oddity lurks in the grounds of Guy's, a hospital founded in 1721 by Thomas Guy. Guy was a publisher who made his fortune in the South Sea Bubble (before it burst). The oddity is a round-headed Portland stone alcove from the old London Bridge (not the one shipped to Arizona in 1968) containing a bronze statue of a seated figure.

The alcove comes from the bridge that was taken down in 1831 and was installed at the hospital in 1861 – ten guineas was paid for it – to be used as a shelter for convalescing patients. It's been in its present position since 1926 and is named after the old Lunatick House (which originally stood near by), built in 1744 as a 20-bed facility for mentally ill patients.

36   THE HANGING GARDENS OF LONDON

> **Address:** The Oval Cricket Ground, Harleyford Street, SE11 5SS (kiaoval.com).
> **Transport:** Oval tube.

If Lords is the spiritual home of cricket (see Lords Cricket Ground Media Centre on page 222), the Oval probably has the more interesting history. It dates from 1845, when ten acres of what had been a market garden was leased as a cricket club. The ground was the scene of the first ever Test Match, in 1880, and the first FA

Cup final was also played here. During World War II it was briefly a prisoner-of-war camp.

The Oval recently doffed its cap to its agricultural origins: as part of a £25m development, the futuristic stand at the Vauxhall end opened in 2005, and its street side has its own hanging garden, providing an unexpected splash of green in this still-gritty part of London.

THE LOST THAMES FORD   37

Address: St Thomas's Steps, by Westminster Bridge, SE1.
Transport: Westminster tube.

It's long been thought that there's a ford across the Thames by Westminster Bridge, its use dating back thousands of years. The Romans, in particular, were said to wade across the river here – at a spot in front of St Thomas's Hospital – although in 1909 the remains of a Roman boat were found nearby, so, obviously, they sometimes liked to keep their sandals dry.

The late, eccentric Labour peer Lord Rufus Noel-Buxton was keen to demonstrate that the ford still existed and walked into the Thames at low tide on March 25th 1952, wearing ordinary clothes. When the water reached his neck – he stood 6ft 3in – and was still rising, he admitted defeat and had to swim. He blamed heavy rain in the Cotswolds for the situation.

38 PECKHAM LIBRARY

Address: 122 Peckham Hill Street, SE15 5JR (020-7525 2000).
Opening hours: Mon, Tue, Thu and Fri, 9am-8pm; Wed, 10am-8pm; Sat, 10am-5pm;
Sun, noon-4pm.
Transport: Peckham Rye rail.

This four-storey library and community centre is an unexpected splash of glamour in inner-city Peckham. Strikingly coloured and unusually shaped, the building was designed by Alsop and Stormer, and won the RIBA Stirling Prize for Architecture in 2000, the year it opened. It's been described as resembling an inverted capital letter L and its upper section is supported by thin steel pillars that appear to have been positioned and angled randomly.

The colourful, varied exterior cladding consists of pre-patinated copper, steel mesh and coloured glass, making it resemble a giant wrapped sweet. It has become popular with the local community and was designed to be part of the area's on-going regeneration.

---

39 RAISED WALKWAYS

Address: Shad Thames, SE1.
Transport: Tower Hill tube.

Shad Thames is a narrow riverside street of converted warehouses. Its most unusual feature is a series of latticed, wrought-iron walkways that crisscross it high overhead. Most of them connect the Butlers Wharf Building and the Cardamom Building, originally used to roll barrels and other items between warehouses. They're an example of the Victorians' great eye for design, which they applied even to functional items.

The name Shad Thames may be a corruption of St-John-at-Thames, a church that once stood in the area. In Victorian times, this neighbourhood included London's largest warehouse complex, completed in 1873. The last warehouse closed in 1972 and the area was subsequently regenerated. Many of the warehouses now house upmarket apartments, bars, restaurants and shops.

WILLIAM BLAKE'S MOSAICS 40

Address: Centaur Street Tunnel, Centaur Street, SE1 7EG.
Transport: Lambeth North tube.

1757 1827 William Blake

Lambeth has an unusual shrine of sorts to the artist, etcher, illustrator, innovator, poet, printer and visionary William Blake (1757-1827). It's here because Blake lived nearby – at 13 Hercules Buildings, Hercules Road – from 1790 to 1800. This was his so-called 'Lambeth Period', which was arguably the most important and productive of his life.

Underneath a railway tunnel on Centaur Street are around 24 mosaics based on Blake's output. One side of the street has works from *Songs of Innocence and Experience*, the other features images from other books and drawings. There's also a sound installation of readings of Blake's poetry by locals and noted figures, including author Philip Pullman, whose trilogy *His Dark Materials* was influenced by Blake's *The Marriage of Heaven and Hell*.

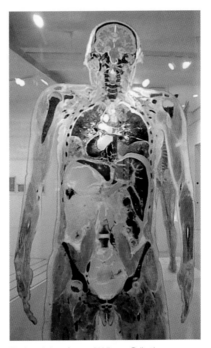

Plastinated slice of a man, Wellcome Collection

INDEX

D

E

F

G

H

Living and Working in London

ISBN: 978-1-907339-50-9

6th edition

Graeme Chesters & David Hampshire

L iving and Working in London, first
published in 2000 and now in its 6th
edition, is the most comprehensive book
available about daily life – and essential
reading for newcomers. What's it really
like Living and Working in London? Not
surprisingly there's a lot more to life than
bobbies, beefeaters and busbys! This book
is guaranteed to hasten your introduction
to the London way of life, irrespective of
whether you're planning to stay for a few
months or indefinitely. Adjusting to day
to day life in London just got a whole lot
simpler!

£14.95

Where to Live in London

ISBN: 978-1-907339-13-4

David Hampshire & Graeme Chesters

E ssential reading for newcomers
planning to live in London,
containing detailed surveys of all 33
boroughs including property prices
and rental costs, schools, health
services, shopping, social services,
crime rates, public transport, parking,
leisure facilities, local taxes, places
of worship and much more. Interest
in living in London and investing
in property in London has never
been higher, both from Britons and
foreigners.

£15.95

£10.95

London Sketchbook

ISBN: 978-1-907339-37-0, 96 pages, hardback.

Jim Watson

London Sketchbook is a unique guide to the most celebrated
landmarks of one of the world's major cities. In ten easy walks
it takes you on a fascinating journey around the most famous of
London's huge variety of vistas, with identification of the panoramic
views and relevant historical background along the way.

Jim Watson's illustration technique is traditional line and wash,
but his approach is that of a curious neighbour, seeking out the
scenes which give each area its individual character – while
keeping a keen eye open for the quirky and unusual.

London's Secrets

LONDON'S HIDDEN SECRETS

ISBN: 978-1-907339-40-0, £10.95

Graeme Chesters

A guide to London's hidden and lesser-known sights not found in standard guidebooks. Step beyond the chaos, cliches and queues of London's tourist-clogged attractions to its quirkier side.

Discover its loveliest ancient buildings, secret gardens, strangest museums, most atmospheric pubs, cutting-edge art and design, and much more: some 140 destinations in all corners of the city.

LONDON'S HIDDEN SECRETS VOL 2

ISBN: 978-1-907339-79-0, £10.95

Graeme Chesters & David Hampshire

Hot on the heels of London's Hidden Secrets comes another volume of the city's largely undiscovered sights, many of which we were unable to include in the original book. In fact, the more research we did the more treasures we found, until eventually a second volume was inevitable.

Written by two experienced London writers, LHS 2 is for both those who already know the metropolis and newcomers wishing to learn more about its hidden and unusual charms.

LONDON'S SECRET WALKS

ISBN: 978-1-907339-51-6, £11.9

Graeme Chesters

London is a great city for walking – whether for pleas exercise or simply to get fro to B. Despite the city's exten sive public transport system walking is also often the quickest and most enjoyable way to get around – at least the centre – and it's also fre and healthy!

Many attractions are off th beaten track, away from the major thoroughfares and pu transport hubs. This favours walking as the best way to explore them, as does the fact that London is a visually interesting city with a wealth of stimulating sights in ever 'nook and cranny'.

320 PAGES, PRINTED IN COLOUR